Material Cultures, Material Minds

Material culture has been part of a distinctively human way of life for more than two million years. Recent symbolic and social analyses have drawn much attention to the role of material culture in human society, emphasising the representational and ideological aspects of the material world. These studies have, nonetheless, often overlooked how the very physicality of material culture and our material surroundings makes them unique and distinctive from text and discourse. In this study, Nicole Boivin explores how the physicality of the material world shapes our thoughts, emotions, cosmological frameworks, social relations, and even our bodies. Focusing on the agency of material culture, she draws on the work of a diverse range of thinkers, from Marx and Merleau-Ponty to Darwin, while highlighting a wide selection of new studies in archaeology, cultural anthropology, history, cognitive science, and evolutionary biology. She asks what is distinctive about material culture compared with other aspects of human culture and presents a comprehensive overview of material agency that has much to offer to both scholars and students.

Nicole Boivin is senior research associate at the McDonald Institute for Archaeological Research, University of Cambridge. She is editor, with Mary Ann Owoc, of *Soils, Stones, and Symbols: Cultural Perceptions of the Mineral World*.

Material Cultures, Material Minds

The Impact of Things on Human Thought, Society, and Evolution

NICOLE BOIVIN
University of Cambridge

CAMBRIDGE
UNIVERSITY PRESS

CAMBRIDGE UNIVERSITY PRESS
Cambridge, New York, Melbourne, Madrid, Cape Town,
Singapore, São Paulo, Delhi, Tokyo, Mexico City

Cambridge University Press
32 Avenue of the Americas, New York, NY 10013-2473, USA

www.cambridge.org
Information on this title: www.cambridge.org/9780521176132

First published 2008
First paperback edition 2010
Reprinted 2011 (twice)

A catalog record for this publication is available from the British Library.

Library of Congress Cataloging in Publication Data

Boivin, Nicole, Ph.D.
Material cultures, material minds: the impact of things on human thought, society,
and evolution / Nicole Boivin.
    p.   cm.
Includes bibliographical references and index.
ISBN 978-0-521-87397-0 (hardback)
1. Material culture.   2. Intellectual life – History.
3. Civilization – History.   4. Social evolution.   5. Human evolution.   6. Social
archaeology.   7. Ethnology.   8. Social history.   9. Cognitive science.
10. Evolution (Biology)   I. Title.
GN406.B65   2009
306–dc22   2007052895

ISBN 978-0-521-87397-0 Hardback
ISBN 978-0-521-17613-2 Paperback

To my parents, Janet and Joseph Boivin

Contents

Members of the Australian Aboriginal community are respectfully advised that this book contains reference to a deceased Indigenous person.

List of Tables and Figures

Tables

Figures

Acknowledgements

As those close to me will know, this book has been a long time in the making. Its origins lie in ideas that emerged during the writing of my PhD thesis, and its main thesis has evolved dramatically in subsequent years. I am grateful for the many 'homes' I have had during its conception, research, and writing. The book proposal for Cambridge University Press was generated during my time as a Research Fellow in Cognitive Archaeology at the McDonald Institute for Archaeological Research in Cambridge from 2002 to 2004. I am very grateful to Colin Renfrew and Chris Scarre for their support and encouragement during my time at the Institute. The conference entitled Rethinking Materiality, organised by Chris Gosden, Elizabeth DeMarrais, and Colin Renfrew in March 2003, and published by the McDonald Institute, provided an important venue for me to test out and develop some of my ideas at an early stage.

Much of the research and early writing of the book was carried out while I was a Fyssen Foundation Post-Doctoral Research Fellow in Paris in 2005. The Laboratoire de Préhistoire et Technologie at the Maison René Ginouvès de l'Archéologie et de l'Ethnologie, University of Paris X, Nanterre, provided a warm and friendly work atmosphere, and I am particularly grateful to Valentine Roux, Hélène Roche, Jacques Pelegrin, and Isabelle Sidéra for helping me to settle in and feel at home there. The book was completed during my residence at the Leverhulme Centre for Human Evolutionary Studies in Cambridge. I am indebted to Rob Foley and Marta Mirazón Lahr for inviting me to be part of the Centre, and for expanding my horizons in so many ways.

This book would not have been written without the encouragement and support of Richard Bradley, who as one of my PhD examiners, and the original Cambridge editor of the book, saw something to get excited about in my PhD thesis. Richard's enthusiasm is contagious, and it inspired me to develop some fledgling ideas into a long book proposal. Richard played an active role in driving the early stages of my research on the book, and his encouragement, advice, and support have been invaluable. I am also indebted to Andy Jones for playing a pivotal role in promoting my work and for endlessly encouraging and inspiring me along the way.

I am grateful to the many colleagues and friends who have helped out with this book in various ways over the years – whether stimulating ideas, providing a forum for my thoughts to be aired, sharing information, or advising me on practicalities – including Paul Devereux, Mark Devitt, Rob Foley, Dorian Fuller, Chris Gosden, Ian Hodder, Andy Jones, Toomas Kivisild, Carl Knappett, Marta Mirazón Lahr, Bill McGrew, Sven Ouzman, Mike Parker Pearson, Michael Petraglia, Valentine Roux, Jay Stock, Marc Verhoeven, Dave Wengrow, Howard Williams, and the members of the Cambridge Archaeological Theory Discussion Group.

I am exceedingly grateful to those who, once the book was completed, took time to read and comment on it or on particular chapters: Joseph Boivin, Paul Devereux, Rob Foley, Dorian Fuller, Clive Gamble, Matthew Johnson, Bill McGrew, Michael Petraglia, and Colin Renfrew. They have provided valuable feedback and editorial advice, and the book is a better one for their efforts. I bear full responsibility for any errors or inconsistencies that may remain.

I would also like to thank those who played a less direct, but still important, role in this work. I am grateful to the people of Balathal village, whose lives and material culture I discuss at various points in this book. They welcomed a stranger into their midst, endlessly and patiently dealt with her strange questions and even stranger ways, and had the generosity to not only feed, house, and shelter me, but also make me feel at home. I am grateful also to the many other people who helped me to accomplish my ethnoarchaeological and archaeological research in India, including in particular Bridget and Raymond Allchin, Raj Bhanti, B. R. Chauhan, Lorraine

Fernandes, Rima Hooja, Jheevan Kharakwal, Ravi Korisettar, V. N. Misra, R. K. Mohanty, Lalit Pandey, Vasante Shinde, Rabindra Nath Vyas, and S. R. Walimbe.

A number of friends and colleagues have helped in locating, providing, or making the illustrations that appear in this book, and I gratefully acknowledge their assistance: Ted Banning, Ofer Bar-Yosef, Maurice Bloch, Susana Carvalho, Chris Clarkson, Mark Devitt, Michael Dietler, Shahina Farid, Dorian Fuller, Ingrid Herbich, Ian Hodder, Lisa Maher, Bill McGrew, Steve Mithen, Howard Morphy, Sven Ouzman, Michael Petraglia, Tom Plummer, Jason Quinlan, and Christine Watson. I am also grateful to the many independent and professional photographers who agreed to let me use their photos, and to the various people who helped with photos that ultimately could not appear herein, including Joakim Goldhahn, Janet Hoskins, Tim Insoll, and Paul Stoller.

For various forms of technical support and assistance, I would like to thank Fabio Lahr and Aidan Baker. I am also grateful to the team at Cambridge for their enthusiasm for the book, particularly to my editors, Simon Whitmore and Beatrice Rehl, for their hard work in bringing it to publication. Mary Paden at Aptara was very patient and supportive during the copyediting stage, and a pleasure to work with.

I raced with my daughter Eva to see which would be born first, her or this book, and my daughter won. I am grateful to her for bringing so much joy to my life, and equally grateful to the many friends and family members who have taken such wonderful care of her so that I could slip off, worry free, for a few peaceful hours of work over the past months. That time was instrumental to my completing this book. In particular, I would like to thank Marc Boivin, Federica Crivellaro, Joanne Horton, Fabio Lahr, Marta Mirazón Lahr, Natasja Windsor, the Petraglia family (especially Catherine, Maria, Larry, and Roseanne), the Young family, and my parents.

Last, but certainly not least, I would like to specially thank the three individuals who, more than anyone else, have supported, encouraged, and inspired me, and who have done so much to make this book possible. The first is my husband, Michael Petraglia, whose endless optimism and excitement I thrive on, and who, over the past year, has sacrificed much to ensure I can continue to do the research I love. The other two are my parents, Janet and Joseph Boivin, who have never wavered in their support, their love, or their belief in me. Though I have often been far away, they have always been present, in the most important of ways, giving me the stability, security, and encouragement to pursue my dreams. It is for this reason that I dedicate this book, born out of the PhD research they played such a role in supporting, to both of them. Thank you.

CHAPTER 1

Introduction

In Pursuit of Symbols in Western India

The origins of this book lie in a small rural village in the Indian state of Rajasthan. The village, called Balathal, sits next to an ancient mound bearing the archaeological remains of one of the earliest villages in western India. The ancient site is also known as Balathal, and it is to study this archaeological site, rather than the contemporary village, that I originally went to Rajasthan in 1997. I was a PhD student, and I went armed with a new technique, called soil micromorphology, and a, by then, relatively well-established archaeological theoretical framework, called post-processualism. I planned to combine the two to try to understand more about architecture and spatial use at the Chalcolithic period site. Soil micromorphology is a geoarchaeological technique that involves the microscopic examination of ancient buildings, particularly the materials used to construct them and the waste materials that build up on their floors, in order to understand how the structures were built, used, and transformed through time. It is a high-resolution technique that is aptly suited to creating the kind of rich ethnographic image of a site that post-processualist archaeologists, who are often interested in the social and symbolic aspects of everyday life and material culture use, aim to generate.

My interest in the present-day village of Balathal arose out of some relatively minor archaeological questions. I saw that the floors of the mud structures in the early levels of the neighbouring archaeological site were made up of a variety of materials, and I had no idea why. I initially visited the mud houses in the modern village next to the mound to learn more about why particular types of sediment or clay rather than other types might have been used to make the ancient floors. My early visits to the village demonstrated that there was so much to know about how people made floors and houses, and why they did so, that it would be difficult to use the still pioneer-phase method of soil micromorphology to analyse ancient spaces until more background research had been done. My interests therefore shifted to ethnoarchaeology, and to the study of the mud houses in modern-day Balathal village using ethnographic and soil micromorphological techniques. I was keen to try to see how the rich ethnographic detail of everyday domestic life related to the soils, sediments, and debris that archaeologists dig up and that archaeological soil micromorphologists look at under the microscope.

The approach I took is aptly illustrated by one particular link I noted in the early days of my fieldwork. One of the things I had observed in the village houses was that they inevitably contained a large red rectangular patch above the main hearth, as well as sometimes above other hearths (Figure 1.1). I had been asking about the red patches, but had generally received similar banal and unsatisfying answers in response to my questions about their meaning. "They are painted on to look nice" I was told repeatedly, and some people argued that the red covered up the black soot caused by cooking. I was deeply suspicious of these answers, especially since the red patches and the sooty black areas only ever partially overlapped. I therefore tried changing how I phrased my question, and instead of asking what the squares meant, I asked why red soil (called *pili mitti*) had been used to make the squares.

With this change in tack, things got more interesting because when I asked the question this way, I was repeatedly given a very different answer: that the red soil was used because it contained Laksmi. The deity Laksmi is the Hindu goddess of wealth and good fortune. More specifically, I was often told that *pili mitti was* Laksmi. This was exciting not only because it helped me to understand the red patches, but more importantly because it was

Figure 1.1: Red patch above the hearth in a Balathal house. Trying to determine the meaning of the patches posed a challenge. Photo Nicole Boivin.

the first indication of a pattern that would become increasingly clear to me: soils were often selected for use because they possessed some meaningful significance – and this was the case not just when it came to making decorative features, but even when much more mundane aspects of plastering and construction were undertaken. While the literature on traditional mud-build architecture inevitably described building and plastering out of mud as a kind of scientific enterprise involving the maximisation of efficiency, strength, and durability, Balathal villagers were often doing things that did not make much sense from such a perspective. They plastered floors using bright red soil even though it was not strong and rubbed off on everyone's clothes, because *pili mitti* was Laksmi, and using the soil made the house auspicious. They used pure white soil brought from far away by visiting relatives to plaster over the outside of the house not because it was the most resistant to weathering, which it was not, but because white soil was beautiful and symbolised purity (Figure 1.2).

The more I looked into the creation of mud houses and the choices made concerning when and how to construct, plaster, and replaster them, the more I saw that symbolic thought pervaded many seemingly mundane aspects of construction technology. The house was a world of symbols that shaped the habits and understanding of those who built it, used it, and grew up in it. This was of course not a new finding (Bourdieu (1973, 1977, 1990) in particular has emphasised it), but what I was able to contribute was an understanding that even the materials that make up the house are meaningful, and add to its power as a symbol. This of course has implications for geoarchaeologists, who tend, like the architects who study traditional mud-built architecture, to interpret architectural choices as rational and efficient in the modern Western sense. It was exciting to be able to show microscopic images of floors and sediments and describe how they had been built up as a result of complex social and symbolic practices that drew on the cosmological understandings and strategic manoeuvrings of social agents. It was also important to realise that floors and sediments could be used by archaeologists to help reconstruct not just the functional, but also the social and symbolic aspects, of ancient societies.

In the late 1990s, my ideas were new ones in the sub-disciplinary field of geoarchaeology, as was my relatively novel attempt to examine the links between archaeological science and archaeological theory (though see also Evans 2003; Jones 2002). But in terms of its emphasis on symbolism, the social aspects of technology, and agency, my thesis research (Boivin 2000, 2001, 2004b) was very much part of a wider post-processual or interpretive turn within archaeology. Symbolism and meaning, drawn upon by agents during the production and reproduction of social practices as well as the negotiation of social change, was very much the order of the day in archaeology, and I was relatively content to serve them up. The only tensions emerged when, encouraged by an archaeological science perspective that continually prevented the physical world

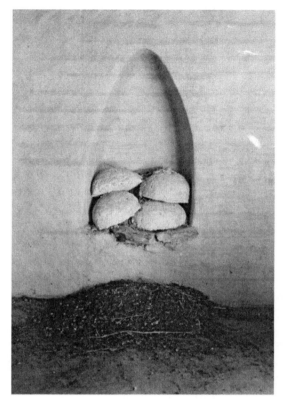

Figure 1.2: Valuable pure white soil is often formed into cakes and carefully stored for future use in Balathal village. Its value is aesthetic and symbolic rather than strictly functional. Photo Nicole Boivin.

from being completely swallowed up by the abstractions of social and symbolic theory, I began to consider the implications of the physicality of soil for its role in society. I recognised that soil has particular properties of malleability and plasticity that permitted it to be used in specific ways in Balathal village homes. Those homes, and the way that they were constantly transformed in concert with the temporal rhythms of the year, the individual lifecycle, and the domestic group cycle, were very different from my own, much more solid house of concrete, steel, wood, and drywall.

They were also different from the much more temporary types of structures that were generally built in the period preceding sedentism. I therefore also began to consider how building with soil, as people started to do in a major way in the Near East and Eastern Mediterranean at the start of the Neolithic period, may have helped the Neolithic sedentarisation process along in particular ways because of the specific physical properties of soil (discussed in Chapter 4 and Boivin 2001, 2004d). The enormous Neolithic and Chalcolithic period tells of these regions attest to a major experiment with soil that was likely implicated in these first conversions to sedentary living (Figure 1.3). The shift to using soil is of course very unlikely to have caused sedentism, but it almost certainly encouraged it because soil is so untransportable and breakable when converted into houses and pots. It cannot be attributed with having caused radical changes in social organisation, communication, material representation, and cooking and building technologies, but its physical properties can be said to have enabled and perhaps even encouraged these changes by virtue of soil's ability to be divided up into houses, rooms, walls, and courtyards and shaped into furnishings, decorations, jewellery, pots, and symbols. As humans shaped soil, so it likely shaped them and their world. Thus, the material world impacts on the social world in a real way, not just because of its ability to act as a carrier of ideas and concepts, but also because its very materiality exerts a force that in human hands becomes a social force.

It was this recognition that material culture is in some ways distinctive from other aspects of the cultural world that led me to begin to question the focus on symbolism and meaning that had become the orthodoxy within British archaeological theory. At the same time, I also began to see problems with the symbolic account that I had constructed in my thesis. I had seen symbols everywhere, but what proof did I really have that they existed? My account was attractive, in that it made sense of a wide variety of facts, and brought order to a complex assortment of statements, observations, practices, and material patterns, but it also seemed in some ways far from the reality of everyday living that I had been part of while staying in Balathal. I attributed even colours and textures with meanings, so that the women who plastered and transformed houses became the creators of complex, abstract, coded messages that they were nonetheless insufficiently aware of

Figure 1.3: Prehistoric to historic period tell in Jordan in the Near East. Tells are composed primarily of the clay brought to make mud-built houses. Photo Steve Mithen.

to describe to me. The following passage from my PhD thesis is symptomatic:

> It is only with such a nuanced understanding of the colour red that we can begin to understand the use of *pili mitti* as a plastering material. For while the application of *pili mitti* is strongly associated with weddings and festivals (and particularly first fruits festivals), it is also, as we have seen, associated with spatial boundaries, cooking and death. These associations cannot be fully explained through the discursive argument that *pili mitti* symbolises auspiciousness and protection. They can, however, be understood when we recognise that all these divergent uses of *pili mitti* have in common an association with liminality, and, in particular, transformations. It is the transition between states then – the transition from married to unmarried, from virgin to mother, from alive to dead, from raw to cooked, from out to

in, and from production to consumption – that is actually symbolised by *pili mitti*. Like the colour red then, *pili mitti* seems, at least at one level, to be about the processes that are necessary for life to carry forward. (Boivin 2001: 92)

Such abstract constructions were never described to me by informants of course, but were rather pieced together out of a myriad of separate observations and statements. These days, going back to rural India as I regularly do for archaeological fieldwork, it is abundantly clear to me that this ordered, sterile world of structural oppositions, no matter how much I claimed that it was used by knowing agents, has little if anything to do with the real world of smells, crying babies, joy, hardship, animals, dirt, money, conflict, and passion that is living in a rural Indian village, or indeed any place on Earth.

Looking back now, I question this focus on order and many other aspects of my understanding of material culture in Balathal village. I question, for example, my interpretation of *pili mitti* as a symbol of Laksmi. In my notes, I clearly record many people stating that *pili mitti* was considered *to be* Laksmi, and yet I preceded with my analysis as though *pili mitti represented* Laksmi. In doing so, I betrayed my inclination to interpret everything in the material world as a symbol, as something that represents something else. I have also returned to those original answers to my queries about the red patches, which was that they looked nice. I received what I felt were similarly banal answers when I asked ordinary women and men about the meaning of particular domestic rituals (Figure 1.4). The response was inevitably a list of the food and other material items that were used in conducting the ritual, as well as a description of the practices that were carried out, rather than any attempt at presenting an insight into the reasons *why* such items and practices were used. These kinds of answers suggest that, for the people living in the houses and conducting the rituals, there is no abstract meaning behind specific practices, or at the very least, there is not abstract meaning behind every aspect of practice. It is highly likely that the material world – the red patches of *pili mitti* and the myriad of items used in domestic rituals – evoke experiences that lie beyond the verbal, beyond the conceptual, and

Figure 1.4: A domestic ritual underway in Balathal village. Questions about the meaning of particular rituals were frequently met with a description of the objects and foods employed in them. Photo Nicole Boivin.

beyond even the conscious. These items of the material world do not necessarily symbolise anything else: their very power may lie in the fact that they are part of the realm of the sensual, of experience, and of emotion, rather than a world of concepts, codes, and meaning.

This very brief summary of the evolution of my thoughts concerning Balathal village and its material culture tracks what was not only a major shift in my own thinking, but also a crucial transformation in the social sciences and humanities. This transformation concerns the way that we understand society, culture, and our own minds. It also, specifically, concerns the way that we understand the material world, and its relationship to the mind, to culture, and to society. This book is about that transformation, and its implications. In critiquing here a focus on representation, I am not only critiquing my own work, or even the work of British archaeologists, but also important aspects of the history of Western thought since the Enlightenment.

The Model of the Text

"Material culture is like a text." A radical and, to some at least, counterintuitive statement, this became the banner for a new and highly influential movement that arose within British archaeology in the early 1980s. This new approach, which was first promulgated in a series of articles and books starting in 1982 (Hodder 1982a, 1982b, 1985; Miller & Tilley 1984; Shanks & Tilley 1987), was highly critical of the then dominant archaeological models for understanding material culture, which it derided as 'functionalist', 'adaptive', and 'scientistic'. It argued instead that material culture needed to be understood as 'meaningful' and 'symbolic'. The new movement even critiqued previous attempts to link material culture to social aspects of society, asserting that they portrayed material culture as passive and simply *reflective* of social realities. Material culture, the proponents of the new movement asserted, needed rather to be recognised as *active* in constituting those very realities (Hodder 1982b, 1991, 1992; Shanks & Tilley 1987; Tilley 1989). Material culture was argued to be a symbolic medium for social practice that was used at times habitually to reproduce social and symbolic structures, and at other times strategically to challenge them. The archaeologist Ian Hodder, for example, studied the domestic material culture of the Ilchamus tribe of Kenya, and argued that women decorated calabashes (Figure 1.5) in order to draw attention to their own important roles in child-rearing and looking after milk (a symbolically important resource) and to challenge their status within a patriarchal society (Hodder 1991). Material culture was strategically used by the Ilchamus during the course of social practice and did not simply and passively reflect social realities.

These and other critiques by a group of young British archaeologists were aimed at what was known as the 'processual' school in archaeology, an influential movement that had emerged in the 1960s and 1970s, and that argued that archaeology needed to be more rigorous, scientific, and systems oriented. The radical new critique against this school therefore became known as post-processualism (Hodder 1985). Its tenor was decidedly social,

Figure 1.5: Decorated calabashes from Kenya. Ian Hodder argued that women of the Ilchamus tribe decorate calabashes to challenge their status in a patriarchal society. Photo Ian Hodder.

cultural, and interpretive. As indicated, it came to adopt a model of the text for understanding material culture (Hodder 1988, 1989, 1991; Patrik 1985), drawing on such varied fields as structuralism, semiotics, hermeneutics, and post-structuralism for inspiration. Assertions like this one by Chris Tilley were therefore common:

> Speech and writing signify – they communicate meaning and in an analogous way material culture constitutes a significative structure of meanings. (Tilley 1991: 20)

One of the primary concerns of post-processual archaeology thus became the search for meaning, and the interpretation of past material culture symbols – "archaeology" as Tilley described "as ... a pursuit of sign systems" (Tilley 1989: 188).

While the ideas of post-processual archaeology seemed radical, and indeed were radical within the context of the discipline of archaeology in the 1980s, it is important to recognise that they were not entirely new. The powerful school that post-processualism eventually became very clearly constituted part of a wider movement within the social sciences and humanities, and if anything, archaeology had been slow to take these ideas on board. Its neighbouring discipline, anthropology, had already embraced the so-called symbolic or linguistic turn for several decades by the time that archaeology got around to giving it any significant attention. Indeed, the work of an anthropologist – Claude Lévi-Strauss – had played a vital role in the generation of this new movement by demonstrating the applicability of models developed in linguistics to a wider range of social phenomena (Chandler 2002). Lévi-Strauss had shown that the kinds of 'deep structures' identified by linguists like Saussure and Jacobson for language also seemed to underlie things like kinship rules and myth systems in human society. Across the Atlantic Ocean, in America, other anthropologists drew on a different, culture-inspired tradition to arrive at a similar interest in symbols and semiotics. Clifford Geertz, one of the leading proponents of this new symbolic anthropology, summed up its aims as follows:

> Believing, with Max Weber, that man is an animal suspended in webs of significance he himself has spun, I take culture to be these webs, and the analysis of it to be therefore not an experimental science in search of law, but an interpretive one in search of meaning. (Geertz 1973: 5)

It is with Geertz that we find the textual metaphor (Ricoeur 1971) entering anthropology: he argued, for example, that "the culture of people is an ensemble of texts" (Geertz 1973: 448). In the 1960s and 1970s then, the anthropologist's job became one of interpreting and understanding those texts. By the time archaeologists began to adopt these various symbolic strands in the early 1980s, anthropologists were already dealing with the problems they posed, and attempting to resolve them through post-structural, hermeneutic, or practice approaches, all of which also entered archaeology at around the same time.

Idealism in Western Thought

In embracing an interest in language and symbolism, anthropology itself was not of course following an original path. The 'linguistic turn' had a major impact in the second half of the twentieth century on a range of disciplines from philosophy to history to literary criticism (Derrida 1978; Foucault 1972; Rabinow & Sullivan 1979; Rorty 1967). Throughout the humanities and social sciences, language has become a core model for understanding many aspects of human action, thinking, and society, and this orientation has led to an emphasis on meaning, symbolism, representation, signification, and interpretation. A wide variety of phenomena have been demonstrated to be 'language-like' in diverse ways, and multiple fields have drawn upon the work of linguists like Saussure and Jacobson, and the methods that they developed to examine, model, and understand language. Thus, relationships – or webs of meaning – have become key: words and concepts are understood not relative to things in the world, but rather through comparison to other words and concepts. Meaning is constructed rather than given. This has led to an interest in representation, and its power to shape action and thought. Post-modernism has stressed the role of language and discourse in shaping subjectivity, social institutions, and politics (Seidman 1994). Language is increasingly understood less as a neutral medium for representing and understanding the world, and more as a key way through which the world is constructed. Other 'language-like' systems are recognised to share the same partiality.

While the twentieth-century preoccupation with language has been distinctive, it is also clear that the roots of the linguistic turn in many ways go back a long way in Western thought. In particular, we can trace several major trends in the history of Western philosophy that foreshadow the post-war interest in language. These include a focus on order, a distinction between thought and world, and a ranking of the two in hierarchical order. As many have noted, Plato was instrumental in establishing these trends – indeed the history of Western philosophy has been described as "a series of footnotes to Plato" (Whitehead 1978: 39). Plato famously distinguished between forms and instances of forms; the former, he argued, were universals that existed outside of space and time, while the latter were the innumerable instances of these forms that we encounter in the world (Heil 2004). Thus, for Plato, something else – forms – lay behind the real world, and was responsible for it. The job of philosophers was to attend not to the multiplicity of instances (perceptible things), but rather to seek knowledge by using reason to discern the ultimate forms that underlie them (Lakoff & Johnson 1999: 365). Plato's idealism is also clear from his views on knowledge. He asserted that, while things were outside the mind and thus not directly perceptible, ideas were directly present in the mind and thus have more reality than things (ibid.: 367). Ideas were not only transcendent but also the basis of reality.

Descartes is another influential figure in the idealist tradition. As Heil has argued, it is Descartes, more than any other historical figure, who is responsible for the modern conception of mind (Heil 2004: 16). Descartes' model of the mind is famously dualistic: it holds that mind and material are distinct substances. Minds, or mental substances, think, while things, or material substances, are extended in space (Heil 2004). The outcome of this conceptualisation is a mind–body split that has been influential since the Enlightenment (Csordas 1990; Freund 1988; Jackson 1983; Kirmayer 1992). For Descartes, thoughts were representations in an 'inner' realm (of the mind) of objects existing in the 'external' world (Lakoff & Johnson 1999: 391). Thus, thoughts were once again more real for us than the world they represent, and rational thinking became the key to knowledge. This lineage continues thereafter, tracing itself through Kant and Hegel, who continued to build on Platonic foundations, and to emphasise the power of pure thought over such human faculties as feeling and action (Stoller 1989: 151). In the twentieth century, analytic philosophy, characterised as it was by the linguistic turn, continued to share many aspects of this tradition, even as it challenged others. With analytic philosophy, language was made the unique, or at least most central and fundamental, object of philosophical investigation. With its advent, we witness a continued stress on the mind and its products over the body and the world, and a far from novel emphasis on the underlying order behind the apparent chaos of life and world (Jackson 1996a).

While this simple sketch of a few main stepping-stones belies the complexity and richness of Western philosophical thought, it nonetheless demonstrates something of the intense preoccupation that it has maintained with order, the mind, thought and ideas, language, rationality, the transcendent, and culture. These have continually been emphasised over and above the body, the material, the world, the emotional, the subjective, the everyday, and nature. Western thought not only divides and dichotomises, but also inevitably values and ranks. Not only are mind and body, culture and nature, ideal and material, and the objective and the subjective distinguished and held apart, but they are differentially valued. And in the long, drawn out contest between the two, it is inevitably the mind and its apparent objectivity that have been favoured, and with it a view of humans as apart from nature, categorically different from other animals, and defined, inevitably and irrefutably, by a capacity for symbolism, language, and the creation of a unique, cultural order.

Anthropology and the Superorganic

The linguistic turn in anthropology, and by extension archaeology, is in every way as natural an outcome in these disciplines as it was in philosophy. Anthropology, almost by definition, has been concerned with finding order behind apparent chaos – defining kinship *systems*, discovering the *structures* that lie behind myth, and above all, building *general* theories about human society (Stoller 1989). It has also furthered the notion that something transcendent and immaterial – be it culture or society – is at the base of the human world. The anthropologist Michael Jackson has described how the term culture evolved from an original Latin term that "did not imply any separation of conceptual and moral qualities from practical life and social activity", including its material aspects, into an eighteenth- and nineteenth-century European term denoting a realm of authentic spiritual values radically opposed to the world of social utility and material means (Jackson 1996b: 16–17). This transition allowed anthropology, several centuries later, to adopt a view of culture as the 'Superorganic' (Kroeber 1917), that is, a set of attributes that are not only extrasomatic, but also mark humans as fundamentally different from animals. The transition is summarised by Jackson:

> Whether we consider the idealist traditions of the eighteenth and nineteenth centuries which "etherealized" the body or anthropological definitions of culture which play up conceptual and linguistic dimensions of human existence to the exclusion of somatic, sensory, and biological dimensions, one finds that science since the Englightenment has been pervaded by a popular bourgeois conception of culture as something "superorganic" and *sui generis* – a self contained world of unique qualities and manners divorced from the world of materiality and biology. (Jackson 1996b: 18)

If it has not been culture that is transcendent in anthropology, it has been society. Durkheim, in particular, exemplifies this tradition, drawing, as Gell has noted, on Kantian rationalism to argue that the phenomenal world is structured by mind-contrived conceptual underpinnings – Durkheim's collective representations (Gell 1992: 9). The current vogue for social and cultural construction in anthropology – for example, the social construction of emotions (e.g., Lutz 1988; Rosaldo 1984) – is heir to this tradition (Morton 1995). Morton critiques anthropology's "frantic need to define humans as cultural or social rather than natural" (ibid.: 103), and expresses doubt that

> current anthropology has actually moved far beyond Durkheim's collective conscience, Kroeber's superorganic or White's realm of the symbol in attempting to establish a site for anthropological metaphysics, a site in which nature and culture exist as mutually exclusive and exhaustive categories. (Horigan 1988 as cited in Morton 1995: 103)

The Marginalisation of the Material

It is clear then that Western thinking, including anthropological thinking, has passed down very few ways of theorising and understanding the material world. Philosophers have been overwhelmingly concerned with the mind, language, truth, rationality, and objectivity, and have not usually been inclined to link these to the material and biological worlds. Anthropologists have conceptualised society and culture as mental products that transcend nature and biology, and have more recently followed other disciplines in taking up language as a key area of interest. Archaeologists, meanwhile, have embraced the dualism implicit in all of these disciplines, and recreated within their own field the human and natural studies split that has been the outcome of dichotomous Western thought. Torn between the material and biological remains that are their data and the disappeared abstract social formations and cultural entities they feel they should be reconstructing, they have chosen one of two pathways: either they have turned for inspiration to the natural sciences (or natural science-inspired anthropological paradigms like cultural ecology and ecological anthropology (Harris 1966; Rappaport 1967; Steward 1955)) because these at least provide conceptual models that take proper account of the physicality of their data sets, or they have attempted to find ways to link the idealist, constructivist tradition of the humanities and social sciences to the material and biological remains they encounter in the archaeological record. The former approach characterises much of processual archaeology, while the latter is an appropriate description of much of the work that has taken place within the postprocessual tradition. Both, not surprisingly, re-create the dualistic thinking that generated them.

Fortunately, in recent years, the dualisms that have led Western scholars in the humanities and social sciences to ignore the material, the world, biology, and the environment have begun to be seriously and systematically challenged across a wide range of disciplines. While much of this discussion has focused on the body and a critique of the way that it has traditionally been written out of humanistic accounts (Csordas 1990; Frank 1990; Freund 1988; Jackson 1983), some of it has also drawn attention to the way that the material world, including material culture and technology, has been overlooked in most models of culture, society, and thought. Joerges, for example, has argued that:

> The social sciences have no concepts for dealing with technology because they have no concepts of things and tangible

events in general. They have left the world of matter and tis-
sues, the material-organismic world, to use Popper's term,
to the natural and engineering sciences, and have constructed themselves a world of actors devoid of things.
(Joerges 1988: 220)

This same recognition has taken place within a variety of disciplines. For example, the social anthropologist Michael Jackson has
highlighted the lack of attention that has been given to material
culture within anthropology (Jackson 1989: 205, 1996b). His critique is by no means unique within the discipline, and is part of
larger anthropological recognition that the social and cultural have
a material and ecological dimension that has been marginalised
within anthropological accounts (Descola & Pálsson 1996; Ellen &
Fukui 1996; Gell 1999; Ingold 2000). The psychologist Alan Costall
has observed that psychology too has normally taken little notice
of the role of things and the environment in human thought processes. He notes that the traditional understanding within the discipline is that "psychology . . . is about people, the natural sciences
about things" (Costall 1997: 76). Scholars like Daniel Miller and
Paul Graves-Brown, meanwhile, have drawn attention to the way
that material culture has been ignored in studies of modern culture
(Graves-Brown 2000; Miller 1998a). Graves-Brown points out that it
is the "very familiarity, mundanity of the material world around us
[that] leads us to leave it unquestioned" (Figure 1.6; Graves-Brown
2000: 1).

Such critiques have led to an increased acknowledgement of the
role of the material in the social, cultural, and mental processes
that are the focus of scholars in the humanities and social sciences. Social anthropology has in recent decades seen the emergence of studies of goods and consumption (Appadurai 1986;
Miller 1995, 1998b; Pfaffenberger 1988) and technology (Lemonnier 1992; Miller 1995; Pfaffenberger 1992), the latter influenced
in particular by an already well-established French interest in the
ethnology of gestures and techniques (Haudricourt 1968; Leroi-
Gourhan 1943, 1945, 1964, 1965; Mauss 1979; Michea 1968). In
addition, a new interdisciplinary forum, material culture studies,
has brought together scholars from a range of social sciences and

Figure 1.6: Street in downtown Halifax, Canada. As Paul Graves-Brown has noted, the very familiarity of the material world can lead us to overlook it. Photo Nicole Boivin.

humanities backgrounds to address the topic of material culture (see in particular studies in the *Journal of Material Culture Studies*). Much of this recent interest in material culture arguably stems from the attempts of a more interpretive and social archaeology to grapple with the link between material culture and the social and cultural aspects of society. Materially inclined anthropologists like Daniel Miller (1985, 1995, 1998a), Henrietta Moore (1986), Victor Buchli (2002), and Barbara Bender (1993, 1998) have either emerged directly out of the post-processual tradition in archaeology or repeatedly trespassed the boundaries between archaeology and anthropology. As discussed previously, a serious interest in attempting to reconcile the material and socio-cultural dimensions of human activity also began to take shape in archaeology in the early 1980s, and despite being sidelined in some accounts and inter-disciplinary ventures (e.g., a volume of the journal *Social Analysis* (March 1997) dedicated to technology), archaeology continues to play an influential and leading role in the struggle to define a clear place for material culture in the humanities. Archaeologists have very much led the way in attempting to show that the world of ideas, practices, concepts, and thoughts is also a material world in which things and environments have a crucial role to play (Hodder 1991; Miller 1985; Miller & Tilley 1984; Shanks & Tilley 1992; Thomas 1996; Tilley 1990). While other fields have often focused on particularly obvious examples of material culture's role in human society – on shopping (Miller 1998b) or on modern technology (Jackson 2002a; McLuhan 1964; Winner 1986), for example – archaeology has aimed to integrate material culture more systematically into the very theoretical models according to which we understand society.

Despite all of this new interest in material culture, however, there is in much of this work, commendable as it is in spirit, a very serious flaw: it often continues to overlook the actual materiality of the material world. What we frequently find instead is a far from novel emphasis on ideas, on human thought, and on representation. What we often find is a model, either implicit or explicit, of material culture as a text or as a language, as something that represents something else, and that is there to be interpreted. Thus, despite frequent claims to the effect that such studies are breaking down inherited Western dichotomies between ideal and material, between subject and object, and between culture and nature, many of them in fact simply re-impose traditional dualistic frameworks. The physicality of the material world continues to be ignored, as does the way that engagement with that materiality is at the crux of the human enterprise. Instead, what is presented is a world of material surfaces, to which concepts emerging from a higher plane are attached. What is presented is a notion of material entities as things that represent. Meanwhile, the real action – what is represented – continues to take place well away from the material world, in the realms of human thought, social activity, and cultural conceptualisation. The material world then is little more than a theatre, with objects as kinds of props (Graves-Brown 2000), in a story that has already been written by human agents. While scholars have attempted to argue that the new studies of material culture demonstrate how it is active in constituting human society (Hodder 1982b; Shanks & Tilley 1992), in fact material culture often continues to be understood in as passive a way as ever.

This paradoxical view of the material world is already inherent, it can be argued, in the very term 'material culture'. As Jules Prown points out, "material is a word we associate with base and pragmatic things; culture... with lofty, intellectual, abstract things" (Prown 1996: 19). In using material as a qualifier of the base noun culture, we might argue that we reveal an underlying propensity towards understanding the cultural and the abstract as pre-eminent, and the material as little more than a manifestation of these pre-existing phenomena. Such a view is summed up in the assertion that "goods... are the visible part of culture" (Douglas & Isherwood 1996: 44). Seen in this light, we are not at all far removed from Plato's 2,000-year-old notion of forms that transcend and are imposed on the everyday world of substances. Mind once again supersedes matter, and the substantive, physical, real, sensual, and visceral nature of life is omitted from theoretical accounts of human beings and society.

The continued subordination of matter to mind, even in many very recent studies of material culture, has not escaped the notice of all scholars, however, and we find in the literature signs of a growing unease with idealist and constructivist accounts of material culture. One early critic is Bernward Joerges, who commended Mary Douglas and Baron Isherwood for drawing attention to the material world in their study *The World of Goods*, but also critiqued the way they saw goods as little more than social 'markers' that serve symbolic and expressive functions (Joerges 1988: 224). As Joerges noted, "things do more than speak. A washing machine or a central heating system or a car do much more than mark the social place of their owners. They do work, among other things" (ibid.). Similar criticism has been directed at post-processual accounts of material culture in archaeology (Boivin 2004d; Lemonnier 1992; Olsen 2003; Schiffer 1999). Commenting on the often narrow focus on the meaning of stylistic and formal aspects of material culture, Pierre Lemonnier, for example, warned that post-processual discussions of stylistic meaning are "far from being the only anthropological statements that can be made about material culture" (Lemonnier 1992: 97).

More recently, attention has been drawn to the way that discussions of material culture frequently overlook its actual materiality (Boivin 2004d; DeMarrais et al. 2004; Ingold 2000; Knappett 2005; Olsen 2003; Schiffer 1999). Joseph Corn, for example, notes that the history of technology does not actually pay much attention to real material evidence (Figure 1.7; Corn 1996). Based on a survey of the field's pre-eminent journal, *Technology and Culture*, between the years 1986 and 1996, Corn observes that slightly more than half of the authors publishing in the journal did not write about objects, and less than 15 percent employed any material evidence at all (ibid.). Writing from the perspective of archaeology meanwhile, Bjørnar Olsen has similarly noted a failure to take account of the physical, the 'thingly' aspects of material culture (Olsen 2003: 87), and the "properties and competences possessed by the material world" (ibid.: 91). He argues that:

> Contrary to the accusation of being too concerned with things . . . I claim that archaeology rather suffers from being undermaterialized. The materiality of past societies is mostly seen as the outcome of historical and social processes that are not in themselves material, leaving materiality itself with little or no causal or explanatory power for these processes. (ibid.: 90)

I would argue in turn that what the thrust of these various disciplinary and interdisciplinary – and increasingly vocal – critiques amounts to is a call for a new kind of social and cultural theory, and a new model of the mind. What is called for are new approaches that not only take account of the material world, but also recognise that it is integral to the human story and must be at the core of any

Figure 1.7: Steam tractor. Joseph Corn notes that many historians of technology do not actually pay much attention to objects themselves. Photo Philip MacKenzie.

realistic and practical theory or model of how human individuals and societies operate (Figure 1.8). This book constitutes an attempt to respond to this call, and to move a little closer towards these goals.

Uniting Mind and Matter

In this book, I will undertake an exploration of the ways in which culture, society, and mind, the things we think of as most abstract and transcendent in our lives, are in fact far more material, visceral, and sensual than most of our academic models acknowledge. I will attempt to show that the history of human engagement with the material world is not so clearly one of mind being imposed on matter, or form on substance, but rather a history in which mind and matter, and form and substance continually bring each other into being. Indeed, I will attempt to collapse these very dichotomies, even if the language in which I write complicates this by continually imposing them through its very terms and definitions. While I recognise the very significant role of language in constituting and reproducing the dualisms that require breaking down, however, I do not feel that they demand that we continue to overlook the material and the biological in the humanities. Such a course narrows the ability of scholars to understand human beings and their history, and reinforces a rather remarkable lack of communication between the humanities and social sciences on the one hand, and the natural sciences on the other (Ingold 2000; Morell 1993).

Western thought is of course not without approaches that take into account the reality and materiality of human existence. If we have had Plato grounding reality in a realm of transcendent forms or universals, we have also had Aristotle grounding it in the material world (Heil 2004). Thus, in addressing the material world in this book, I will draw on the work of many other scholars who have also been interested in the material world. Some have presented materialist theories, while others have been keen to subvert idealist–materialist dichotomies. Some have presented new models and approaches; others have generated new data. Many are situated clearly within the humanities or social sciences, but, in an attempt to subvert traditional dualisms, I also draw on work carried out firmly within the natural sciences. More rarely, I have been able to take inspiration from a minority of scholars who have seriously attempted to overcome this problematic divide.

This book presents no new over-arching theory of society, the mind, or material culture. Whether such a goal is appropriate is unclear, but even if it is, it is even less clear that it is possible at this time. Rather, this book may be considered an exploration, drawing upon diverse sources from the humanities and natural sciences, of some of the ways in which the material world impacts upon our lives, and is part of, rather than separate from, our cognitive processes, cultural concepts, and social activities. Its aim is to draw attention to the material component of human social and cultural existence, which has so often been overlooked by those seeking to understand the 'cultural' rather than the 'natural' world. As such, it may be predicted that it will at times err in over-emphasising the material, and by focusing upon it, reinforce the dichotomy between

Figure 1.8: Skyscrapers in Hong Kong. More than just an expression of culture, material culture is instead fundamental to the human story. Photo Edwin Stemp.

ideal and material. But what is ultimately sought is a recognition that, much as our language prevents us from naming it, human involvement with the world reflects a unity of mind and material, and of culture and nature. While dividing up academic labour into natural and cultural domains may seem useful, and setting off humans from nature may seem logical, these epistemological and metaphysical acts are in fact fraught with problems.

A word on definitions: when I speak here of the material and the material world, it is in the broad sense implied when material is opposed to ideal. Thus, *material* incorporates objects, landscapes, environments, and bodies – in short all that is tangible rather than abstract. *Materiality*, meanwhile, is a word that I will use to emphasise the physicality of the material world – the fact that it has dimensions, that it resists and constrains, and that it offers possibilities for the human agent (or organism) by virtue of a set of physical properties. *Material culture* is a problematic word that I use out of necessity – its implied emphasis on culture makes it a less than ideal term relative to the points I am making, but it is hard to avoid when it is used so widely and systematically, particularly by archaeologists, to refer to the things, objects, and artefacts made by people. As implied by my use of the term material, this book will also address the body. What it ultimately argues for is a synthesis of mind, body, and material, but often the concept of the body is simply incorporated into the term 'material'. In addition, given that the body has been abundantly dealt with, and its materiality increasingly recognised in recent publications, less attention is given to the materiality of our bodies than the materiality of objects and physical environments.

The remainder of the book is organised into five chapters. Chapter 2 addresses the issue of representation and the way in which the material world comes to signify cultural concepts. It takes issue with the notion that there is an arbitrary relationship between concepts that are represented and the specific material entity that is used to represent them in human society. Instead, it argues, using in particular examples drawn from anthropology, not only that material signifiers are often linked in concrete ways to the notions they signify, but furthermore that cultural cosmologies and understandings are very much rooted in the material and biological worlds. It then shifts to a more general consideration of human cognition, and considers evidence from linguistics and the cognitive sciences that our concepts are shaped by our experience of the world, and in particular its physical dimensions. It examines more recent trends in cognitive science, which seek to reformulate understanding of the relationship between mind, body, and the surrounding world. It will be demonstrated that the empirical data collected by these disciplines, and the new mind–body models they are generating, have much to offer those scholars interested in integrating the material world into humanistic paradigms. It will also be shown that these

studies are paralleled by others in medicine and in medical anthropology that demonstrate the clear relationship between body, mind,
and environment, despite the dominance of a biomedical paradigm
that prefers to hold them separate.

Hereafter the book moves beyond the issue of representation, and
shifts from a discussion of how material signifies to how it effects.
Chapter 3 looks in particular at the ways in which material culture
and other aspects of the material world impact on human experience of the world and on social relationships, not because of their
representative qualities, but because of their sensual, emotional,
and aesthetic properties. The chapter opens by looking at the ways
in which two different anthropologists began, in recent decades, to
question semiotic and symbolic approaches to culture and material culture, and examines the different routes each anthropologist
travelled in searching for alternative approaches, with one drawing
upon the phenomenological tradition within philosophy, and the
other the cognitive sciences. Much of the remainder of the chapter
then draws heavily on examples – from archaeology, anthropology,
history, and cognitive science amongst others – to explore the ways
that material culture impacts people sensually, experientially, and
emotionally. It looks, for example, at how rock art research has
been altered by a consideration of the sensual aspects of prehistoric art production, and how some new studies of material culture
address its emotional and experiential dimensions. It concludes by
looking briefly at the emerging interest in neurophenomenology,
an approach that brings together the very different ideas and methods of cognitive science and phenomenology in order to examine
human experience, and accordingly offers one new way of potentially bridging the divide between the sciences and humanities.

Chapter 4 then looks at the agency of matter. It examines the
means by which the material world plays an active role in constituting human society because of its material qualities, and the
ways these both constrain certain possibilities and enable others.
Matter is not simply at the mercy of human design. To illustrate
this point, the chapter draws heavily upon historical case studies, as well as the ideas of a range of thinkers, from Karl Marx
to Marshall McLuhan. Much of the chapter's discussion focuses

on technology, whose role in shaping society has fascinated scholars for many centuries. Thus, it examines the impact upon society of a range of technologies, from snowmobiles to overpasses,
and nuclear reactors to vacuum cleaners. It explores the notion of
technological determinism, and the way that more recent studies
have tried to explore both the technological aspects of society and
the social aspects of technology. Such studies draw attention to
the ways in which both humans and material things have agency,
and are accordingly linked in complex networks of interaction. The
chapter ultimately attempts to demonstrate that the kinds of material artefacts archaeologists and others study are therefore not an
epiphenomenon of human history, but an integral aspect of the
human story.

In Chapter 5, the argument that material culture shapes us is
extended even further back in time, and is used to explore our evolutionary past. In this chapter, the impact of material culture on the
very physical make-up of our bodies and minds is examined. The
chapter draws upon innovative theoretical ideas within evolutionary biology, as well as new pioneering work in molecular genetics,
to argue that human beings have shaped their own evolutionary trajectories by making and using material culture. In particular, the
chapter explores the implications of niche construction theory, and
the idea that humans have shaped the niches they occupy, and thus
the selection pressures to which they are exposed. The chapter also
looks at evidence from primatology and evolutionary anthropology that supports the idea that humans are a 'self-made species'. It
notes more recent archaeological and osteological evidence indicating that this process of human self-modification continued into the
Holocene, taking the form of a kind of self-domestication, in which
many of the morphological changes that took place in domesticated animals also impacted humans. New findings from molecular genetics, which show ample evidence for very recent, potentially Holocene period, change in the human genome are taken
to support the notion of a self-domestication process. Finally, the
chapter concludes by examining, more speculatively, the potential
impact of material niche construction on the evolution of human
cognition. Ultimately, the chapter tries to demonstrate that the
opposition commonly drawn between evolution and history is a

false one, since our past has always been, and our future will for-ever continue to be, defined by integrated changes in genes, bodies, environments, and cultures.

Chapter 6 is a concluding chapter, which reviews the main argu-ments of the book, and presents a plea not only that humanities-based scholars supplement their current interest in representation and language with attention to the material and visceral aspects of human culture, society, and mind, but also that scholars from both sides of the humanities–sciences divide attempt to break down the debilitating division that has been built up between these realms of study in the previous centuries. While the challenges of doing so are recognised, it is nonetheless one of the fundamental beliefs of this author that we will not get far in understanding human culture, society, cognition, evolution, or biology unless we do.

CHAPTER 2

Representation and Matter

Materiality and the Motivation of Signs

Matter represents. That is, the material world, in all its richness, is frequently used as a medium for the expression or representation of thoughts, concepts, values, and meanings (Figure 2.1). This book does not dispute this fact, and takes no issue with the assertion that the material world symbolises. What it argues, rather, is that the representational aspects of material culture far from exhaust its uses or role within society. There is, it emphasises, more to the relationship between human thought, society, and mind on the one hand, and matter on the other, than representation. However, before moving *beyond* representation, I would like in this chapter to focus *on* representation, and to give some consideration to the precise relationship between material things and the concepts they are used to signify. My argument will be that here, too, there is more of a place for materiality than is commonly assumed.

What is the relationship between a material thing and the concept it is used to represent? How is this relationship normally conceived? In considering the representational or symbolic properties of material culture, many scholars have turned to better studied and more well understood symbolic systems, and in particular language, which is often considered the most paradigmatic of all sign systems. The linguist Ferdinand de Saussure, for example, argued at the beginning of the twentieth century that:

Figure 2.1: Material culture – in this case the designs and jewellery worn by Maasai women in Kenya – is frequently called upon to symbolise group identity. The material world is often used in such ways to signify ideas and meanings. Photo Christine Remy.

> signs which are entirely arbitrary convey better than others
> the ideal semiological process. That is why the most com-
> plex and the most widespread of all systems of expression,
> which is the one we find in human languages, is also the
> most characteristic of all. In this sense, linguistics serves as
> a model for the whole of semiology, even though languages
> represent only one type of semiological system. (Saussure
> 1983: 68)

Saussure's views on signification, and his semiological model for the analysis of signs, have subsequently been extremely influential across many fields in the social sciences and humanities. Saussure's model of the sign was a 'dyadic', or two-part, one that divided the sign into *signifier*, the form the sign takes, and *signified*, that which the sign refers to. Crucially, Saussure's concern was not with the *referential* properties of signs, but rather with their *relational* qualities, such that meaning derived not from the inherent features of signifiers or any reference to material things, but from the systematic relations between signs within a total sign system

(Chandler 2002: 22). Thus, for example, an individual word such as 'girl' derives its meaning from its relationship to other words in the system, such as 'boy' and 'woman'. There is nothing furthermore that specifies that the concept girl needs to be represented by this particular word – it would change nothing if instead of 'girl', the word 'ball' had been historically selected to represent this particular concept. This is what is meant when the relationship between signifier and signified is described as arbitrary. The arbitrariness of the signifier was a key aspect of Saussure's model of the sign.

It has been noted that Saussure's signification model leaves little space for the world. Meanings derive from systems of contrast rather than reference to things, and signs themselves are non-material, 'psychological' forms (Saussure 1983). Not surprisingly, the structuralist and post-structuralist approaches that have emerged out of Saussure's semiology have had a similarly idealist flavour. Structuralists have focused on idealised, abstract, and ahistorical schemes rather than real-life processes, while post-structuralists have done away with reality completely in favour of what they describe as an endless play of signifiers, none of which can be fixed to a signified. With post-structuralist deconstructionists like Jacques Derrida, we find that the arbitrary nature of signifiers means ultimately that there is nothing outside the text (Derrida 1976: 158, 163). Saussure's model has also been used to argue that language constructs reality (Chandler 2002; Sturrock 1986). As Daniel Chandler notes, "[t]he arbitrariness of the sign is a radical concept because it establishes the autonomy of language in relation to reality" (Chandler 2002: 28). Languages differ not only in the signifiers they employ, but also in the way they categorise the world according to a system of signifieds. There are no 'natural' concepts that are simply 'reflected' in language (ibid.: 27; Korzybski 1933). Thus, different languages will construct different understandings of the world, which are not strictly translatable (Whorf 1956).

The semiological model of the sign proposed by Saussure, and the various structuralist and post-structuralist approaches it has spawned, have served as a source of inspiration for many anthropologists and archaeologists interested in the symbolic qualities of material culture. Early work by structural anthropologists like Claude Lévi-Strauss (1972), Mary Douglas (1966), and Edmund

Leach (1976), for example, which brought the material world into a framework of structural oppositions ultimately argued to derive from the mind or society, suggested new approaches to scholars studying material culture. For example, anthropologists have observed materially framed oppositions such as light:dark, high:low, pure:impure, and raw:cooked at play in organising and conceptualising space (Bourdieu 1973; Cunningham 1973; Sahlins 1976; Tambiah 1969), food-related practices (Ferro-Luzzi 1977), and ritual activities (Douglas 1966). These material oppositions were often seen as expressive of more abstract, conceptual, or social oppositions, such as male/female, elite/commoner, life/death, and culture/nature.

Sahlins, to provide an illustration, noted how the people of Moalan Island in eastern Fiji saw the world in terms of a series of structural oppositions (Sahlins 1976). Central to their scheme was the opposition between land and sea, which was used to symbolise the dualism between politically inferior and superior social groups (Land People and Chiefs), women and men, and paternal and maternal clansmen. These distinctions were also mediated through the organisation and use of domestic space, oriented along sea–land and upper–lower axes. These axes, and their relative value, Sahlins observed, structured where women and men worked, where various people sat, and where particular objects and items were placed. According to Sahlins then, space, the house, and other aspects of material culture served amongst the Moalans as mediums that structured action and hence society – they were, in his words, "the medium[s] by which a system of culture is realized as an order of action" (Sahlins 1976: 36). Culture, he argued, made use of the natural binary distinctions of the world to transmit and reproduce its arbitrary values, structures, and beliefs.

Within archaeology, the structural approach was first applied by French scholars like Leroi-Gourhan who were directly influenced by Lévi-Strauss (though see Lewis-Williams (2002) for a discussion of an early form of structuralism in the work of the German art historian Max Raphael). Leroi-Gourhan used a structuralist approach to analyse Upper Palaeolithic cave paintings in southern France, and focused specifically on investigating the spatial distribution of signs and animal figures within the caves (Leroi-Gourhan 1968,

1976). He divided signs and animals into male and female types, and argued that their spatial patterning suggested the expression of a binary opposition between male and female that was fundamental to the Palaeolithic cultural and symbolic world. Archaeological interest in structuralism was substantially revived in the late 1970s and early 1980s, and led to the publication in 1982 of a volume entitled *Symbolic and Structural Archaeology* (Hodder 1982a). In the introduction to the volume, as well as in an ethnoarchaeological study of the Nuba of Sudan published the same year (Hodder 1982b), the archaeologist Ian Hodder outlined with greater specificity how structuralist approaches could be applied to an analysis of material culture symbolism. "Material culture", he argued, "can be examined as a structured set of differences" (Hodder 1982c: 7). Hodder accordingly demonstrated the patterning of Nuba material culture in keeping with a set of rules concerned with purity, boundedness, and categorisation, and argued that such rules enabled individuals within a culture to organise and understand experience (Hodder 1982a, 1982b). Hodder was not unaware of the problems with structuralist approaches, but argued nonetheless that "even if structuralism as a whole is generally rejected, the analysis of structure has a potential which has not been exhausted in archaeology" (Hodder 1982a: 1–16).

Hodder and other post-processualists went on to combine analyses of structured sets of material culture signifiers with theories of practice and with post-structural approaches. Shanks and Tilley, for example, stated in 1987 that "[t]he position we are taking is that material culture as communication is a structured sign system" (Shanks & Tilley 1987: 98). They argued that:

> If we take up Saussure's notion of the diacritical sign – i.e. the sign whose value is independent of denoted objects and rests upon its insertion in a system of signs, and Derrida's deconstruction of the notion of the sign as possessing a plenitude of meaning by virtue of its relation to other signs – we arrive at what might be termed the metacritical sign: the sign whose meaning remains radically dispersed through an essentially open chain of signifieds-signifiers. If we conceive of material culture as embodying a series of metacritical signs then we must regard the meaning of the

archaeological record as being always already irreducible to the elements which go to make up and compose that record, characterized as a system of points or units. What we will be involved with will be a search for the structures, and the principles composing those structures, underlying the visible tangibility of the material culture patterning. Our analysis must try to uncover what lies behind the observable presences, to take account of the absences, the co-presences, and co-absences, the similarities and the differences which constitute the patterning of material culture in a particular spatial and temporal context. (ibid.: 102–03)

Like Hodder, Shanks and Tilley saw material culture meanings as essentially emerging out of the relationships between material signifiers within a system or web of signifiers, related through contrasts, oppositions, and similarities. The archaeologist's job was to focus not so much on specific artefacts as the patterned relationships of artefact types to other artefact types – were certain types of artefacts generally found in association with other types of artefacts or apart, and what kinds of localities were they typically present in or absent from? Based on their *context* within the entire pattern of associations, the meanings of artefacts could begin to be worked out, at least in a general way (Hodder 1987, 1991). Thus, for example, Hodder demonstrated that at the Neolithic site of Çatalhöyük in Anatolia, male burials occurred in the back sacred area of the house, which was also associated with paintings of wild animals (Hodder 1990). Men were buried with hunting points and weapons. Women, in contrast, were buried closer to the hearth and domestic area of the house, and were not buried with the equipment used for hunting wild animals. Hodder (ibid.: 10) argued from these and other material culture associations for the following set of structural oppositions:

male	inner (back)	death	wild
female	outer (front)	life	domestic

These structural oppositions became the basis for an argument concerning the use of material culture in the symbolic 'domestication' of the wild during the Neolithic period (ibid.). Hodder noted that much elaborate symbolism addressed death, the wild, and the fearful (Figure 2.2), and that such 'dangerous' symbols were domesticated spatially within the house, by being separated and controlled by the female area of the house (ibid.: 10). The house, therefore, had an important role to play in domestication, through the representation and manipulation of dyadic material symbols that it was used to achieve.

Shanks and Tilley similarly looked at how structural principles generated the patterning of human remains in communal tombs in Neolithic Wessex in England, and in Skåne in Sweden, and argued that distinctions of individual:group, bounded:unbounded, male:female, right:left, and culture:nature were important in Neolithic society, and particularly mortuary practices (Shanks & Tilley 1982). They argued, amongst other things, that the redistribution of bones into collective (rather than individual) sets was a deliberate treatment that served to assert the collective and deny the differences between individuals. Similarly, the regrouping of disarticulated remains according to basic body symmetries such as body:limbs, upper:lower, and left:right, which created symmetry between body parts, expressed a denial of the asymmetrical relationships that dominated relations of production. Their focus was on the way that material culture, through symmetrical principles, could play an ideological role by both naturalising and misrepresenting social practices.

Such structuralist analyses can be found in the work of many archaeologists in the 1980s and 1990s. Mike Parker Pearson and Colin Richards, for example, like Hodder, looked at houses, this time in Neolithic Orkney, and observed oppositions between left and right, and light and dark that they suggested might link to gender distinctions between male and female (Parker Pearson & Richards 1994). They hypothesised that the left-hand, darker area of the house represented an inner domain associated with domestic reproduction and women. Anne Yentsch also saw gender distinctions being expressed through material culture, this time in the use of pottery in English and Anglo-American society (Yentsch 1996). Yentsch, pursuing an explicitly structuralist analysis, argued that pottery was part of a "symbolic language of objects" that served to reinforce social principles by way of physical analogies (ibid.:

Figure 2.2: The skulls and horns of dead cattle embedded within the plastered walls of a building at the Neolithic site of Çatalhöyük in Turkey. Ian Hodder has noted the way in which much symbolism at the famous site concerns death, the wild, and the fearful. Photo Jason Quinlan, courtesy of the Çatalhöyük Research Project.

316). Her analysis indicated that, over time, ceramic vessels were increasingly employed in 'boundary maintenance', to create and reinforce distinctions between a male, public sphere, and a female, private one. Earth-toned ceramics became the primary vessels used in women's social spaces, while white-toned vessels of different types were confined to male spheres, and employed in social display activities. She observed a whole suite of binary oppositions in ceramic vessels that could be traced through the different spaces, food consumption patterns, and social practices of men and women, and that served to reinforce beliefs about the proper roles of each.

Archaeologists, even in the early 1980s, were not unaware of the problems associated with the application of structuralist methods in archaeology. However, their primary concerns were with the failure of structuralism to account for either agency or history (Hodder 1991; Shanks & Tilley 1987). Its development as a method for analysing the ideal symbols of language, and its focus on the abstract as opposed to material were not immediately recognised as particularly problematic. Thus, while Shanks and Tilley observed that material culture as a 'system of discourse' and 'second order type of writing' was not directly assimilable to or reducible to language (Shanks and Tilley 1987: 99), they did embrace the notion that material culture meaning is entirely relational – that is, based on relationships within a system. This is made particularly clear in the following passage, from Jean Baudrillard's *For a Critique of the Political Economy of the Sign*, cited appreciatively in their 1987 discussion of material culture:

> ... the empirical 'object,' given in its contingency of form, colour, material, function, and discourse ... is a myth. How often it has been wished away! But the object is *nothing*. It is nothing but the different types of relations and significations that converge, contradict themselves, and twist around, as such – the hidden logic that not only arranges this bundle of relations, but directs the manifest discourse that overlays and occludes it. (Baudrillard 1981: 63)

Shanks and Tilley accordingly take no issue with Saussure's assertion that the relationship between signifier and signified is arbitrary, even in the case of material culture signifiers (Shanks and Tilley 1987; see also Tilley 1989).

Not all archaeologists and anthropologists have shared this perspective on the way material things act as symbols, and a number have drawn attention in particular to the way that symbols may be 'motivated' rather than arbitrary. Victor Turner's extensive mid-1960s analysis of ritual symbols among the Ndembu of Zambia, for example, explored in some detail the links between material signifiers and the concepts they signify (Turner 1967). Indeed, his definition of a symbol as "a thing regarded by general consent as naturally typifying or representing or recalling something *by possession of analogous properties* or *by association in fact* or thought" (ibid.: 19; my emphasis) suggests a distinctly non-Saussurean understanding of material signifiers. Turner's discussion of the polarization of symbolic meaning represents an early and admirable attempt to try to understand exactly how material signifiers relate to the concepts they signify. Turner defined two poles of symbolic meaning, the 'ideological' pole and the 'sensory' pole. Clustered at the ideological pole are *significata* that refer to, for example, components of the moral and social orders of society, principles of social organisation, or norms and values, while around the sensory pole are normally found *significata* that refer to natural and physiological phenomena and processes (ibid.: 28). Turner noted that at the sensory pole, meaning content is normally closely related to the outward form of the symbol (ibid.). Thus, the mudyi tree means breast milk for the Ndembu because it exudes a kind of milky white latex (ibid.). The tree as a symbol in Ndembu society refers not only to breastfeeding, but also by extension the social ties between mother and child, and matriliny in general (ibid.: 20–21). The relationship between material signifier and the concepts it signifies, even if not predictable, is far from arbitrary, and draws upon the properties of the signifier.

Even anthropologists whose approaches have been unabashedly structuralist have recognised the non-arbitrariness of material symbols. Mary Douglas, for example, distinguishes between the horizontal and vertical dimensions of symbolic analysis in her book *Natural Symbols* (Douglas 1996). Horizontal analysis concerns the usual structural investigation of the relation of elements within a system. The vertical dimension, on the other hand, concerns references to "physical and social experience" (ibid.: 78) that she argues must be studied if we are to understand the basis of natural symbols. Even Lévi-Strauss, who played a key role in developing the structuralist method, came to recognise that symbolic systems were not, as he had initially thought, completely arbitrary, but were rather motivated by the natural properties of symbolic materials or the way they were commonly used by people (as discussed in Layton 1997: 87).

The views of a number of post-processualist archaeologists concerning material signifiers have demonstrated similar patterns of evolution. Ian Hodder, for example, writing in 1992, referred to a gradual realisation that he had "overemphasised the arbitrary nature of material culture symbolism" in earlier writings (Hodder 1992). Hodder's writings throughout the 1980s show an increasing recognition that Saussure's language model was in a number of important ways not ideal for examining material culture. In an important article published in 1989, for example, Hodder argued that material culture meanings were often far from arbitrary, and pointed out that texts and discourse, which were routed in practice, were a better model for understanding material culture than language. He suggested that "material culture meanings come about partly through experience rather than solely through an arbitrary system of categories" (Hodder 1989: 258).

The archaeologist Christopher Tilley's understanding of material culture symbols can be seen to undergo a similar transformation. While his early writings stress the linguistic model of Saussure and the way material culture meanings are built up through contrasts and similarities with other symbols in complex webs of significance (Shanks & Tilley 1987; Tilley 1989, 1990), his 1999 book *Metaphor and Material Culture* gave significantly more consideration to the ways in which meaning relates to the form and use, in ordinary and ritual practice, of the material entities employed as metaphors (Tilley 1999). Like Hodder, Tilley came to recognise that material culture signifiers are not arbitrary, and are indeed in many respects very different from linguistic signifiers. He stated:

> It can be argued that material metaphors, although inherently polysemous, are always likely to be motivated, or take on meaning, in a manner different from language because, in any given culture, they are relatively constrained. The three questions "what does this artefact mean?" "what does this artefact do?" and "why was this artefact chosen rather than another?" are intimately connected. This is because material forms, unlike words, are not communicating meaning but actively *doing* something in the world. (ibid.: 265)

Tilley's consideration of metaphor is interesting not only because it demonstrates a departure from Saussurean frameworks for understanding material signifiers, but also because it implies an overlap with the competing theories of Charles Sanders Peirce, the founder of semiotics (Peirce 1998). As a number of archaeologists have now pointed out, Peirce's model of the sign is in many ways more appropriate than Saussure's for understanding the representational qualities of material culture (Bauer 2002; Knappett 2005; Preucel & Bauer 2001). While many post-processualists made do with tacking notions of agency and practice onto a semiological model of the sign that did not take people or the world into account, semiotics actually builds both into the sign model. In contrast to Saussure's dyadic sign, Peirce proposed a three-part model that took account of sign users and variable interpretations of the sign's meaning, as well as the process of sign interpretation (Peirce 1998). He also outlined three modes of relationship between sign vehicles and their referents, only one of which – the symbolic – was arbitrary. The iconic mode, which includes metaphor, was non-arbitrary since it featured a formal resemblance between the signifier and that which is signified, as in the case of portraits, cartoons, and scale models. The index mode was non-arbitrary in a different way: it involves a direct connection between the sign and the signified, as, for example, the connection between the moving weathervane and a gust of wind (Figure 2.3), or between smoke and a fire. Understanding of the relationship between material signifiers and the concepts they signify is clearly enriched by recognising these variable modes, and the multiple non-arbitrary ways in which material signs function. As Peirce and other semioticians point out, the modes are not mutually exclusive, and much signification does in fact involve some combination of the three of them.

Abstracting the World

Signs then, particularly material ones, are frequently non-arbitrary. That is, the forms they take often have a non-arbitrary basis in the real, material world. Clay is in many societies a symbol of fertility and of women, for example, because things grow in it and it can be used to create a myriad of new forms (Boivin 2004a). Stone is, in contrast, often a symbol of men and of things, like lineage and ancestors, that transcend time because it is hard, like men's bodies, and resistant to destruction and weathering (Figure 2.4; ibid.; Parker Pearson & Ramilisonina 1998). The meanings of signs are not determined by their physical properties and uses, but they are certainly often motivated by them. This motivation of

Figure 2.3: Weathervane. The semiotic model of Charles Sanders Peirce argues that there are different ways in which signs and ideas can be related. In the index mode – as with a weathervane, for example – there is a direct, non-arbitrary relationship between sign and signified. Photo George Bosela.

material culture meanings is now widely recognised in archaeology and anthropology, sometimes explicitly and other times implicitly. What is not as well recognised, however, is the implications this has for understanding more complex sign systems, involving a myriad of inter-connected signs and meanings. Such sign systems include thought schemas, cosmologies, cultural concepts, and social constructs. While individual, non-linguistic signs are widely recognised as partially motivated by material phenomena, complex sign systems still tend to be conceived as autonomous, abstract constructions of the human mind or of human social relations. Despite frequent assertions to the contrary, much anthropology

Figure 2.4: Stone symbolises particular concepts and ideas, like masculinity and ancestral lineage, for example, because it is physically hard and resistant to weathering. The relationship between sign and signified is not arbitrary. Photo Edwin Pijpe.

and archaeology maintains a firm distinction between culture and nature, between sign systems and the natural and material phenomena whose apparent purpose is to represent them.

The constructivist perspective that sees symbols as a means of projecting pre-existing cultural and social codes onto the material world can be traced back through some of the most prominent names in anthropology, including Émile Durkheim, Claude Lévi-Strauss, Mary Douglas, and Marshall Sahlins. While these scholars disagreed as to where to root the concepts of society – for Durkheim they were socially determined, while for Lévi-Strauss they were the outcome of universal structures of the human brain, for example – all privileged abstract social or cultural concepts over the natural and material worlds. Even when giving specific consideration to the economy and material goods, for example, Mary Douglas, writing with Baron Isherwood, granted priority to the social and cultural. "Forget that commodities are good for eating; forget their usefulness", they advised, "and try instead the idea that commodities are good for thinking" (Douglas & Isherwood 1996: 40–41). Food, space, clothing, transport, sanitation, all were seen primarily as markers of social and cultural categories – the social and cultural world projected onto the material (Figure 2.5; see also Douglas 1966, 1996). Sahlins' views on material things were similar; he saw the 'system of objects' of a society as the "transposition on another plane of the scheme of society" (Sahlins 1976: 37). For Sahlins, as for many other anthropologists, the cultural world subsumed the material, and symbolic or meaningful reason took precedence over practical reason. Cultural schemes and meanings were arbitrary because they could not be predicted.

The introduction of more practice-oriented approaches in anthropology and archaeology, beginning in the 1970s, may have been expected to result in greater attention to the material world, given their critique of the way structuralist approaches ignored history, the real world, and social agency. This was not, however, generally the case. Practice theory frequently drew attention to what people did, rather than the world they did it in, which at best consisted of a series of material props for acting out strategies and creating dispositions (Bourdieu 1977; Moore 1986). Thus, in an extensive theoretical discussion of the role of space in social practice, for example, the anthropologist Henrietta Moore paid virtually no attention at all to the actual materiality of space (Moore 1986: chapters 1 and 5). Moore advocated understanding space as a cultural text, and argued "that spatial and literary texts have similar properties" (ibid.: 82). While action and movement in space were taken into account, they were described as discourse, and compared in detail to speech and writing. Moore's discussion, framed as a challenge to structuralism and traditional semiotic anthropology, nonetheless reproduced their fundamental predisposition to abstraction. She also maintained a firm distinction between culture and nature, asserting that "[t]hrough classifying the world, people separate themselves from nature and in doing so create a cultural order which is not that of nature" (ibid.: 2).

The pre-eminence of the social and cultural world over the material has similarly been stressed by Hodder, who while cautioning that the study of material culture signs cannot be limited to a

Figure 2.5: Pottery for sale in Oaxaca. Mary Douglas argued that commodities were good for thinking. Photo L. M. Powell.

linguistic type of analysis, nonetheless argued that "we need to understand the way in which the biological and physical world *is embedded within* social and cultural meanings" (Hodder 1992: 211; my emphasis). Thus, while Hodder made some very insightful arguments about the role that material culture and the environment could play in generating cultural frameworks of thought in his piece entitled "This Is Not an Article about Material Culture as Text" (Hodder 1989), he also seems to have found it difficult to escape from the notion that the social and culture encompass the material and biological. The archaeologists Shanks and Tilley, writing in the mid-1980s, also gave emphasis to the world created by social and cultural activity, as the following quote suggests:

> The form of social relations provides a grid into which
> the signifying force of material culture becomes inserted to
> extend, define, redefine, bolster up or transform that grid.
> The social relations are themselves articulated into a field
> of meaning partially articulated through thought and lan-
> guage and capable of reinforcement through the objectified
> and reified meanings inscribed in material culture. (Shanks
> & Tilley 1987: 102)

Material culture according to this view is once again a prop, something which does little more than enable or assist social processes. It is 'inserted' into a pre-existing social grid. Shanks and Tilley
echoed Mary Douglas in arguing that the primary significance of
material goods was not their pragmatic, utilitarian or technological
use-value, but their significative exchange value (ibid.: 105).

While Tilley's more recent work, like some of Hodder's, grants
more importance to the material world, and scholars like Tim
Ingold (2000) have strived to incorporate environments and materiality into social theory, it is nonetheless the case that anthropology and post-processual archaeology, along with many other
fields, remain dominated by constructivist approaches that privi-
lege culture over nature. Like material culture and landscapes, for
example, bodies and emotions have also been seen to be culturally
constructed, and by extension arbitrary. Within such formulations,
social and cultural constructions give shape to thoughts and activities, and material and biological entities, if they are recognised at
all, serve a primarily supporting, passive role in the process.

Illuminating the Unknown: Sensual Cosmologies
and Material Thoughts

In the remainder of this chapter, I wish to challenge this view
of the role of materiality and the body in human thought. I do not
accept that it is always the case that ideas, concepts, and social

strategies exist first and are then materialised by attaching them to appropriate symbols, in order to make them more easily understood, or to reinforce, communicate, or enact them. I wish to assert, rather, that a far more interesting argument can be made that, in many cases, ideas and cultural understandings do not precede, but rather are helped into becoming, by the material world and human engagement with it. Like the relationship between material signifiers and signifieds, the relationship between things like material environments, technologies, and bodies, and complex cultural systems of symbols like cosmologies and social constructs is also often far from arbitrary. This is not to make the reverse error of granting priority to the material world, and giving it a determinative role in social and cultural life, but rather to argue that supposedly abstract things like cosmologies can also be deeply material and sensual things. Human thought has not only used the world as a prop for expressing itself, but has, in fact, often been enabled by that world.

Studies that support this view actually go back a long way in anthropology. Turner's analysis of colour symbolism amongst the Ndembu, for example, discussed earlier in this chapter, led him to conclude that colour meaning was embedded in physiological processes (Turner 1967). Colours, according to Turner, were not arbitrary symbols that obtained their meanings purely from their relations to other colours in a colour system (as Sahlins (1976), for example, attempted to argue), but instead derived their meanings from the experience of organic processes, and the fluids, secretions, and waste products released by the human body, including blood, semen, milk, urine, and faeces. Turner hypothesised that the earliest symbols were colour symbols that represented products of the human body whose emission, spilling, or production is associated with heightened emotion. What gave the colour symbols force was the fact that the experience of these organic processes and colours was at the same time the experience of social relationships. Red, for example, was no abstract symbol, but derived its meaning from the implications – for humans, their social relationships and their existential experience – of the appearance of blood during the course of pivotal events like birth and death. "Culture, the superorganic", Turner was led to assert, "has an intimate connection with the organic" (Turner 1967: 89). Turner's recognition of the way ritual systems and symbols were so closely linked to organic processes and material entities led him to argue against the Durkheimian notion that the origin of symbolic systems lay in forms of social organisation: "Against this I would postulate that the human organism and its crucial experiences are the *fons et origo* of all classifications" (ibid.: 90).

While the need to specify some sort of ultimate origin for culture is perhaps outdated, Turner's recognition of the important role played by bodily processes, materials, and experiences in human thought is precociously contemporary. Equally relevant are Fredrik Barth's thoughts on knowledge and ritual systems, which emerged in the context of ethnographic study amongst the Baktaman of highland Papua New Guinea and were published in the mid-1970s (Barth 1975). Barth's findings, based on a detailed analysis of the rituals and ritual symbols of the agricultural/hunter-gatherer Baktaman, led him to several important conclusions. One was that Baktaman symbols or idioms did not derive their meaning from their contrast with other symbols within a system, but rather from certain physical features and qualities that made them appropriate representatives of an idea or abstract thought. Thus, for example, the cassowary feather, a key ritual symbol, was employed as a symbol of senior men not because of its contrast to other types of feathers, but because the cassowary bird is enormous, swift, and elusive, and eats the sacred pandanus fruit. The pandanus fruit is in turn also a symbol of senior men because of its phallic shape. Barth thus argued that the idioms of Baktaman ritual could best be understood not as arbitrary symbols, but rather as metaphors, drawing on some inherent connection between form and meaning. This realisation led him to distinguish between digital and analogic codes. Digital codes, like computer programs and language, involved arbitrary symbols whose meaning derived from their place within the code as a whole and only within it (ibid.: 207–08). Structuralist anthropology had focused entirely on the analysis of such codes. Barth argued that Baktaman ritual involved instead the use of analogic coding, in which inherently independent metaphors were interlinked to create messages or understanding, which were not necessarily internally coherent or consistent. He critiqued the structuralist drive towards order and complete internal consistency. He saw instead in Baktaman ritual codes a loose, analogic structure that was more appropriately compared to the chords and harmonies of music (ibid.: 238) than the binary language of computers.

Perhaps even more important, however, was Barth's assertion that ritual and other symbolic systems did not just re-create codes that were expressed in mythic, spatial, culinary, and other practices, as the structuralists would have it. Instead, Barth argued that "the essence of metaphor is the use of the familiar to grasp the elusive and unrecognised, rather than the mere ordering of phenomena by homology" (ibid.: 199). Metaphor involved the use of something familiar or distinctive as a model or analogy for something less clearly conceptualised, which was thus *illuminated* by the analogy (ibid.). For example, Barth described Baktaman religion as a fertility cult concerned with growth and agriculture. A pervasive group of symbols used in Baktaman rites were dew, fat, fur, and hair (Figure 2.6). He argued that the Baktaman, who lacked calendars and other ways of handling time, as well as scales through which to specify linear measures and cumulative results, possessed few familiar prototypes which could be used as metaphors for the growth process. Specifically, he argued that

> in their ritual expression of the process which they celebrate and desire, the Baktaman seem to be groping for something only diffusely understood, and the metaphors used are such as can provide a minimal cognitive grasp of it: Dew accumulates on leaves. Fat grows inside the pig and makes its skin hard and tight. Hair grows out where it is cut off. Fur covers the body, vegetation covers the ground. All these are images that can evoke the idea of increase; and rubbing with them, extending them as with a wig, or burning them and transferring them by smoke as with the fur of sacrifices, are all operations which serve as concrete symbols for the process. (ibid.: 200–01)

Barth thus demonstrated how the material world helps to create concepts and understanding, and is not just a plane to which these concepts are attached. People use the world and its material richness to think with, not just to re-create thoughts they already have. In a similar manner, rites *do* something rather than just *say* something (ibid.: 209).

These views helped Barth to avoid simple nature–culture dichotomies; he was clear that the Baktaman did not distinguish between nature and culture, and that for them the environment was one in which all places, species, and processes were "understood as being basically of one unitary kind" (ibid.: 195). Accordingly, Barth did not root meaning in either the material or cultural worlds, but rather in the activity of people. He emphasised that symbolic meaning was not determined solely by the formal properties of things, but rather by the way things were used and operated upon in the course of everyday and ritual activity (ibid.: 173, 189). Thus, Barth emphasised human engagement with, as opposed to distanced contemplation of, the material world as critical to the process of meaning production.

Thinking with Metaphors in Everyday Life

We have now seen that both Turner and, more explicitly, Barth recognised the significance of metaphor in understanding ritual and ritual symbols. More recently, the importance of metaphor in general human cognitive and linguistic processes has also been highlighted in a series of groundbreaking and widely influential publications by George Lakoff and Mark Johnson (Lakoff & Johnson 1999, 2003). Lakoff, a linguist, and Johnson, a philosopher, have argued together that metaphor, rather than being a minor poetic or rhetorical device of peripheral, linguistic interest, is in fact key to the way humans think and understand the world. Their work suggests that the insights of Turner and Barth concerning the relationship between the material/organic and the conceptual have relevance well beyond discussions of ritual in anthropology.

Lakoff and Johnson's argument is that metaphors are far more pervasive in our language than traditional linguistic models recognise. They point out that most linguistic metaphors actually fall outside the domain of figurative language, and are part of what

Figure 2.6: Dew on a leaf. Frederic Barth argued that engagement with material elements like dew enabled the Baktaman to model and grasp abstract concepts like growth and increase. Photo Ove Tøpfer.

is called literal language. They give the example of the pervasive TIME IS MONEY metaphor, of which the following expressions are some examples:

> TIME IS MONEY
>
> You're *wasting* my time. This gadget will *save* you hours. I don't *have* the time to *give* you. How do you *spend* your time these days? That flat tire *cost* me an hour. I've *invested* a lot of time in her. You're *running* out of time. You need to *budget* your time. Is that *worth your while*? (Lakoff & Johnson 2003: 7–8)

Lakoff and Johnson argue that metaphors like TIME IS MONEY are not just linguistic metaphors, but also conceptual ones. The TIME IS MONEY metaphor actually structures how we conceive of time – as something that can be spent, wasted, budgeted, invested wisely or poorly, saved, or squandered (ibid.: 8). The metaphor is not arbitrary of course; it has developed out of our experience of living in an industrialised, capitalist society in which work is associated with the time it takes and time is precisely quantified. However, this understanding of the relationship between time and money has come to structure our understanding of time outside of labour contexts; it structures our very understanding of what time – which as a concept evades simple understanding – actually *is*.

Not all metaphors are as apparent as the TIME IS MONEY one. Many metaphors, for example, have to do with spatial orientation, and our basic, physical experience of the world. For example (ibid.: 15):

> HAPPY IS UP; SAD IS DOWN
> I'm feeling *up*. That *boosted* my spirits. My spirits *rose*. You're in *high* spirits. Thinking about her always gives me a *lift*. I'm feeling *down*. I'm *depressed*. He's really *low* these days. I *fell* into a depression. My spirits *sank*.

> CONSCIOUS IS UP; UNCONSCIOUS IS DOWN
> Wake *up*. Get *up*. I'm *up* already. He *rises* early in the morning. He *fell* asleep. He *dropped* off to sleep. He's *under* hypnosis. He *sank* into a coma.

Lakoff and Johnson argue that these spatial metaphors, which pervade our everyday language, have a basis in our physical, bodily experience. Sadness and depression go along with a drooping posture, positive emotional states with a more erect one (ibid.). Humans and most other animals sleep lying down and stand up when they awaken (ibid.).

Conceptual metaphors then are rooted in aspects of both physical and cultural experience – "the kind of beings we are and the way we interact with our physical and cultural environments" (ibid.: 119). What we use metaphor to do is conceptualise one type of experience in terms of another. Usually we use a more physical experience to conceptualise a more abstract one. In *Metaphors We Live By*, we find Barth's arguments about metaphor reiterated in a much more systematic way:

> Because so many of the concepts that are important to us are either abstract or not clearly delineated in our experience (the emotions, ideas, time, etc.), we need to get a grasp on them by means of other concepts that we understand in clearer terms (spatial orientations, objects, etc.). . . . We have tried with examples to give some indication of just how extensive a role metaphor plays in the way we function, the way we conceptualize our experience, and the way we speak. (ibid.: 115)

Lakoff and Johnson describe how our conceptual system is grounded in our experience of the world (ibid.: 117), including experience acquired through our bodies, our interactions with our physical environment, and our interactions with other people.

Bodily and Material Metaphors

While Lakoff and Johnson's work focuses in particular on linguistic metaphors, it is clear from the anthropological examples discussed in this chapter that metaphors can also be bodily and material. Another nice anthropological example of the grounding of a concept in a non-linguistic metaphor can also be found in Arnold Van Gennep's theory of the tripartite structure of rites of passage (Van Gennep 1960). Based on an analysis of rites of passage in various cultural contexts, Van Gennep argued that they often featured a three-part sequence in which initiates are first separated from one social grouping, then shifted to a liminal, "betwixt and between" status, and then incorporated into a new social grouping. This sequence is conceived in terms of actual physical movement, and rites of passage therefore frequently involve changes in the spatial location of those undergoing a social transformation. In terms of Lakoff and Johnson's model, what Van Gennep did was to recognise the cross-cultural significance of the metaphor we could describe as RITES OF PASSAGE ARE A JOURNEY TO A NEW PLACE. The more abstract transformation from one social status to another is conceptualised in terms of the experience of a physical journey to a new place.

My ethnoarchaeological studies of domestic space in Balathal in western India, addressed at the outset of this book, demonstrated some of the ways in which this pervasive metaphor is expressed materially in rural Rajasthan. In Balathal, doorways and entrances are frequently coated with red plaster, red being a colour that I have argued is associated with transformations in rural Rajasthan. Doorways are also frequently embellished with painted designs and various paraphernalia, particularly on the occasion of important ceremonies and festivals (Figure 2.7). These material features highlight the link between passages and transformations. As Helen Lambert has also argued, doorways and entrances in Rajasthan are in some ways also dangerous, liminal places (betwixt and between) that require protection (Lambert 1994), and their embellishment perhaps serves this role as well. These associations with passage, transformation, and liminality are rooted in the physical experience of moving through doorways, between one space and another, and help explain the use of doorways in rites of passage and other rituals in Rajasthan. For example, at weddings, the bride and groom pass under a ritual *toran*, or gate, as part of the process of their social transformation.

Christopher Tilley has also discussed material metaphors at length in his book *Metaphor and Material Culture* (1999). My point here is, however, to emphasise the use of material metaphors as devices not just for expressing, but also for understanding. I wish to stress the way doorways and entrances do not just express or represent social transformations, but also help to conceptualise them and thus effect them. It is not just that the passage from one social status to the next is *expressed* in terms of a passage through a doorway. Passage through doorways as a general physical and cultural experience also helps *to create our understanding* of what a social transformation is, and thus *achieve* such a transformation in a credible and convincing way through a series of ritual activities. The perceptual experience of passing through a doorway from one

Figure 2.7: Embellished entrance in Rajasthan. Doorways, in Rajasthan as elsewhere, often serve as a metaphor for transformation. Photo Nicole Boivin.

space into a different one helps lead to the metaphorical conceptualisation of a social change as a spatial movement from one space to another (Figure 2.8).

This example assists us in understanding why material metaphors can be so powerful. With material metaphors, there is no necessary conversion of an experiential metaphor into a verbal one – indeed, as in the case of doorways, the same kind of embodied and material experience that led to the conceptual metaphor in the first place may subsequently be drawn upon to demonstrate, to evoke, or to understand a concept. Thus, to say that doorways and passage through them *signify* liminality and social transformations is in many ways to ignore the way material metaphors function, even if linguistic restrictions largely demand such a simplification. An important part of the way material metaphors work is by appealing to the experiential and the non-linguistic. Tilley discusses this fact in the theoretical sections of *Metaphor and Material Culture* (1999), but in his case studies, material metaphors are often discussed as though they are simply physically representing pre-existing social and cultural concepts, or acting as a medium for the reproduction, negotiation, or transformation of such concepts. Instead it needs to be recognised that material metaphors do something very unique, by addressing a non-linguistic side to understanding. This recognition will lead the way to a better and fuller comprehension of what often seem to be very strange uses of material items in ritual and other contexts.

What can be recognised from the above discussion is the way that the things in our world – our material environments – play a role in structuring our concepts. This is obviously a very interesting fact, particularly for those working towards understanding how the material world impacts on culture and society. However, it is important to note that culture also has a critical role to play. It is essential not to replace one determinism with another. Neither nature nor culture has a determining role to play in structuring human thought, and it must instead be recognised that they come together in the thought process. As Lakoff and Johnson are careful to point out, things in the world play a role in constraining our conceptual system, but only through our experience of them (Lakoff & Johnson 2003: 154). Thus, while they hypothesise that, for example, the different ecological zones people inhabit will impact on the development of conceptual systems (ibid.: 146), they also stress that culture constrains experience, such that experiences will vary from culture to culture (ibid.: 154). Metaphorical concepts emerge out of our active engagement with a material and social environment in culturally constrained ways (see also Quinn 1991). The resulting metaphors radically shape our understanding of reality.

The emergence of metaphors out of human engagement with a world that is simultaneously natural and cultural is nicely illustrated in an example from Alfred Gell's book *The Anthropology of Time* (Gell 1992). In Chapter 10 of the book, Gell addressed two

Figure 2.8: Moving through a doorway, from one space into another, is a physical transformation that can help us to understand conceptual transformations, for example, from one social stage to another. Photo Ben Mizen.

very different time regimes, one found amongst the Umeda of New Guinea, and the other amongst the Muria Gonds of Central India. The Muria Gonds share a time metaphor similar to that described by Lakoff and Johnson for the capitalist West, which Gell argued is summed up by the word *pabe*, meaning 'disposable time, opportunity'. This word is most frequently encountered as part of the expression *pabe mayon*, which is used to refuse assistance, and essentially means "I have not got time" (ibid.: 87). The Muria thus metaphorically conceive of time as a scarce resource. They divide time up into named months, consult published almanacs detailing the best time to do things, articulate the year with first-fruits and other ceremonies, and are capable of detailing, with precision, the annual cycle of activities. They are able to and frequently do make arrangements for social and ritual events months or even years in advance within a rigid calendrical framework (ibid.: 89). The Umeda concept of time could not be more different. The Umeda have no equivalent to the *pabe* concept, no names for months, and no idea of how many months there are in the year. They do not celebrate first-fruits ceremonies, and only very weakly distinguish the seasons as wet and dry. They lack weeks as well as weekly markets of the type attended by the Muria Gonds.

Muria Gond and Umeda metaphors for and concepts of time are thus radically different, and Gell argued, interestingly, that the difference derives in large part from the contrasting subsistence systems practised by the two societies. The Muria Gonds are rice farmers (Figure 2.9), and producing rice requires the observance of a strict schedule according to which particular operations are carried out at particular times. Rice production is a difficult process in which rice is grown in an artificial environment, and much labour is required to carry out sowing, weeding, and harvesting at particular times. The failure to perform particular activities at particular designated times is essentially equivalent to a failure to perform them at all – they cannot just be postponed. Each season is thus associated with sharply distinctive activities, which gives the year a decidedly heterogeneous aspect. In contrast, the Umeda subsist primarily on sago, a plant that takes up to fifteen years to mature and that is processed year-round. Seasons are only weakly distinguished, and there is no overall sago production schedule. Instead, the sago production process is shifting, improvisatory, and uncoordinated. Autonomous family groups meander through dense forest from one sago stand to another throughout a year that, compared to the Muria Gond year, is remarkably homogeneous. Gell therefore argued that

> different societies or social strata, operating under different ecological circumstances, employing different technologies and faced with different kinds of long-term and short-term planning problems, construct quite different cultural vocabularies for handling temporal relationships. (ibid.)

Figure 2.9: Rice harvesting in India. Alfred Gell argued that rice culti-vation, which requires a very temporally precise schedule, helped lead to a particular notion of time amongst the Muria Gonds. Photo Dorian Fuller.

While Gell's argument, focused as it was on a critique of Bloch's claim that cyclic ideas of time are confined to ritual contexts and hierarchical societies, stressed the ecological and economic basis of time concepts, it is clear that social and cultural factors also have an important role to play. The Muria Gonds are very much part of a market economy and national Indian educational and calendrical systems. It is also unlikely that they have not been influenced by Western notions of time. As Gell noted, one of the few English words to have entered their vocabulary is 'time' (ibid.). Lakoff and Johnson make the important point that the TIME IS MONEY metaphor is spreading globally as part of the Westernisation process (Lakoff & Johnson 2003), and the Muria Gond notion of time as a scarce resource may well have to do in part with cultural influence from the West. How deeply rooted the time-as-a-resource concept may be within Indian civilisation

Table 2.1: Technology and artefact-oriented metaphors discussed by Lakoff and Johnson, together with selected examples of their use in everyday language (more examples of each metaphor can be found in Lakoff and Johnson (2003))

METAPHOR	EXAMPLES
THE MIND IS A MACHINE	We're still trying to *grind out* the solution to this equation. My mind just isn't *operating* today. Boy, the *wheels are turning* now!
THE MIND IS A BRITTLE OBJECT	Her ego is very *fragile*. The experience *shattered* him. I'm *going to pieces*. His mind *snapped*.
IDEAS ARE CUTTING INSTRUMENTS	That's an *incisive* idea. That *cuts right to the heart* of the matter. That was a *cutting* remark. He's *sharp*. He has a *razor* wit.
IDEAS ARE PRODUCTS	We're really *turning (churning, cranking, grinding) out* new ideas. We've *generated* a lot of ideas this week. His *intellectual productivity* has decreased in recent years. It's a rough idea; it needs to be *refined*.
IDEAS ARE COMMODITIES	It's important how you *package* your ideas. He won't *buy* that. That idea won't *sell*. He's been a source of *valuable* ideas.
THEORIES ARE BUILDINGS	The theory needs more *support*. The argument is *shaky*. We need some more facts or the argument will *fall apart*. We need to *construct* a *strong* argument for that. The argument *collapsed*. We will show that theory to be without *foundation*.

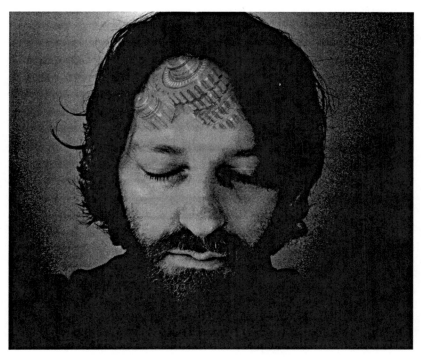

Figure 2.10: The Mind Is a Machine. The metaphor of the mind as some kind of machine is a pervasive one. Artwork Mark Devitt.

itself, which has long featured urban centres, markets, and global trade networks, also of course needs to be considered.

Technological Understanding

The idea that the introduction of new metaphors can also lead to the introduction of new concepts, as with the spread of the TIME IS MONEY metaphor (Lakoff and Johnson 2003), is an interesting one. Given that a number of the metaphors Lakoff and Johnson discuss are based on technology and material culture (see Table 2.1), it is tempting to consider the possible ways in which technological change has impacted on our conceptualisation of the world. For example, has the metaphor THE MIND IS A MACHINE (Figure 2.10) impacted on how we actually understand the mind in our industrial era? Certain observations suggest that it has. For example, structuralists like Lévi-Strauss conceived of the mind as operating according to a binary code similar to a computer. Likewise, the use of robot studies to help understand how the mind functions, as undertaken by some cognitive scientists, rests on the premise that there are real parallels between such artificial machines and the human mind (see 'Ecological embodiment' section later in this chapter). Elizabeth Hallam and Jenny Hockey have furthermore described the way in which understanding of how memory works has altered as the culturally available media for storage have changed – from the chest to the computer, for example (Hallam & Hockey 2001). Thus, our understanding of the still very mysterious functioning of the mind, both at the everyday and academic levels, does seem to draw upon our much more clear understanding of how machines work.

The link between technology, linguistic metaphors, and philosophical and conceptual understandings has also been explored by Bill Sillar (1996). Like Lakoff and Johnson, Sillar notes the dominance in Western thinking of the IDEAS ARE CUTTING INSTRUMENTS metaphor. He goes further than them, however, in linking the linguistic metaphor to a specifically European fascination with metal and blade technology (ibid.: 260). As he observes, such technology was central to much of the region's social and technological development, and was widely applied in a range of processes, including vegetable processing, carpentry, and tailoring (ibid.). He also notes the central importance of aristocratic swordsmen to the development of Iron Age and later feudal society in Europe (Figure 2.11). Sillar suggests that "because blade technology was considered prestigious and associated with 'sharp' ideas it was drawn upon and developed in new directions" in Europe (ibid.). Our understanding of ideas as cutting instruments is therefore not random, or based purely on the physical experience of using cutting technology, but rather arises out of a technological tradition privileged over a long period within our culture.

Sillar suggests that techniques and technologies can serve as cultural metaphors that help to shape society. He discusses 'technology as philosophy' (ibid.: 272), and notes the interdependence of technological practices and philosophical and ideological notions. Different societies will feature different understandings that will

Figure 2.11: Medieval Spanish coat of armour with sword. The distinctive dress of medieval knights underscores the European emphasis on metal and blade technology that Bill Sillar has highlighted. Photo Felix Atsoram.

draw in part on their varying technological traditions. Thus, in the Andes, a very different kind of technology was privileged than was seen in Europe. This technology both shaped and was shaped by a particular set of cultural values and ideas, and involved an emphasis on grinding and crushing. Pre-Hispanic warfare in the Andes, for example, did not involve the use of blades and cutting, but was instead dependent on clubs and missiles to deliver crushing blows (Lechtman 1984). Grinding was also very commonly used in food production, clay production for ceramic making, and other areas of Andean technology. Thus, the same linguistic terms were used to describe the 'grinding' of flour and the 'grinding down' of the enemy.

Sillar argues that this sharing of techniques "reflects a particularly Andean perception of how to process materials, which requires things to be ground down before they can be productive" (Sillar 1996: 267). Crushing is not just a metaphor of destruction, but also of enculturation and re-creation. Andean technology reflected a particular cultural philosophy that was at the same time a technological philosophy. It is difficult – and as with the dilemma of the chicken and the egg, probably pointless – to try to determine which one was the origin of the other.

What these various examples suggest is that understanding the basis of metaphors and their associated concepts will, at least in some cases, involve looking at technological history. To fully understand language and thought today, as well as in the past, it will be necessary to understand the material and technological developments whose history is embedded in them. This fact emphasises even further the relationship between human thinking and the material world. It also draws the historical disciplines into the study of language and culture in a new way, since technological developments are of course primarily recoverable through disciplines like archaeology, history, and ethnohistory. All have something of interest to contribute to the investigation of the metaphorical underpinnings of human thought. It is also clear from the previous discussion that metaphors, as many have now argued, are not just linguistic but also material. The cultural concepts they clarify and create are therefore also material concepts, the result of a coming together of the abstract and the material.

Modelling the Mind: Bringing Back the Body

So symbols are not arbitrary, and symbolic systems – concepts and cosmologies, for example, that bring together multiple symbols – are not arbitrary either. Both are clearly motivated, to some degree, by the world that symbol-making humans inhabit, and by their engagement with that world. Culture does not hover, 'superorganically', above nature, nor can culture and nature be clearly delineated. Instead, culture and nature are intermeshed and mutually constituting. "The realm of symbols", as the cultural psychiatrist

Laurence Kirmayer writes, "lives in and among the world of things" (Kirmayer 1992: 342). What is suggested, therefore, is that in order to understand how human beings communicate symbolically and how they think, it is necessary to understand not just minds and brains, but also bodies and environments. And, indeed, this is what a whole range of disciplines from medical anthropology to cognitive science are discovering. To conclude this chapter, I will therefore briefly address some examples of theoretical and empirical studies of the mind and of cognitive thought that take into account its organic and material context. I will first explore studies that take account of the body's role in cognitive processes, and then consider even more holistic perspectives that also attempt to recognise the equally important role of the material world in cognition, and that stress the need to study the *ecological* facets of embodiment.

"Bodies are in." So declared Arthur Frank in 1990, in a discussion of the emergence of the body as a major topic of interest within the social sciences and humanities. Faced with the recognition that the body had been effectively ignored in most work on human thought and society, practitioners in a range of subjects from sociology (Bourdieu 1977), philosophy (Foucault 1977, 1980; Lakoff & Johnson 2003), and anthropology (Csordas 1990; Jackson 1989), to history (Connerton 1989) and archaeology (Hamilakis et al. 2002; Meskell 1996, 1999), began to devote attention to it. This surge of interest can be traced back to the 1970s, and the work of scholars like Mary Douglas, Pierre Bourdieu, and Lakoff and Johnson, which in various ways drew new attention to the body. However, recognition of the importance of the body had also preceded these works, and can be found in particular in the writings of several French scholars: the sociologist Marcel Mauss (1979), and the post-war philosopher Maurice Merleau-Ponty (1962). Merleau-Ponty especially is a major figure in the story of the body's career beyond the natural sciences. Over-turning an inherited dualistic conception of the mind and body as separate, as promulgated most explicitly by Descartes, Merleau-Ponty argued that the world was not on the outside, beyond some separate and interior mind. Instead, consciousness and mind were projections of the body into the world. As Merleau-Ponty argued, "there is no inner man, man is in the world, and only in the world does he know himself" (ibid.: xi). Merleau-Ponty thus attacked traditional distinctions between subject and object, which reduced the body to the mechanical object of a subjective mind. He argued instead that the body was the only way of being conscious of the world, that subject and object were one.

Merleau-Ponty's writings on the embodiment of mind have in recent decades received significant attention within the social sciences. However, during much of their previous history, and even up to the present day, the social sciences have often embraced a peculiarly 'disembodied' view of human beings. Peter Freund attributes this to their revolt against the "biological imperialism" (Hirst & Wooley 1982) of natural sciences approaches (Freund 1988: 839), and an attempt on the part of social science to establish its own autonomous discourse, "which unfortunately often ignores the bio-physical properties of its subjects" (ibid.). As a result, the social sciences, ironically, share with biologically deterministic approaches the assumption of mind–body dualism (ibid.). While the latter grant priority to the human body, the social sciences demonstrate equal short-sightedness in attributing primacy to the mind. Thus, "[m]ind and body never interpenetrate each other and persons stand in opposition to the environment in which they are a part. Social science eliminates any consideration of continuities between humans and the biological, natural world" (ibid.).

Whatever its origins, the social science view of the human subject was so disembodied that even when it finally began to recognise the fact that bodies might somehow be important to social theory, it nonetheless managed to overlook their very 'bodily-ness'. The same abstractions that had led to a disembodied social theory continued to play out in conceptualisations of the body. While bodies were now taken into consideration, interest focused on the ways in which they were socially and culturally constructed (e.g., Douglas 1996; Foucault 1977, 1980). They were understood primarily as expressive media for the representation of social identities and cultural beliefs. What was pursued was a primarily semiotic or textualist approach that understood the body as an inscribed surface that received and transmitted pre-existing cultural messages. The body was effectively 'etherealised' (Jackson 1983: 327). Increasingly, however, and especially since the late 1980s and early 1990s, the shortcomings of this idealist approach to understanding the body have been recognised, and new approaches promoted. This has led to a renewal of interest in the work of Merleau-Ponty on embodiment, and the phenomenological approach advocated by him and others. This approach emphasises the continuity between mind and body, and the experience of 'being in the world'. Also important has been the work of Pierre Bourdieu, which similarly drew early interest to the body, and the very active role it plays in creating and reproducing socio-cultural knowledge and values (Bourdieu 1977, 1990). Bourdieu stressed in particular the way that habitual bodily practices, including movements and postures, inculcate cultural values and dispositions. He drew interest to the role of space and also time in creating culturally and socially appropriate bodily practices that are unconsciously adapted through childhood mimesis and engagement with the material world.

Within anthropology, this new approach to the body is exemplified in the work of Michael Jackson (1983, 1989, 1996b). Starting in the early 1980s, Jackson began critiquing the overly abstract approach to the body taken in much anthropological work, and he is thus an important pioneer of more embodied approaches within that discipline. Writing about the Kuranko people of Sierra Leone, Jackson stressed the embodied nature of their knowledge (Jackson 1989). He noted that amongst the Kuranko, much learning is achieved through bodily practice, which imparts knowledge directly. Thus, even when the Kuranko supply verbal exegesis, it tends to centre on root metaphors which refer to bodily and practical activity, such that initiation, for example, is seen to be a process of taming (unruly emotions and bodies), of moulding (as of clay), of making dry or cool (as in cooking, smoking, and curing), of ripening (as of grain and fruit), of strengthening (of the heart), and of hardening or straightening (the body). Jackson argued that such "allusions to domestic and agricultural life are not mere figures of speech, for they disclose real connections between personal maturity and the ability to provide food for and give support to others" (ibid.: 132).

Jackson took a similar position on the Kuranko use of the word *kile*, meaning 'path' or 'road', as a metaphor for social relationships. He pointed out how natural this metaphor seems as soon as one enters a Kuranko village, where little clusters of thatched houses are interconnected by a labyrinth of lanes and paths. But he emphasised that the metaphor is not just descriptive, since the physical movement of people is largely determined by social, economic, and moral imperatives, such as visiting and greeting, sharing food, cooperating in food production and holding festivals, and giving gifts or services in accordance with kinship and other commitments. Drawing on Lakoff and Johnson's work, and his own ethnographic research amongst the Kuranko, Jackson stressed the inseparability of conceptual and bodily activity (ibid.: 148). However, he differed from Lakoff and Johnson in arguing against the traditional notion that metaphors express one thing in terms of another, and emphasises instead that they reveal unities, the "true interdependency of mind and body" (ibid.: 142). While Jackson argued that the relationship between thought, language, and activity is intrinsically closer in a preliterate society like the Kuranko than in a modern literate society where knowledge is often abstracted and separated from bodily skills and material processes (ibid.: 132), he also recognised that such a relationship is not confined to preliterate peoples, and that all human thought is to some degree rooted in somatic processes and embodied activity.

Some of the most interesting work on embodiment has taken place within the field of medical anthropology. These approaches have been less concerned with bringing the body into the mind, than the mind into the body. Attention has focused on the critique of Western biomedicine, and its failure to appreciate the very real connections between mind and body, and the many ways in which bodily states are linked to mental ones. Indeed, medical anthropologists frequently argue against the dichotomous conception underlying the very use of such separate terms. An influential paper by Scheper-Hughes and Lock identified the problem as follows:

> As both medical anthropologists and clinicians struggle to view humans and the experience of illness and suffering from an integrated perspective, they often find themselves trapped by the Cartesian legacy. We lack a precise vocabulary with which to deal with mind-body-society interactions and so are left suspended in hyphens. (1987: 10)

Despite these terminological limitations, many studies in medical anthropology over the past few decades have successfully demonstrated the unity of mind and body. Some have done so through an examination of patterns or case studies within Western biomedicine. For example, studies comparing the effectiveness of real coronary bypass operations and sham operations, in which the entire operation procedure was carried out except that the arteries were not ligated, demonstrated that bypass surgery was successful for reasons that were only partially related to physical intervention, and that had as much or more to do with patients' beliefs (Moerman 1983). Examples of such placebo effects, of which there are many, have presented a serious challenge to scientific understandings within Western medicine (Hahn & Kleinman 1983; Moerman 1983). As Hahn and Kleinman emphasised some time ago now, however, "these effects should be surprising only following a Cartesian principal that regards mental events as nonphysical and physical events as mindless" (Hahn & Kleinman 1983: 18). They emphasise that all human events have physical and mental aspects: "The mind is embodied, the body mindful" (ibid.).

Medical anthropological studies have looked not only at Western biomedicine, but also at non-Western medical systems, whose practices have been drawn upon to demonstrate that the dualistic conception of mind and body integral to Western medical intervention is absent in many other cultures (Lyon 1990; Scheper-Hughes & Lock 1987). Studies of native pharmacologies inevitably emphasise that neither native therapists nor their patients see pharmaceuticals as any more important to the success of therapy than the song, dance, and other symbolic and performative practices that often attend healing procedures (Moerman 1983). Non-Western therapeutic approaches, once seen as irrational and non-sensical, are increasingly recognised as holistic approaches that often derive remarkable effectiveness from the attention they devote to the patient's mental and social well-being. Indeed, the rise of the specialist area of psychoneuroimmunology (Ader & Cohen 1993; Solomon 1987) reflects an increasing recognition within Western biomedicine of the importance of mental states to the ability of the body to heal itself. Various psychoneuroimmunological studies have now convincingly demonstrated the association, for example, between what

is described as 'psychosocial stress' and such biomedical phenomena as slowed wound healing, increased likelihood of infection,
and impaired result after vaccination (McDade 2005). And while
such studies make it clear that minds impact bodies, other non-
Western traditions are also being drawn upon to effect the converse:
the impact of body on mind. For example, as Jackson emphasised,
altered patterns of body use, a balanced pose, and steadying of the
breath (as effected through traditional yoga practices, for example),
can induce tranquillity of mind and a sense of equanimity (Jackson
1989: 129). The popularity of non-Western healing and yogic practices in contemporary Western society demonstrates the degree to
which they address major lacunae in Western biomedical and psychological approaches.

Recognition of the essentially unified nature of mind and body
has also begun to take place in the field of cognitive science, an area
where a number of disciplines, including neuroscience, psychology, linguistics, anthropology, philosophy, and computer science,
overlap and engage in the study of the mind. The work of Lakoff
and Johnson falls within this sphere, and their study of metaphor
has repeatedly demonstrated the links between bodily experience
and more 'abstract' aspects of thought. This link is perhaps most
explicitly formulated in Lakoff's discussion of the metaphorical
understanding of emotion, and particularly anger (Lakoff 1987).
Lakoff demonstrates that the common usage of metaphors like
"He lost his cool", "I almost burst a blood vessel", and "You make
my blood boil" are all drawn very clearly from the bodily experience of the physical effects of anger. Anger leads to increased
body heat (hence, "don't get hot under the collar"), increased internal pressure (blood pressure, muscular pressure; thus, "he almost
had a hemorrhage"), agitation ("he was shaking with anger"), and
interference with accurate perception ("she was blind with rage").
Thus, our concept of anger, which is elaborated in various ways to
make complex statements and abstractions, is rooted in our very
physiology.

Lakoff and Johnson's concept of the mind is also embodied in
that it takes into account the fact that the mind is related to the
wet mass of dense, neuron-rich tissue that is the brain. Thus, Lakoff
and Johnson attempt, in addition, to link their work on linguistic

Figure 2.12: Father holding baby. George Lakoff and Mark Johnson link the metaphor AFFECTION IS WARMTH to our experience of affection when we are babies. Photo © Tracy Toh.

metaphor to neuroscientific studies of the brain (Lakoff & Johnson 1999, 2003). Taking the example of the metaphor AFFECTION IS WARMTH ("He's a warm person" or "She's a block of ice"), they argue (drawing upon the work of Christopher Johnson) that affection and warmth may be conflated because as babies, while being held, we experience affection as warmth (Figure 2.12; Lakoff & Johnson 2003). This conflation relates, they argue (based on the work of Srinivas Narayanan), to a neural learning system that causes neuronal activation occurring simultaneously in two parts of the brain – one devoted to emotions and the other to temperature – to lead to neural connections between brain regions. "Neurons that fire together wire together" is a common understanding in neuroscience (ibid.: 256). They argue that it is also behind the creation of linguistic metaphors rooted in bodily physiology and experience of the world. Thus, Lakoff and Johnson make a rare attempt to bridge "the enormous gap between physical brain structures and the level of human concepts and language" (Lakoff & Johnson 1999: 570; see also, for example, Ramachandran & Hubbard 2003). Such a bridge is arguably essential to any proper and full understanding of the human mind.

Andy Clark is another cognitive scientist who has devoted significant attention to the embodied nature of human cognition. Drawing on empirical studies from scientific fields as diverse as artificial intelligence, psychology, and biology, Clark has argued convincingly for recognition of the way in which cognition often extends out beyond the brain and into the body (Clark 1997, 1998, 1999; see also Varela et al. 1991). This perspective contrasts sharply with the more traditional model of the brain or mind as a kind of 'control panel' that receives information from the senses, and on that basis, sends messages to the body concerning how it should act. Take, as an illustration, the example of vision. What has been referred to as the 'pure vision' scenario understands the task of vision as one of building rich inner models of a surrounding three-dimensional reality (Churchland et al. 1994; Clark 1999). Reason and thought are then focused on the inner model, and action functions only to implement solutions arrived at by pure cognition. This scenario has recently been overturned by research in interactive or animate vision, demonstrating that action is integral to vision itself, which works in a very efficient way to serve immediate, real-world aims (Churchland et al. 1994). Visual data are not passively received, but actively retrieved, as they are needed. Thus, computer imaging studies show that people looking at scenes can fail to notice quite large changes made in areas of the scene they are not focusing on (ibid.). They are not building rich inner representations of the scene, but gathering information as they need it. And motor activity is not initiated upon conclusion of visual activity, but is integral to it. Head, eye, and whole-body movements are part of the process of seeing and make the entire process more economical. "[P]erception and action engage in a kind of incremental game of tag in which motor assembly begins long before sensory signals reach the top level" (Clark 1998: 265). This understanding is consistent with neurophysiological and neuroanatomical data showing, for example, that neurons sensitive to eye position seem to know in advance about planned visual saccades (shifts in focus).

Clark also discusses the example of catching a fly ball (Figure 2.13; Clark 1999). He notes that understanding of how this

Figure 2.13: Boy trying to catch a baseball. Andy Clark argued that catching a fly ball involves not complex calculations of the mind, but real-time adjustments of the body. Photo Bruce Grigg.

occurs cognitively has changed as a result of recent research in cognitive psychology. While it was once believed that the cognitive process involved in knowing where to stand to catch a fly ball was the result of complex calculations of the arc, acceleration, and distance of the ball, it is now clear that a much more computationally simple strategy is at work (see McBeath et al. 1995). This involves the outfielder continually adjusting his or her run so that the ball never seems to curve towards the ground, but instead appears to move in a straight line in his or her visual field. Thus, instead of the brain taking sense data, performing a complex calculation, and then instructing the body where to go, what occurs instead is a series of real-time adjustments to the run that maintain a coordination between the inner and outer worlds. The problem is not solved ahead of time, nor is any rich representation of the outside world constructed in the mind. Clark describes instead "a kind of adaptively potent equilibrium that couples the agent and the world together" (Clark 1999: 346).

Ecological Embodiment: Uniting Mind, Matter, and World

Clark's work, as this example suggests, stresses the mutuality not only of mind and body, but also of mind–body and environment. The environment, or material world, forms the final component of what amounts to a linguistically separated but deeply interpenetrated triad composed of mind, matter, and body. As I suggested earlier, the importance of building the world into models of perception and cognition has increasingly been recognised in research within a range of fields. A number of these ultimately owe much to the pioneering insights made by the psychologist James Gibson in the 1950s through to 1970s.

Gibson was an original thinker who challenged mainstream representationalist theories of perception, and forwarded a radically novel understanding of how perception occurs (Gibson 1966, 1986). Instead of passive channels that merely transmitted meaningless inputs from 'outside' to 'inside', Gibson recognised the senses as active systems for perception. In doing so, he removed the need for some sort of mediating representational structure to fill the gap between sensation and perception – that is, to 'process' senses into perceptions. He also challenged the appropriateness of the laboratory as a place for studying perception. If perception was about the active retrieval of information from the environment, then what must be studied, argued Gibson and his fellow ecological psychologists, was the coordination of organism and environment. Gibson accordingly focused on how perception had evolved as a means for organisms to acquire information about and act within their environments. His was a model of perception far removed from the ideal world described by physics, which cognitive psychologists had used as the theoretical setting for an isolated and autonomous subject set apart from its real environment (Costall 1984).

The insights of ecological psychology have subsequently been substantiated through work in a range of disciplines. Artificial intelligence research – which is aimed not only at the construction of useful intelligence systems, but also at understanding human intelligence (Winston 1984) – has demonstrated, for example, that "explicit representations and models of the world simply get in the way" (Brooks 1991b: 139) when researchers attempt to create intelligent machines. Rodney Brooks, Director of the Computer Science and Artificial Intelligence Laboratory at the Massachusetts Institute of Technology, has pointed out that because traditional artificial intelligence research (AI) has tackled intelligence through notions of thought and reason, it is unable to account for significant aspects of what goes into intelligence (Brooks 1991a). In addition, traditional AI offers solutions to intelligence that bear almost no resemblance at all to how biological systems of intelligence work, and that fail to take into account how evolution occurred. Brooks (1991b) points out that evolution has concentrated its time on the difficult task of creating organisms that have the ability to move around a dynamic environment, sensing the surroundings to a degree sufficient to achieve the necessary maintenance of life and reproduction (Figure 2.14). He has suggested that problem-solving behaviour, language, expert knowledge and application, and reason are all relatively easily achieved once the essence of being and reacting become available.

Brooks and others thus argue for a new approach in which situatedness and embodiment are prime considerations when creating intelligent machines. The stress on situatedness is remarkably reminiscent of Gibson. While traditional AI built machines that work in symbolically abstracted domains not situated in the real world, new approaches try to understand and re-create intelligence by making machines that can function in real contexts. And while traditional AI created robots that constructed models of the world, then planned and executed actions on the basis of these models, the new approach to AI creates robots that use the world as their own model, referring continuously to their senses rather than any internal world model. The creation of machines with improved performance as well as decreased computation requirements has demonstrated the success of this approach (Brooks 1991a).

What Gibson highlighted and others have demonstrated or rediscovered then is that the workings of the mind cannot be understood independently of the environment. Just as thinking is a bodily activity, it is also an ecological or situated activity (Chiel & Beer 1997; Clark 1997, 1998, 1999; Varela et al. 1991). Models of the mind that dismiss or abstract the environmental setting of the thinking organism will fail to do justice to the way in which real cognition occurs. Sensations, perceptions, and thoughts are not separate,

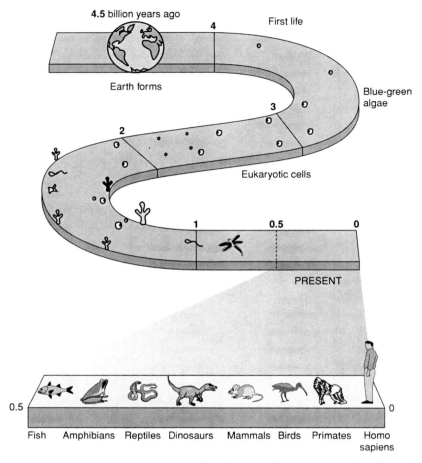

Figure 2.14: Approximate time scale of major achievements in biological evolution. Diagram Nicole Boivin.

linearly organised entities, but artificial categories that distinguish what are often in effect combined processes. These processes or activities involve engagement of the embodied mind with its surroundings, a tight coupling that has led philosopher Barry Smith to compare living organisms to highly complex tuning forks – beings "tuned through our batteries of sensors to the environment which surrounds us in complex ways" (Smith 2003).

Gibson was critical of the way that fields like anthropology and ecology distinguished the study of the natural environment from the study of the cultural environment, which he argued were not sharply divided. He furthermore argued against the separation of cultural environment into 'material' culture and 'non-material' culture: "This is a seriously misleading distinction", wrote Gibson, "for it seems to imply that language, tradition, art, music, law and religion are immaterial, insubstantial, or intangible, whereas tools, shelter, clothing, vehicles and books are not" (Gibson 1966: 26). The materiality of even the most apparently intellectual and abstract aspects of culture, as well as the importance of environment and ecology to thought, language, and music, are fortunately matters that some anthropologists at least are coming to appreciate nowadays. While earlier ecological anthropology defined its project within the compass of the idealism versus materialism debate (Biersack 1999: 5), and focused on the questionable project of demonstrating the environmental adaptiveness of culture (e.g., Harris 1966; Rappaport 1967), the diversity of 'new ecologies' in anthropology (Biersack 1999) has taken account of environment without reverting to either functionalism or sterile dichotomies (e.g., Descola 1996; Ingold 2000; Soper 1995). Some of the most interesting examples of this work, within the context of the present discussion, are those that have explored the interplay between environments and so-called 'higher' realms of culture, such as language, ritual, and cosmology.

Alfred Gell, for example, has explored the way that language form might be related to ecology, drawing on the example of the phonological iconisms prevalent in some of the languages of Papua New Guinea (see Gell 1995). Gell argues that phonological iconism, in which the sounds of words are related to their semantic meaning (as, for example, in onomatopoeia – a rare English example of phonological iconism – with words like 'hiss', 'buzz', and 'crunch'), may be linked to the landscape inhabited by speakers of these languages. The Umeda, the Kaluli, and the Foi, all of whom commonly employ phonological iconisms in their languages, live in sparsely inhabited and thickly forested areas of Papua New Guinea. Gell argues that this primary forest environment has imposed a closely tailored organisation of sensibility that gives pride of place to the auditory sense. As Gell discovered to his consternation, it is simply impossible to see over long distances in these landscapes, and hearing is instead the primary tool for long-distance sensing. In addition, the closed canopy of the forest creates a dark, intimate space in which the acoustic sense is far more important than vision in most day-to-day activities. The forest landscape privileges audition and de-emphasises vision, and the relative dominance of hearing as the sensory modality for coding the environment as a whole has likely favoured a language subtly attuned to the potential relationships between sounds and concepts. This acoustic orientation is likely also responsible for the great importance placed by the Umeda, Kaluli, and Foi on music, song, and oral poetry (ibid.), as documented in several detailed ethnographic studies (Feld 1982; Weiner 1991).

At the close of his paper, Gell also, perhaps more controversially, suggests a possible link between the overall acoustic tendency of these 'poetic' societies and a particular set of social attitudes, which might be labelled as 'sympathetic' (Gell 1995: 251). Gell points out that detailed field research by both Weiner and Feld has indicated that 'sociality', in Foi and Kaluli terms, is crucially bound up with the demonstration of sympathy (ibid.). He suggests that this 'culture of sympathy' might derive in part from the inherent intimacy of sound relative to vision (which promotes a more abstracted orientation), as well as, arguably, the social necessity of sympathy in a context where the vicissitudes of forest existence impose an inescapable instability on the collective institutions on which life depends. Gell concludes by noting that:

> This is a narrow, and, if you like, environmental-determinist theory of ethno-poetics. I insist on it only so far as I believe cultural theories ought to be anchored in the specifics of physical localities, technologies, lifestyles, rather than seeking to appeal to absolutes and essences. (ibid.: 252)

Gell is not the only anthropologist to flirt with theories that risk being branded as environmentally determinist. Constance Classen has also, more briefly, considered the relationship between senses and the environment in her analysis of the way in which cosmologies can differ in terms of their sensory orientation (Classen 1991). Classen notes that the cosmology of the Amazonian lowlands makes more symbolic use of the proximity senses (taste, smell, and touch) than does that of the Central Andean highlands, which places more emphasis on sight and sound. She suggests that

Figure 2.15: Thick clothing and open landscape characteristic of the Central Andean highlands. Constance Classen has argued that such features of the sensory landscape have shaped Andean cosmologies, which tend to emphasise sound and sight. Photo Rebeca Hoyos Ortiz.

in the barren Andean highlands, touch is dulled by the cold and layers of clothing (Figure 2.15), odours are poorly diffused through the thin atmosphere, and the range of foods is limited. In contrast, hearing is heightened by the acoustics of the mountains, and sight is engaged by the open sky and vista of mountain peaks. Thus, it is perhaps natural to find that Andean cosmologies orient around the symbolic aspects of sound and sight. Meanwhile, the frequent employment of symbolism relating to the proximity senses in Amazonian cosmology is perhaps equally understandable in terms of the rich odours, tastes, and textures that abound in the dense tropical Amazonian rain forest, where, as pointed out for the Papua New Guinea forest, vision is limited.

While, as Gell's concluding statement highlighted, anthropologists who suggested a role for the environment in shaping 'higher' aspects of culture once risked being charged with environmental determinism, it is clear that such fears are increasingly anachronistic in an academic context in which the tight grip of a dominant textual, anti-materialist approaches is showing signs of loosening. In the current, changing climate, anthropologists, like Simon Harrison, for example, are recognising that people are not just embodied, but 'ecologically embodied' (Harrison 2004: 596). Harrison's study of the relationship between ritual, seasonality, and mood disorders like seasonal affective disorder (SAD) across a wide range of societies provides a subtle account of the way that biology, culture, and environment interact in complex ways to produce globally diverse approaches to change and the human lifecycle. Harrison neither discounts nor sees as determinative the role of neurophysiology in producing seasonally linked mood disorders, but instead views SAD as the particular expression of a 'lived' or 'embodied' metaphor conceived not only in a specific bodily and cultural milieu, but also a specific environmental setting. Harrison argues that SAD needs to be understood within the context of a particular culturally construed link between seasonality and emotion, but also argues that this cultural model is far from arbitrary:

> People are, of course, not merely embodied, but embodied in environments, with characteristics of seasonality, geographical latitude, climate, and so forth. In its effects on the body, and on sensory experience, an environment is part of the complex of physiological possibilities and constraints shaping the symbolisms with which those who live in that environment give meaning to their affective states.... In this sense, embodiment does not end at the skin, but extends beyond it into the physical world. To put this differently, people are not just embodied, but also embodied *ecologically*. This has implications for our understanding of the cultural metaphors with which they communicate, and perhaps also experience, their emotions. These imageries may often indeed be motivated physiologically. But the motivations come not from the body but from the body-connected-to-a-particular-environment. (ibid.)

Analyses like that by Harrison are to be commended for seeking to draw a balance between the cultural and the material, and point the way toward a new, less fractured anthropology. It is also clear that in a range of other fields on either side of the humanities–sciences divide, it will be critical, if progress is to be made, to take account of both body and environment in attempts to understand a range of human properties – language, thought, culture, intelligence, and mind – that were once thought to float above the lowly, earthly morass of breathing, growing, crawling, oozing things. Instead of a two-tiered world, neatly matched by major academic divisions, what we have instead is a much more complicated world in which the multiple, interwoven connections between 'higher' and 'lower', mind and matter, culture and biology preclude any simple academic division of labour.

Beyond Representation

Matter represents, but it does not do so in an arbitrary manner. Symbols and symbolic systems do not draw randomly on the material world to create, define and express themselves, as though they constituted a divine font of self-creation. Rather, the rich representational systems that humans create draw heavily upon the realities of engagement with a world that they spent millions of years adapting to, using bodies that have similarly been millions of years in the making. The idea that humans have somehow been able to extricate themselves, in contrast to all other creatures, from this material, biological, and ecological reality may have a very long and distinguished history, but it is one that it does us little credit to embrace in a self-reflexive, post-modern era.

This chapter has focused on the material, ecological, and biological aspects of representation and thought, and in exploring them has already hinted at some of the issues that will arise in subsequent chapters. For now, having focused on representation, I wish to move beyond it, in order to explore how the material world does not just represent, but also moves us, in a whole myriad of ways. This is a theme that has already begun to be explored in this chapter, but now I wish to explore it more fully by examining in detail a whole range of diverse topics – the senses, emotionality, social change, and biological evolution amongst them – that I have but briefly touched upon here.

CHAPTER 3

Words Are Not Enough

Rajasthan Revisited

In the introduction to this book, I described how I began, late in the process of writing up the results of my Rajasthani ethnoarchaeological study, to question the textual orientation and overwhelming emphasis on symbols that had characterised my analysis of material culture in rural India. Thinking more about the soil called *pili mitti*, and paying closer attention to anthropological accounts of how minerals are perceived in various cultures (Boivin & Owoc 2004), I started to wonder whether *pili mitti* really *represented* the goddess Laksmi. My informants had in fact told me that *pili mitti was* Laksmi, and in other accounts of how people understand minerals (and indeed other aspects of the material world), it was also clear that things were often perceived as spirits, deities, demons, or other beings, rather than mere representations of them. Furthermore, in trying to understand the red squares painted on house walls, as with my attempts to understand the materials used in rituals, I had focused on decoding their meaning, and had been frustrated by what I felt were banal statements about their function – as coats of plaster that covered up stains and made spaces look nicer. The discovery that *pili mitti*, the red soil used to plaster the squares, was Laksmi became the key I needed to unlock a complex symbolic code that enabled space and the materials used to create it to be understood. Only later did it really worry me that the very complex, abstract symbolic formulation I had worked out seemed to have departed

Figure 3.1: Painting designs, like other activities in rural India, and elsewhere in the world, involves meeting practical goals as well as representing abstract concepts. Photo Nicole Boivin.

significantly from the ways people talked about and used domestic materials. As I drove through and stopped in hundreds of Indian villages during the course of subsequent archaeological fieldwork in the south peninsula, I contemplated how far my post-fieldwork theory-building had drawn me from the lived reality of village life, which – like all life – was so clearly chaotic, emotional, sensual, and immediate. I had created an abstract and ordered symbolic universe when really what was there was desire, need, pleasure, pain, and people striving to accomplish practical goals, whether by sowing crops and building houses, or painting red squares and other designs, and undertaking ritual activities (Figure 3.1).

I have subsequently been comforted to discover that other anthropologists have experienced similar doubts, reappraisals, and even

wholehearted reversals when reconsidering their earlier accounts
of symbolic and representational meaning. Michael Jackson, in particular, has penned a very eloquent reversal of his earlier analysis
of a girls' initiation rite in a Kuranko village in northern Sierra
Leone. Writing over half a decade after the initial analysis was published, and over a decade after witnessing the rite in question, Jackson (1977) admitted that despite perhaps some unease, he initially
applied a fairly standard symbolic interpretation to the mysterious
rites he had seen in Firawa, in which women and girls dressed,
danced, and behaved like men (Jackson 1983). He describes "the
fervor with which I sought clues to hidden meanings" (ibid.: 331)
and his analysis of the ritual activities as if they were symbolic representations of unconscious concerns (ibid.). Jackson comes to see
this symbol-oriented interpretation as deeply misguided: "I now
realize the absurdity of this analytical procedure" (ibid.), he wrote
in 1983. Jackson describes how in spending much of his time trying to find out what the initiation rites were about, and ignoring
Kuranko advice that they were not about anything beyond enter-
tainment and people taking part, he managed to entirely miss their
point:

> My bourgeois conception of culture as something "super-
> organic," something separable from the quotidian world of
> bodily movements and practical tasks, had led me to seek
> the script, the director, and the interpretation in a rite which
> had none. This quest for semantic truths also explained my
> inability to participate in the spirit of the performances and
> why I spent my time asking people to tell me what was
> going on, what it all meant, as if the painted bodies and
> mimetic dances were only the insipid remnants of what
> had perhaps once been a symbolically coherent structure
> of myths and masks. . . . But to hold that every act signifies
> something is an extravagant form of abstraction, so long as
> this implies that the action stands for something other than
> itself, beyond the here and now. (ibid.: 332)

Jackson's subsequent analysis admits that rites like the Kuranko
girls' initiation can give expression to ideas and symbolic meanings,

Figure 3.2: Carving from a Zafimaniry house. Zafimaniry wood carvings serve to "honour the wood" rather than represent things or concepts. Photo Maurice Bloch.

but stresses that this is only part of the story. As suggested in the introduction to Jackson's work in the previous chapter, he argues that rites also involve an important bodily and experiential dimension that lies beyond abstract conceptualisation, and that rites frequently make sense for people at the level of experience (ibid.). Much understanding in the Kuranko girls' initiation rites is achieved through embodied practice, rather than verbal exegesis or symbolic representation.

Another anthropologist who has engaged in similar self-critique is Maurice Bloch. During the course of ethnographic fieldwork amongst the Zafimaniry of Madagascar, Bloch became interested, like many professional and amateur anthropologists and archaeologists before him, in the traditional carvings that cover the wooden parts of their traditional houses (Figure 3.2; Bloch 1992, 1993, 1995).

Like these earlier visitors, he admits that he too spent much time initially 'bothering' the Zafimaniry by asking them what their carvings 'mean' (Bloch 1995). Like Jackson and me, Bloch was also initially disappointed by – and ignored – his informants' assertions that there was no meaning to be found. The carvings, argued the Zafimaniry, do not represent anything at all, and serve instead to 'make the wood beautiful' or, as some put it, to 'honour the wood' (ibid.: 214). While such statements initially struck Bloch as bland and frustrating, he eventually – within the context of a wider re-evaluation of Zafiminary thought – came to find them revealing instead. For Bloch realised, like Jackson, that while some human thought and knowledge can be expressed in language, much of it is in fact "anchored in practice and material experience" (Bloch 1992: 132). Zafiminary houses, and their exquisite carvings, are not an expression of abstract ideas, Bloch came to argue, but are rather the material embodiment of those ideas, and cannot be separated from them. People's understanding of processes of maturation and of marriage are tied up on Madagascar with their understanding of wood and the process of hardening it undergoes through time. Just as wood and bodies harden over time, so do marriages, and, through the process of continued building and carving, so do the houses that married couples inhabit. As Bloch describes:

> The aesthetic and moral value of the hardness of such wood, especially the fact that it is a hardness produced from an original softness (the young plant), totally dominates Zafimaniry discourse in a way which would be almost impossible to overemphasise. This house and this wood can be seen as material culture, but to an extent this is misleading in that such a phrase suggests something different from non-material culture. It would be quite misleading to see Zafimaniry houses as expressing Zafimaniry marriage and society or containing married pairs. The house is the marriage. (Bloch 1995: 215)

Within this context, carving can be understood as a continuation of the process of hardening, and as a practice that 'honours' the wood, and makes its hardness more evident and beautiful. Bloch is emphatic that the carvings do not signify, and that they must be understood as part of an ongoing process, and a conceptualisation of the world that does not precede, but is rather rooted in, its materiality.

Culture, Thought, and Language

[I]f culture were all words, how laborious it would be – like the famous philosophers' Cup Final in Monty Python, in which the ball was never kicked at all! (Gell 1996: 165)

Jackson's and Bloch's reappraisals are not minor points in the history of anthropology. Both anthropologists drew on their insights to propose major changes in how anthropology conceives of thought and activity in human society, and both have had an influential role to play in encouraging the growing challenge to symbolic and representation-based accounts of culture and society to be found in contemporary anthropology. However, while the two anthropologists have expressed similar doubts about the privileged place granted to language and symbolism in contemporary anthropological models of society, they have also turned to very different sources in seeking alternative perspectives for the discipline. Bloch became interested in what cognitive science had to say about thought and the acquisition of knowledge, while Jackson has drawn heavily upon philosophy, and particularly phenomenology, in proposing a more experience-based anthropology. In fact, as this chapter will clarify, the very different perspectives offered by both of these disciplines not only have important insights to offer anthropologists but also all scholars seeking to understand the role of the material world in human thought and society. That the perspectives are not altogether incompatible is furthermore demonstrated by the recent birth of a hybrid sub-discipline known as neurophenomenology, which marries the methodologies of both.

Bloch's interest in cognitive science developed out of a conviction that recent findings in this field were of substantial relevance to anthropology (Bloch 1991). In particular, Bloch noted that while anthropologists were emphasising the importance of language to culture and cultural concepts, research in cognitive science, particularly on learning in children, had demonstrated that concepts are in fact not language dependent, and appear in many cases to precede language acquisition. Bloch argued, on the basis of the findings of cognitive science, that much of our knowledge is non-linguistic, and that while such knowledge may be rendered in linguistic form, it is fundamentally transformed in the process (e.g., Damasio 1994; Hollan 2000). Accordingly, he pointed out that "when our informants honestly say 'this is why we do such things' or 'this is what this means', or 'this is how we do such things', instead of being pleased we should be suspicious and ask what kind of *peculiar* knowledge is this which can take such an explicit, linguistic form?" (Bloch 1991: 194). Bloch emphasised the need to treat all explicit knowledge as problematic, and as likely to be remote from the kind of knowledge employed in everyday, practical activities. Bloch also went further, however, in arguing not only that knowledge is not formulated in natural language, but also that it is in no way even 'language-like'. Against the folk model of thought that holds that thought occurs in a sequential, linear way, broadly similar to the semantics of natural language, Bloch contrasted the connectionist model embraced by some cognitive scientists, which argued for 'multiple parallel processing' and, according to Bloch, better accounted for the speed and efficiency with which we perform everyday acts.

Bloch's argument regarding language is not new. Both Turner and Barth, for example, whose ideas were introduced in the previous chapter, expressed suspicions about the ability of linguistic statements to adequately reflect culture. Barth argued that the ritual symbols of the Baktaman were 'good to act', not 'good to think' (Barth 1975: 221), and noted the absence of an exegetical tradition amongst the Papua New Guinean group. Barth observed in his ethnography that "in translating [ritual experience] into this entirely different medium of language, I have of necessity transformed this material drastically" (ibid.: 224). Like Bloch, Barth went further and argued that Baktaman ritual symbols were in some ways not even language-like. He emphasised that rites were not cast in the digital code of computers and language, that they do not

Figure 3.3. An Indian bride's hands. Symbolic accounts of rituals often overlook the sensuous and emotional aspects of ritual. Photo Mohammed Asif Akbar.

merely communicate messages, and that they were not necessarily logically consistent. Instead, Barth addressed the role of emotion and the senses in ritual, in a way that, as we shall see, anticipated some of the concerns of contemporary anthropology (Figure 3.3).

Bloch's emphasis on the knowledge used in everyday, practical activities is also of course highly reminiscent of Bourdieu, whose influential practice theory was essentially an argument against the abstraction of practice into "the intellectualist language of representation" (Bourdieu 1977: 116). Bourdieu emphasised the way that cultural knowledge was passed on through practical, embodied activity that did not require either discourse or conscious awareness. His comments on ritual parallel Barth's in many ways, and he argued that "rites, more than any other type of practice, serve to underline the mistake of enclosing in concepts a logic meant to dispense with concepts" (ibid.). However, while Barth addressed the material world and its sensual nature, Bourdieu's primary concern has been with the body:

The language of the body, whether articulated in gestures or, *a fortiori*, in what psychosomatic medicine calls "the language of the organs", is incomparably more ambiguous and more overdetermined than the most overdetermined uses of ordinary language. This is why ritual "roots" are always broader and vaguer than linguistic roots, and why the gymnastics of ritual, like dreams, always seems richer than verbal translations, at once unilateral and arbitrary, that may be given of it. Words, however charged with connotation, limit the range of choices and render difficult or impossible, and in any case explicit and therefore "falsifiable", the relations which the language of the body suggests. It follows simply that by bringing to the level of discourse . . . a practice which owes a number of its properties to the fact that it falls short of discourse . . . one subjects it to nothing less than a change in ontological status. (ibid.: 120)

Bloch, however, while acknowledging his debts to Bourdieu (Bloch 1992: 128), remained convinced that Bourdieu was trapped by a logic-sequential model of thought – as exemplified by his discussion of the Berber house (Bourdieu 1973), which describes an ordered system of structural oppositions (Bloch 1992: 145). He has furthermore not been altogether persuaded that practice theory is the Holy Grail that many anthropologists perceive it to be, pointing out that:

[a]lthough the general intention behind the study of practice in anthropology is probably useful, the work we have had so far, including my own, is so vague and lazy as to merit being considered, at best, as merely preliminary. Indeed, one cannot help but suspect that anthropologists' repeated recent emphasis on the importance of 'practice' is merely a way of excusing themselves from thinking hard about it. (Bloch 1998: 150)

Bloch argued that more detailed studies of practice and its link to thought are required. Indeed, he believes that both long-term ethnographic fieldwork and participant-observation are advantages that anthropology has over cognitive science. If cognition is in fact largely anchored in the material world and in practical activities, then it is difficult, if not impossible, to study in the laboratory (cf. Gibson 1966), and the cognitive scientist's preference for 'hard' laboratory data is misguided. What Bloch argued is needed then is continuous and intimate contact and cooperation with subjects of study, and real participation, all of which define the traditional anthropological exercise. Only prolonged fieldwork will enable anthropologists to acquire the kind of embodied knowledge that constitutes the majority of cultural knowledge, and that no amount of questioning will reveal.

This stress on long-term and participatory fieldwork is another similarity that links the work of Bloch and Jackson, and is also found in the writings of the anthropologist Paul Stoller. For Jackson, the embodied character of knowledge means that participation is often likely to be the only route to understanding. Furthermore, participation is not simply a means for gathering data that will then be subject to interpretation after the event (Jackson 1989: 135), but is rather an end in itself. Jackson argued, for example, in *Paths towards a Clearing* that only true participation without ulterior motive will yield understanding of a people. Stoller's emphasis is meanwhile on fieldwork over the long term. He has pointed out that Anglo-American anthropologists have often been content to visit the field once, twice, or perhaps three times during their academic careers, and he argues that this is not enough. "One can discover a great many 'ethnographic facts' in one year of fieldwork", he writes, "but it takes years, no matter the perspicacity of the observer, to develop a deep comprehension of others" (Stoller 1989: 6–7).

Unlike Bloch, however, Jackson and Stoller do not draw on cognitive science, but on philosophy, and in particular the traditions of radical empiricism and phenomenology. Both philosophical schools stress experience over rational, disembodied thought, but it is phenomenology that has had the most significant impact on anthropology and other social science fields. Phenomenology may be found in many forms, but essentially involves the study of the structures of conscious experience – referred to by some phenomenologists as 'being-in-the-world'. Sometimes phenomenology is narrowly defined as the characterisation of the sensory qualities of seeing, hearing, and such, but more commonly it includes various kinds of experience, including perception, thought, memory, imagination, emotion, desire, volition, bodily awareness, embodied activity, and social and linguistic activity (Smith 2005). Jackson, Stoller, and many other anthropologists have drawn inspiration in particular from the version of phenomenology propounded by Maurice Merleau-Ponty, who focused on the phenomenology of embodied experience, and of active engagement with the world (Merleau-Ponty 1962). For these anthropologists, as well as others like Thomas Csordas, phenomenology offers a corrective to the often overwhelming focus on abstract symbolic systems, language, and representation within anthropology and the social sciences in general (Csordas 1994; Weiner 2001). Phenomenology has emerged as a key methodology for scholars at the vanguard of the important 'critique of representation' that has taken shape within the humanities and social sciences (Csordas 1994).

For the anthropologist Csordas, this critique is aimed at the dominance of rules and principles in social anthropology, signs and symbols in semiotic/symbolic anthropology, text and discourse in structural and post-structural anthropology, and knowledge and models in cognitive anthropology (ibid.: 9). These "abstract systematics so beloved of Enlightenment approaches to human life" (Weiner 1996: 173) are described by Jackson as less "mirror images of social reality" than "defenses we build against the unsystematic, unstructured nature of our experiences within reality" (Jackson 1989: 3). Valorisation of the search for order is, according to Stoller, a clear illustration of anthropology's membership in the Platonic tradition (Stoller 1989: 135), against which he calls for a humanistic anthropology – a meaningful description of "human being" (ibid.: 140). Lived experience, the "brute and wild being" that Merleau-Ponty encouraged philosophers to try to bring readers into contact with (see ibid.: 139), always surpasses the concepts we use to grasp it (Jackson 1989: 2). Thus, we need to study sensation, embodiment, feeling, emotion, subjectivity – much of what has been previously dismissed as pre-cognitive or irrational. However, this is not to replace one pole of a dichotomy with another. Csordas emphasises that the aim of the new critique of representation is not to use a concern with experience and being-in-the-world to supplant the textualist concern with representation, but rather to complement it (Csordas 1994). It is not that informants' statements are meaningless, or that language and concepts do not impose themselves on experience, but rather that there is a need to ensure that anthropology makes more of an attempt to capture the lived, embodied, material reality of human experience.

Given the emerging challenge to representationalist models that is also found within the discipline of cognitive science (touched upon above, but outlined more fully in the previous chapter), it is thus clear that the move is on to put representation and language in their place within studies of human thought and society. This is the case not only within philosophy, anthropology, and cognitive science, but also sociology, geography, cultural studies, psychology, archaeology, and various other disciplines. The lived, embodied, and existentially committed experience of being human is an increasing focus of interest, and has opened up new realms of investigation, as well as novel intersections of multidisciplinary study. This new frame of interest has also drawn attention to the need to re-evaluate the role of the material world in human thought and society. The representationalist tradition has suggested interesting new ways of thinking about the material world at the same time that it has slammed the door on a myriad of others. An experienced-based approach reopens many of them, and furthermore shows the way to entirely new ways of understanding the relationship between humans and the world they inhabit.

This is not to say that the material world has been a focus of scholars attempting to move beyond the textualist and representationalist biases of earlier studies. This is very far from being the case. Despite the fact that approaches aimed at unravelling embodiment and experience virtually demand attention to the material world that embodied, experiencing humans inhabit, the material world has generally been the extremely poor cousin of the body in studies of practice, phenomenological experience, and embodied cognition. Even in ostensibly phenomenological studies of the material world, scholars like Chris Tilley have frequently found it difficult to escape a semiotic urge, and have often simply linked detailed descriptions of material traits (the so-called phenomenological part) with final interpretations that are blatantly symbolic and textual in orientation (see Tilley 2004). Nonetheless, there exist within the anthropological, cognitive science, and also archaeological literatures a range of studies – both predating and coinciding with the critique of representation – that not only demonstrate new ways of understanding the material world, but also open the way towards a more holistic understanding of cognition, society, and culture. These studies address the sensual and emotional aspects of material engagement, and suggest that studies of the *meaning* of the material world need also to be accompanied by studies of its *effect* (Pollard 2001). It is to such studies that I turn in the remainder of this chapter, with the aim of demonstrating how a shift towards the investigation of concrete, sensuous experience and lived reality helps scholars to more fully understand the relationship between people and the endless richness of things with which they are surrounded. These studies do not constitute a completed project, but rather the beginnings of a more systematic investigation into the materiality of human existence.

Reawakening the Senses

Subsequent to completing my ethnographically oriented PhD on the material culture of Balathal village, I returned to the study of India's prehistoric societies, and began a project investigating the origins of domestication and sedentism in South India's Deccan plateau. Here, several thousands of years ago, people started to relate differently to place, and to the plant and animal world, ultimately resulting in the development of South India's first agricultural communities. They also began to undertake a distinctive and somewhat puzzling practice: they accumulated extremely large quantities of cow dung at particular places in the landscape that they then periodically burnt in very large, very hot fires. These practices often resulted over time in the formation of large 'ashmounds' in the landscape (Figure 3.4), many of which have survived to this day despite the intrusion of agricultural land, and their frequent mining for construction material. These ashmound fires were clearly started deliberately, and do not appear to have had any straightforwardly functional purpose. Indeed, there is increasingly good reason to see the fires as ritual events (Allchin 1963;

Figure 3.4: The Neolithic ashmound at Kudatini in South India (the truncated hill just behind the wall). The mounds, which are found throughout the south Deccan plateau, appear to have been created as a result of the ritual burning of cattle dung, and may have constituted kinds of monuments in the Neolithic landscape. Photo Dorian Fuller.

Boivin 2004c; Johansen 2004; Paddayya 2004–2005), related to the importance of cattle in Southern Neolithic society, and a spatio-temporal rhythm to life that periodically brought together communities of people, along with their herds of cattle, for social and ritual gatherings, and exchange. The resulting durable mounds, some of which compare to the largest of the North American Hopewell mounds in size, also suggest comparison to monuments – such as earth mounds and megaliths – found in other Neolithic societies.

While it is clear that the ashmound practices can be interpreted symbolically – there is, for example, some suggestive evidence linking transformations between states of hot and cold, and colours like red and white in the ashmound fires to social and lifecycle transformations in Southern Neolithic society (Boivin 2004c) – it is also the case that the ashmound fires invite consideration of less abstract and more embodied aspects of Neolithic life (ibid.). For certainly the fires would have been major, deeply sensual events in the Neolithic lifeworld. The vitrified ash layers within the mounds suggest enormous, incredibly hot bonfires that must have been major events for communities of shifting, village-dwelling farmers lacking exposure to cities, electrical light, and constructed monuments. Accordingly, I have given some consideration to the role that embodied experience and sensuous feeling may have played in ashmound rituals (Boivin 2003, 2004c). I have suggested that to properly understand the ashmound rituals, archaeologists will need to consider the noise, smell, heat, and brightness of the ashmound fires, and the way that the experience of these qualities would have impacted Neolithic peoples. Ashmound events would have involved an intense sensory experience in which ritual participants would have been assailed by the powerful smells of cattle and dung, the bright, leaping flames of the fire, the roar of consuming flames, and any other sensations that might have been produced through singing, dancing, and other activities potentially associated with the fire rituals. Whatever the activities associated with ashmound fires were meant to accomplish – whether memorialising events, for example, or transforming social statuses or relationships – they must certainly have been greatly assisted, if not enabled, by the embodied, sensuous experience of these richly material and physical events. Consideration of the sensuousness of these events also helps us, if only to a minor extent, to regain some of the strangeness of the ashmound rituals, which is all too easily tamed in discourses that stress their role as monuments. Monuments they may in some sense be, but they are also unlike any other monuments we know. Consideration of the unfamiliar sensory experiences that would have been associated with ashmound production reminds us that ashmound practices should not be too easily subsumed into known anthropological categories.

While this summary of ideas has been brief, it is enough to demonstrate that my growing dissatisfaction with symbolic analyses of material culture has gradually shifted me away from the type of representation-focused analysis I undertook during my PhD research. While I still recognise that material culture can express ideas and concepts, I am increasingly interested in the way that the material world, by virtue of its physical nature and the complementary sensory awareness of the human body, can impact people in very different ways that have nothing to do with the communication of abstract notions. While such phenomenological studies in archaeology are not without problems – in particular the necessary assumption of at least a certain degree of basic universality in sensory experience across human groups, which not all anthropologists would agree with – they are nonetheless essential in bringing to archaeology a more sophisticated and multifaceted understanding of the material remains it deals with. In addition, they align archaeology more closely with the critique of representation, and the inherent, if not always explicit, material implications of alternative phenomenological and experiential approaches.

While archaeologists, dealing as we do with the sensual, physical world of material culture on a daily basis, should have been some of the first to draw importance to the senses, most work relating to the senses in archaeology is of recent vintage and ultimately inspired by studies in history and anthropology. These studies have drawn attention in particular to the dominance and privileging of vision (and text) in contemporary and recent Western societies (Innis 1951; Levin 1993; McLuhan 1964; Ong 1969, 2002). While different views are often expressed concerning the origins of this visualism – that it can be traced to the Classical world (Ong 2002; Stoller 1989; Watson 2003), to the fostering of quantification and visualisation within medieval scholasticism (Ong 1969), or to the development of linear perspective during the Renaissance (Howes 1991; Watson 2003), for example – the 'view' shared by most scholars is that its outcome was the creation of a more distanced and observational mode of understanding. While the so-called lower senses invite and sometimes demand bodily engagement, vision promotes distance and abstraction, and was therefore the privileged sense in the Enlightenment quest for rationality, truth, and objectivity. Vision continues to top the hierarchy of senses in the West, and its prominence in the generation of knowledge and understanding is exemplified by the dominance of visual metaphors like "I see", "The evidence shows", and "It is apparent that" (Ouzman 2001: 238). Walter Ong drew early attention to the visual bias in the West, and its links with literacy (Ong 1969, 2002). More recently, Paul

Stoller has played a key role in focusing anthropological attention on senses other than vision (Stoller 1989). His book, *The Taste of Ethnographic Things*, drew upon ethnographic research amongst the Songhay of Niger – amongst whom he argued taste, smell, and hearing were often more important than sight – to make a plea for greater attention to the senses within anthropology. The early 1990s saw this call being responded to by a variety of studies demonstrating the cultural construction of sensory experience. It has increasingly been recognised that sensory tuning is conditioned by culture, environment, technology, and experience.

While these studies have been critical in drawing attention to a much overlooked area of human experience, and generated interesting insights into cultural learning, they have not gone uncritiqued. It has been pointed out, in particular, that, like studies suggesting cultural variation in notions of personhood, they simply create new ways of differentiating 'Us' and 'Them', and of exoticising the Other. Nadia Seremetakis, for example, highlights the theme of sensory 'loss' that is common to many studies of the senses, and that assumes a once whole sensory state. Such studies, she argues, suggest "modernity's separation from a primal and originary sensory experience which can now be relocated in and recovered from a cultural or historical Other" (Seremetakis 1994: 724). Lived experience becomes synonymous with a more deeply sensory realm and one which is to be found predominantly amongst non-Western cultures. Another critique has addressed the bodilessness of much work on the senses, in which cultural construction is emphasised to the exclusion of any physiological aspect, in ways that simply reassert standard dualistic conceptions of mind and body (Morton 1995). We may also note the absence of systematic attention to the material world with which senses engage (as argued by Hamilakis et al. 2002; Seremetakis 1994).

If archaeology has made little attempt to address the first two problems, it has at least made inroads into the project of understanding the relationship between the senses and the material world. This can be seen by examining one specific area of study within the field of archaeology – rock art studies – and the way in which it has been transformed in recent years by a more sensorily aware approach.

Figure 3.5: Use of the term 'rock art' has encouraged parallels to be drawn between rock art and the art that hangs on gallery walls. This may be a problematic comparison. Photo Daniel Kwok.

Rock Art and Sensory Experience

Rock art constitutes one of the most fascinating and yet enigmatic material remnants of the archaeological past. Until recently, attempts to understand ancient and also more recent rock art have generally focused on understanding images. Indeed, the designation 'art' has encouraged this (Goldhahn 2002; Watson 2003), by drawing rock art in line with the art that hangs on museum walls – images meant to be contemplated, interpreted, and aesthetically appreciated by a distanced observer (Figure 3.5). Thus, early attempts to make sense of the paintings and engravings found on cave and rockshelter walls worldwide honed in on images and their careful recording through tracing procedures. Archaeologists tried to understand rock art by studying the imagery, and trying to determine why people would have chosen to paint or engrave the scenes or figures that they did. Indeed, this may seem to be the obvious way to go about studying rock art, and it has been for many decades. Even innovative approaches like that undertaken by the French archaeologist Leroi-Ghouran focused on images. Leroi-Ghouran's structural approach involved determining the distribution of images within Palaeolithic caves in France, and analysing rock art in a syntactic way – as the reflection of systematic structures of meaning within the human mind (Leroi-Gourhan 1968, 1976). Symbolic and linguistic-derived models were further developed under the post-processual paradigm, in which analysts like Chris Tilley undertook to 'read' decontextualised rock art images like texts (Tilley 1991, 1999). Despite multiple revolutions in archaeological theory, rock art continued to be construed as 'art' and, more specifically, as image.

Now, however, numerous archaeologists have began to pay systematic attention to the 'rock' part of the rock art equation – that is, the material substrate upon and into which images have been inscribed. This perspective, which focuses at last on the materiality of rock art imagery, has given a whole new life to rock art studies, and drawn rock art specialists into an engagement with issues of experience and the senses. It has now increasingly been recognised that in rock art studies, the 'rock' is often just as important as the 'art', and that, accordingly, in many ways, rock art is not directly comparable to the art that hangs on the walls of traditional Western museums. Careful contextual studies, and attention to the macro-landscape of the surrounding vegetation, topography, and geological features, as well as the micro-landscape of the rock surface itself, have now revealed that rock art imagery often engages in interesting ways with both rock and place. That is, the rock is not a neutral canvas for image creation, but a fundamental aspect of a process in which the final image may even play only a relatively minor role. These types of studies demand an attention to the senses – to the texture and feel of a rock surface, the play of light across it, and the sounds made while making the art, as well as the sensations brought to bear through the location of the rock art site within the surrounding landscape. Many suggest that notions of representation are inadequate and even unhelpful in understanding a significant number of rock art traditions.

One particularly interesting rock art study that has highlighted the role of the senses is Joakim Goldhahn's examination of the relationship between water and prehistoric engravings from northern Sweden and Scandinavia (Goldhahn 2002). Goldhahn's study demonstrates that a significant portion of Neolithic rock art sites in this region are situated next to waterfalls and places in river channels that, prior to hydroelectrical transformation of the river system, were particularly noisy and raucous, and sometimes even dangerous places. Goldhahn argues that this situation of sites was deliberate, and related to an attempt to encourage particular sensory experiences at rock art sites. The spectacular noise of the nearby rapids, as well as the watery mist that would have been created as water slamming into the rock wall shattered into tiny droplets, would, Goldhahn argues, have encouraged feelings of disengagement with the everyday world. Prolonged exposure may even have resulted in disorientation and hallucinations. Visits to rock art sites thus involved changes in perception and experience, suggesting that rock art production and/or perception was part of a ritualistic process that perhaps only certain members of society participated in.

Various other studies highlight the role that sound likely played at many rock art sites. My own examination of Neolithic rock art in South India indicated that rock art sites in the south Deccan plateau frequently coincide with natural ringing rocks, for example (Figure 3.6; Boivin 2004e; Boivin et al. 2007). These rocks exhibit cupules indicative of percussion, suggesting that sound and possibly music production may have been essential components of the activities carried out at some rock art sites. The pervasive association, in many parts of the world, of rock art sites with ringing rocks (Fagg 1997; Hedges 1993; Rainbird 2002a, 2002b) supports such an interpretation, and may be linked to the role of percussion in transforming experience in ritual practice (Needham 1967).

However, senses other than sound have also been found to be important at many sites. Many scholars who have taken a sensorily aware approach to rock art sites have discovered that rock art patterning demonstrates deliberate situating of rock art in association with cracks in the rock surface, particular textures and mineral inclusions, places where water flow or patination leads to periodic or permanent covering of the rock, and places where reflection or absorption of light is maximised, for example. Rock

Figure 3.6: Ramdas, a local village inhabitant, ringing rocks at the Hiregudda (Kupgal Hill) rock art site in South India. Rock art sites in the region are frequently associated with ringing rocks. Photo Nicole Boivin.

art sites may be intentionally situated in windy places, wet places, dangerous places, dark places, or quiet places. What this patterning means is not always easy to discern, particularly, as is often the case, in the absence of any associated ethnographic tradition. However, there is interesting research linking some sites to places of access to an underworld or spirit world, and some rock art experiences to transitional experiences aimed at achieving alternate states of consciousness that would enable entry into such a world (Lewis-Williams 2002; Lewis-Williams & Dowson 1988, 1990). Some researchers argue that the sensory experience of site location and rock topography, as well as activities carried out at sites, would have had key roles to play in transforming consciousness. Sven Ouzman, for example, has discussed how evidence of the hammering, rubbing, cutting, and flaking of rock surfaces at San

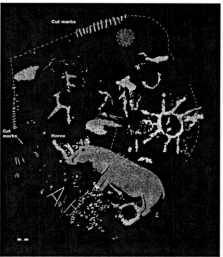

Figure 3.7: A 'San' rock engraving from North-West Province, South Africa. As Sven Ouzman points out, the original image of a hippopotamus has been rubbed smooth, and horns have subsequently been added to create a 'rain animal'. In addition, the rock substrate has been cut on the edges and bears numerous non-representational hammer marks, which may be the result of hammering of the rock to release its potency, take a piece of it, or create sound. Ouzman has emphasised the non-representational aspects of rock art. Photo and redrawing Sven Ouzman.

rock engraving sites in southern Africa (Figure 3.7) may indicate attempts to cross the boundary between the Ordinary World and the Spirit World, maintain contact between the worlds, or access the power attached to such portals to the Spirit World (Ouzman 2001). The secondary marks left at rock art sites by such practices have also been overlooked in traditional rock art studies, but reinforce the notion that markings on rock may have little to do with representation. Ouzman is careful to point out that even traditional rock art imagery may not be representational, however. He has emphasised, for example, that San rock engravings of spiritually pre-eminent animals did not represent these animals – "rather, these rock-engravings *were* the Spirit World animals and beings emergent" (ibid.: 245). Visceral contact with the engravings, through rubbing, for example, allowed people to access the potency they embodied (ibid.).

Christine Watson, in studying image-making amongst the Kutjungka of the Australian Western Desert, has drawn conclusions
that overlap with these. Her work indicates that image-making in
the Western Desert involves the totality of the senses, including
touch as well as bodily and sonic elements (Watson 2003). Watson
describes Kutjungka image-making (Figure 3.8) as a system of marking the skin or surface of both land and people as part of ceremonial
activities. She argues that it is thus unlike art in the Western sense,
and is not primarily representational in nature. And while the land
itself is seen as alive, and embodying various Ancestral Beings, it
does not represent these Ancestors either. Paul Taçon's study into
the 'power of stone' in Australian Aboriginal culture similarly highlights the way stone used for such purposes as tool and art production may have symbolic value, but also embodies power in a way
that has little to do with representation (Taçon 1991). Many ethnographic comments concerning people's understanding of the material world suggest that such understandings are widespread. *Pili
mitti* in rural Rajasthan does not represent Laksmi, for example; it
is Laksmi. Christian religious relics do not represent the saint; they
are the saint (Pels 1998: 104). Huichol art does not represent the
deities, but becomes a manifestation of them (Shelton 1992: 240).

Such examples of 'untranscended materiality' (Pietz 1985: 7), in
which notions of matter as an empty signifier are challenged, link
studies of the senses with those of fetishism and aesthetics. Recent
discussion of both fetishism and aesthetics in anthropology and
related disciplines has also encouraged more systematic attention
to materiality and the sensuous experience of the material world
within the humanities. The fetish, as a West African material entity
that did not fit easily into the classificatory and understanding
systems of Western traders in the seventeenth century, has become
emblematic of the resistance of certain types of human–material
relations to normal subject–object frameworks of intentionality.
Discussions of the application of the notion of the fetish within
anthropology, psychoanalysis, and Marxism have drawn attention
to its ability to demonstrate the way in which objects can reverse
the flow of agency and intention from humans to artefacts (Ellen
1988; Olsen 2003; Pels 1998; Pietz 1985). Peter Pels points out that
"[a] crucial point of the different discourses on fetishism is precisely
to outline the possibility that the materiality of things can stand in

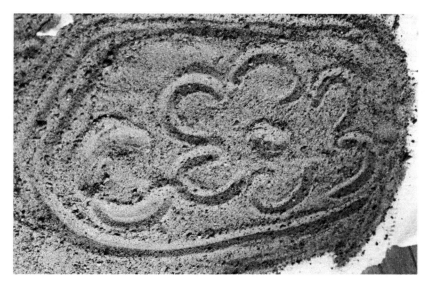

Figure 3.8: An example of the sand drawings made by the Kutjungka of Western Australia. Christine Watson has emphasised that Kutjungka sand paintings are not primarily representational in nature. Sand drawing by Tjama Freda Napanangka, photo Christine Watson.

the way of, and deflect, the course of human traffic" (Pels 1998: 95). He has furthermore highlighted the way that fetishism, "[a]s part of an aesthetics of untranscended materiality, . . . tells us to move in, rather than escape, the sensuous border zone between our selves and the things around us, between mind and matter" (ibid.: 102).

The study of aesthetics within anthropology has also encouraged consideration of the sensuous relationship between people and things in various cultural contexts, and of the way such relationships can bypass notions of representation. While the cause of aesthetics is sometimes hindered by notions of a universal sensory response to which variable cultural readings are subsequently attached (e.g., Morphy 1989), aesthetic studies within anthropology have nonetheless been useful in drawing attention to the sensual experience of the material world. Indeed the sensual is often pivotal to definitions of aesthetics, no matter how variable they may be. The *Oxford English Dictionary*, for example, defines aesthetics as "the science which treats of the conditions of sensuous perception" (Shelton 1992), while Howard Morphy describes aesthetics as "concerned with how something appeals to the senses" (Morphy

1989: 21). Those arguing in favour of a place for aesthetics in anthropology have drawn attention to the way that predominant functional and semiotic studies of art objects – studies that have highlighted the role of art in maintaining the social structure and that have focused on the interpretation of its meaning – have often overlooked the 'artness' of art, that is, the importance of art objects as objects (Coote & Shelton 1992: 3). Such anthropological studies of aesthetics have not been confined to examination of the sensuous experience and appreciation of art objects, however, but have also explored the aesthetics of more everyday objects. Coote, for example, arguing that "[a]ll human activity has a sensuous aspect" (Coote 1992: 246), has focused on unravelling the cattle-oriented aesthetics of the cattle-keeping Nilotes of the southern Sudan. He has demonstrated that despite a lack of art objects as defined in a narrow Western sense, the Nilotes have a well-developed aesthetic that is focused on and influenced by the sensual experience and valuation of cattle features, like hump and horn shape and coat colour and patterning. Coote's analysis highlights the role that sensuous valuation plays in everyday experience amongst the Nilotes, and challenges traditional understandings of aesthetics as narrowly concerned with art and beauty.

How Matter Moves Us: Emotion and the Material World

If the discussion up to this point has succeeded, as I hope it has, in demonstrating that considerations of experience have become more central in many of the human sciences, and have also helped in some cases to draw attention to more material aspects of human life, it has also overlooked a crucial dimension of experience: emotion. In reality, sensual experience is closely entangled with emotional experience, and considerations of experience must acknowledge both. The senses often assume a pivotal role in eliciting emotional feelings, while emotion itself acts back on the senses, and can heighten sensory awareness. Like the senses, emotions also draw us into consideration of the body. Indeed definitions of emotion, either those that stress the opposition between thought and emotion, or those that see emotions as thoughts that are just

Figure 3.9: Emotion is often understood as opposed to rationality. Photo Alessandro Paiva.

somehow more embodied, inevitably emphasise their fundamental bodilyness. However, if as discussed in the previous chapter, much thought is now recognised as embodied and non-representational in orientation, it becomes increasingly difficult to see how emotion is different from thought, or stands out as any special kind of class of thought. In addition, the stress on the bodily dimension of emotion in comparison to other types of human experience, like thought, also perpetuates a mind–matter split. It suggests that some aspects of our experience are very bodily, and others are not. It also separates cognition, consciousness, and thought from emotion, senses, and the subconscious in a way that prepares the ground very neatly for a rational versus irrational split in our understanding of experience.

The idea that emotion is irrational has a deep history, and indeed remains widespread (Figure 3.9). Emotion has long been seen as a threat to reason, and a particular danger to philosophers, whose goal has traditionally been seen as the pursuit of reason (Solomon 2000). As Robert Solomon points out, one of the most enduring metaphors of reason and emotion has been that of master and slave, "with the wisdom of reason firmly in control and the dangerous impulses of emotion safely suppressed, channeled, or (ideally) in harmony with reason" (ibid.: 3). But not all early thinkers divided emotion from rationality, and Aristotle, Baruch Spinoza, and David Hume are amongst those who have believed that at least some emotions are rational (Damasio 2003: 150; Solomon 2000).

While emotion continues to be given short shift, both in terms of ideas about its positive role, and the quantity of research and thought devoted to it within the contemporary academic setting, it is nonetheless the case that modern studies of the workings of the brain are beginning to challenge the deep-seated notion that emotion is opposed to reason, and a minor aspect of human behaviour. The work of the cognitive scientist Antonio Damasio stands out in this regard. In his recent book *Looking for Spinoza*, Damasio, one of cognitive science's main advocates of a more holistic approach to mind, brain, and body (Damasio 1994), has argued forcefully in favour of the view that emotion is in fact inherently rational (Damasio 2003). Damasio's view is that emotion is part of evolution's strategy for making organisms more adept at responding to environmental changes and challenges. Emotion enables us to make more sensible decisions about how to act, both with respect to others and our environment.

The source of Damasio's interpretations is a variety of detailed and very interesting studies of the brain, and especially what happens to people when specific parts of the brain are injured through accident or disease. In particular, cognitive scientists have discovered that when parts of the brain linked to emotional behaviour are damaged, people can continue to perform well on IQ tests, and appear intellectually intact, and yet consistently fail to make decisions that are advantageous to themselves and those close to them. Social behaviour is particularly impaired. Patients cannot determine who is trustworthy, they lack a sense of what kind of behaviour is socially appropriate, and they may violate ethical rules. Nonetheless, in a laboratory situation, they are able to remember the conventions and rules that they break every day, and realise, when someone calls their attention to the fact, that they have broken these conventions and rules. As Damasio describes, these emotionally impaired patients are able to:

> ... solve successfully a specific social problem when the problem is presented in the laboratory, as a test, in the form of a hypothetical situation. The problem may be precisely the same kind the patient has just failed to solve in real life and real time. These patients exhibit extensive knowledge about the social situations that they so egregiously mismanaged in reality. They know the premises of the problem, the options of action, the likely consequences of those actions immediately and in the long-term, and how to navigate such knowledge logically. But all of this is to no avail when they need it most in the real world. (ibid.: 143–44)

Damasio argues that this is because emotions are actually crucial to successful, real-life reasoning – not merely associated players in the process of reasoning, but indispensable players (ibid.: 145). Experience creates links between emotions and social knowledge that are brought into play when similar social situations arise in the future. Emotion then plays the role, not of substituting reasoning, but of increasing its efficiency and speed. It can also make the reasoning process almost superfluous, such as when we make a decision based on a 'gut feeling' or hunch. Emotion also accentuates reasoning processes by producing "alterations in working memory, attention and reasoning so that the decision-making process is biased toward selecting the action most likely to lead to the best possible outcome, given prior experience" (ibid.: 148). Damasio argues that emotion not only helps with reasoning, but also allows us to empathise and be ethical beings. In the latter, he virtually echoes Hume, who in making this point, observed that "it is not against reason to prefer the destruction of half the world to the scratching of my finger" (Solomon 2000: 7). Thus, while straightforward, intellectually distanced reason may dictate selfish, self-interested behaviour, emotion acts to make reason ethical, and indeed rational from a social point of view.

Like cognitive science, anthropology has also recently taken greater interest in the emotions. In particular, anthropology has explored the way that emotion, rather than being 'hard-wired' and universal as some early biological studies argued, is actually remarkably culturally variable (Lutz 1988; Rosaldo 1984). Anthropological studies of emotion have demonstrated in particular the role of language in the construction of the emotions – rather than being reflective of differently coded but essentially similar emotional experiences, linguistically variable emotion terms have been shown to actually reflect cultural differences in emotion construction. It has been argued that the way emotion is talked about, and also acted out in culturally prescribed ways, are factors that play a key role in the way that emotion is constituted and experienced in different cultural settings.

While such work has been valuable in many ways, Damasio's model takes into account the two key considerations that, as Margot Lyon has pointed out, such 'cultural constructionist' accounts often leave out: the body and the social (Lyon 1995). Lyon has argued against the way that cultural constructionist accounts treat emotions as purely mental events in which the body has little if any role. Michelle Rosaldo, for example, has stated that "feelings are not substances to be discovered in our blood but social practices organized by stories that we both enact and tell" (Rosaldo 1984: 143). Catherine Lutz has described emotions as "forms of symbolic action" (Lutz 1988: 6). Lyon and others have taken exception to such a disembodied understanding of emotion within the social sciences. They have also objected to the lack of real exploration, within constructivist accounts, of how emotions are deeply implicated in social relationships. As Lyon has pointed out, and as Damasio's analysis makes clear, emotions are social phenomena that have much to do with our relations, real, anticipated, imagined, or recollected, with other people (Kemper 1978; Lyon 1995). Lyon observes that this is suggested in Rosaldo's recognition that what separates emotion from certain other forms of thought is the sense that something is at stake (Rosaldo 1984), but argues that the social and bodily bases of this sense remain largely unexplored in most cultural constructionist accounts (Lyon 1995). Meanwhile, though Damasio's discussion of emotions is based within medical research and cognitive science, and hence not specifically concerned with cultural variation in emotional experience, it does clearly account for the fact that thoughts about emotion will influence emotional experience. Indeed, Damasio's model of emotional experience clearly specifies a continual feedback between emotions and thoughts about emotions (which he calls feelings), as well as prior experience and learning. It strives, in a way that cultural constructivist accounts do not, for a non-dualistic understanding of mind and body.

From the point of view of this book, however, Damasio is perhaps most interesting for what he has to say about the material world. For Damasio not only notes that material objects can elicit an emotional response, but he also argues that this process is of fundamental importance. He claims that "one of the main aspects of the history of human development pertains to how most objects that surround our brains become capable of triggering some form of emotion or another" (Damasio 2003: 55). These emotions, he points out, can be weak or strong, good or bad, and conscious or unconscious. And while some are set by evolution, others are the result of personal experience. For example, a house that you were frightened in as a child can continue to make you feel uncomfortable long after the negative emotional experience occurred (Figure 3.10). Indeed it is possible for all houses of a certain type to elicit such an emotional reaction. Damasio argues that "by the time we are old enough to write books, few if any objects in the world are emotionally neutral" (ibid.: 56; Figure 3.11). We do not of course respond to all objects to the same degree, however: while some evoke strong emotional reactions, others will evoke weak, even barely perceptible responses. Damasio has pursued such associations all the way to level of the brain structure, and demonstrated that an important triggering site for reactions to objects of emotional significance is to be found in the frontal lobe region of the brain (ibid.: 61).

If Damasio's discussion of the emotional resonancy of objects, and the way that our material surroundings are painted by the colourful brush of emotion, is limited, it is to be praised for at least taking the material world into account. The idealist bias of many cultural constructivist accounts often precludes such attention

Figure 3.10: A house in shadows. As Antonio Damasio has noted, objects or places associated with an emotional response can continue to trigger an emotional reaction for years to come. Photo Frédéric Dupont (sxc.hu/patator).

to the relationship between mind, body, and physical surroundings. The same oversight is even present in archaeology, a discipline specifically and self-consciously concerned with the material world. An important attempt to introduce systematic concern with the emotions into archaeology by Sarah Tarlow (2000), for example, contains surprisingly little discussion of material culture. Nonetheless, while consideration of the emotional impact of the material world is rare within anthropology and archaeology, some more materially and bodily oriented studies within these and related disciplines have drawn attention to the emotional facets of material objects and environments. These have demonstrated that consideration of emotion is often crucial to understanding the role that objects and environments can have in human affairs, and particularly in processes of memory, identity, and personhood.

The archaeologist Chris Gosden has given some recent consideration to emotion, and argued, like Damasio, that emotion is critical not only to our relationships with other people, but also with objects. "Our main reactions to each other and the material

Figure 3.11: An evocative photo of an old truck highlights Damasio's observation that few if any things in the world are emotionally neutral. Photo Paul Oberlin.

world", observes Gosden, "are emotional" (Gosden 2004: 34). For Gosden, it is the multi-sensory nature of the material world that gives it such emotional resonancy – the way that, as addressed in the previous section, the material world impacts on our various senses, creating rich sensations and experiences. Gosden refers to the "dense intermingling" that takes place between our emotional life and our physical and sensual relationships with our bodies and material culture. It is recognition of this dense intermingling that has led Jean-Pierre Warnier to critique the separation of material culture studies and studies of the body – the way in which, for example, "one journal is devoted to material culture and another to the body, as if they were clearly distinct entities" (Warnier 2001: 10). For Warnier as well, both sensory and emotional experience are integral to the relationship between people and the material world – indeed they, rather than any kind of abstract knowledge, are the reason that material culture "reaches deep into the psyche of the subject" (ibid.).

Morphy, in examining the aesthetics of the art of the Yol-ngu of northern Australia, displays similar interest in the links between sensory and emotional experience. Morphy argues that Yolngu artists create in their paintings a particular visual effect – a kind of shimmering effect called *Bir'yun* (Figure 3.12) – that generates an emotional response in Yolngu viewers that they perceive as a manifestation of Ancestral power (Morphy 1989). Recent cognitive science investigations of the mirror neuron system in human beings have also emphasised the degree to which aesthetic responses can be linked to sensual experience and emotion. David Freedberg, an art historian and Vittorio Gallese, a neuroscientist, for example, have discussed studies that show that simply looking at objects, whether everyday or artistic, activates motor centres of the brain, generating an embodied and empathetic response (Freedberg & Gallese 2007). These studies of art and aesthetics highlight the play between sensual experience and emotion that characterises human relationships to material culture in general.

Abstract thought, symbolic representation, and language are not divorced from this equation of course. But, in some cases, their role is much more apparent than in others. Indeed the relative roles played by abstract representational thought and emotional feeling in mediating the relationship between people and material objects and surroundings could be conceived along a scale. In some cases, objects do actually represent abstract ideas or collective values, and are simply assisted in doing so by the emotional valences that attach to them. A national flag may represent a nation or the idea of a nation, but it can also – hung in house windows and storefronts during a time of war in particular – express ideas of patriotism and duty that derive from the emotional feelings that it engenders. In other cases, however, it is difficult to describe objects (or other aspects of the material world) as representing anything. Instead of being a medium for the expression or representation of an idea or meaning, the object has a different kind of value, one that is often personal, idiosyncratic, and linked very closely to the emotions the object elicits. The emotional significance *is* the object's significance. One can take as an example here the "charge of psychic energy" that sometimes imbues people's personal possessions, and especially the things that belonged to someone who has passed away (Hoskins 1998: 22). In between these two extremes, we find objects that *do* represent but, drawing on emotional associations,

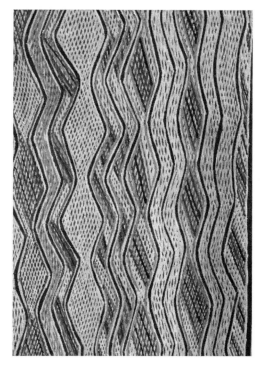

Figure 3.12: The shimmering effect called Bir'yun. *Detail of The Marawili Tree at Djarrakpi, 1976, a painting by Narritjin Maymuru. Photo Howard Morphy.*

represent less conventional meanings. For example, objects may be used idiosyncratically as a metaphor of self (ibid.: 3). They represent, but do not represent abstract or collective notions. Whatever the place on the imaginary scale I have described, however, emotion is crucial to understanding the experience of objects, and the power that they hold in the world we have created.

The emotional resonance of objects is often highlighted in discussions of the relationship between identity or personhood and material culture. While earlier studies tended to focus on the relationship between material style and collective identity – for example, ethnic or cultural identity (Sackett 1977; Wiessner 1984) – and saw material objects, particularly objects of dress, as abstract signifiers of identity, more recent work has given more attention to the experience and creation of identity and personhood through emotionally imbued objects. This is particularly true of the work of Janet Hoskins, who has explored in detail the personal and emotional links between objects and people in Eastern Indonesia (Hoskins 1998). Hoskins' approach is both inspired by and critical of Marilyn Strathern's pioneering studies of the relationship between persons and objects in Pacific societies (Strathern 1988). Strathern famously argued that Melanesians viewed objects differently than Westerners – as detached parts of distributed persons, rather than as things that exist in themselves. Personhood in Melanesia is thus created in part through the circulation of objects, which 'enchain' people into relations with others. Hoskins finds Strathern's work both inspirational and "frustratingly abstract" (Hoskins 1998: 9). Strathern, Hoskins argues, "deliberately excludes considerations of individual subjectivity or biographic experience from her accounts" and does not include emotional affect or trauma as part of the process of enchainment she describes (ibid.: 10). Hoskins' own experience in Eastern Indonesia suggests that these factors are nonetheless critical to the creation of relationships between people and things, which are often far more personal and idiosyncratic than Strathern's model acknowledges.

Hoskins notes that for the Kodi of Samba, for example, objects are invested with great significance, serving as both 'history objects' that provide a collective representation of the past, and also, at a more intimate level, as biographical objects that become entangled in people's lives, and in the process become vehicles of selfhood. She focuses on the latter types of objects, and observes how the Kodi draw objects into biographical narratives in a way that allows complex and often challenging personal and social events in people's lives to be addressed and discussed indirectly. Hoskins records the narratives various people provide about their lives, and the role that biographical objects play within them: for example, a spindle that allows a young woman to describe the story of her romantic longing and later disappointment, or a woven betel bag that becomes a source of identity for a man and a way also for his wives to discuss their disappointment with him. These objects are not the depersonalised objects of earlier accounts, many of which were drawn into totalising schemes of gender opposition – objects "lined up neatly in two columns according to their gender attributes", which were then used to deduce notions of 'male' and 'female' (ibid.: 14). Instead, Hoskins focuses on what she argues is an equally important use of objects to constitute the personal self; not only to express it, however, but also to understand it. The objects used are personally meaningful possessions, and often domestic objects. They are things that gain significance through their association with personal experiences and events that are often highly emotional in nature, and that invest objects with emotion as well.

While Hoskins' work may stress the unique role that objects have in Kodi society, and the way that the emotional significance of certain objects allows them to construct and understand aspects of personhood, she is also keen to avoid contrasting Kodi and Western concepts of material culture in the way that Melanesian and Western understandings of objects have often contrasted (see Strathern 1988; for a critique see Thomas 1991). She notes that while people in the industrialised West are often described as alienated from commodities, these objects are nonetheless also at times invested with emotional significance and used in the idiosyncratic construction of identity. She highlights in particular the way objects can become filled with idiosyncratic meaning through their association with a life-transforming event:

> The last shirt a man wore before his death, the plates used at a wedding dinner, the glass broken in response to shocking news – such events can attach themselves to ordinary objects and fix them in memory as markers of the extraordinary. (Hoskins 1998: 195)

Jackson has similarly described how even highly technological objects in Western society can be imbued with emotional resonance (Jackson 2002b). This occurs in particular when people extend notions of subjectivity not only to others but also, as commonly occurs, the extra-human world. Thus, we regularly anthropomorphise computers, and direct towards new technologies the same kind of anxieties that cause us to construct other peoples as alien, dirty, or dangerous. We also fall in love with a jacket or a new car, or mourn the loss of a teddy bear (Olsen 2003: 95) – all emotion-imbued relationships that suggest that Western commodities are not as clearly alienable as we like to think (Figure 3.13).

Another area of study that has sometimes highlighted the relationship between objects and emotion is that dealing with memory. Studies have demonstrated that memory and emotion are closely coupled (Parrott & Spackman 2000). Not only are emotional stimuli better remembered than unemotional stimuli, but intensely experienced emotions will also cause some details to be better remembered than others. Constructivist researchers – who argue that memories are constructed rather than retrieved – have further emphasised that current emotional state has an important bearing on the kinds of memories one constructs. Very few researchers have, however, systematically explored the relationship between material culture and memory.

Nonetheless, Elizabeth Hallam and Jenny Hockey make some useful beginnings towards such a project. Their recent book, *Death, Memory and Material Culture*, addresses to some degree the role of emotional experience, and particularly emotionally imbued objects, in mediating the relations between the living and the dead, and in producing and sustaining memory (Hallam & Hockey 2001). They describe how objects that play a role in remembering the dead often possess emotional significance, due to their close personal association with the deceased or with the death itself. However, the sensations and emotions associated with death-related objects are not all equally intense – they range from the "powerfully felt to the diffuse and barely perceived" (ibid.: 13). Memory, material culture, and emotion are brought together in varying constellations depending on the nature of the death, the object, and its relationship to the deceased. The key point that emerges from their book is that while material culture can sometimes be used to represent the dead, it can also fulfil various other functions that have less to do with straightforward signification, and much more to do with emotion and experience. Personal, everyday items of material culture in particular may allow tangible, felt links with the dead, rather than the more abstracted links that are formed through the use of public objects like plaques and gravestones – they may bring the

Figure 3.13: Many examples of human–material relations in the West, like the one suggested by this tombstone bearing a Harley-Davidson insignia, indicate that Western commodities are not as alienable as we often like to think. Photo Nicole Boivin.

deceased 'to life' in some sense, rather than just represent them in the lives of the living (Figure 3.14).

Another area of investigation that has given consideration to emotion and the senses, and also at times their relationship to memory, is the study of ritual. In particular, studies of ritual performance since the 1970s (Fernandez 1972; Turner 1982) have drawn attention from what ritual *says* to what it *does*, and addressed the role of ritual experience in changing perceptions and interpretations (Bell 1997). A forerunner to such studies can be found in Barth's analysis of ritual experience amongst the Baktaman of New Guinea (Barth 1975), which is particularly notable for its attention to material culture and the material environment. Barth highlights the strong sensory and emotional experiences often associated with

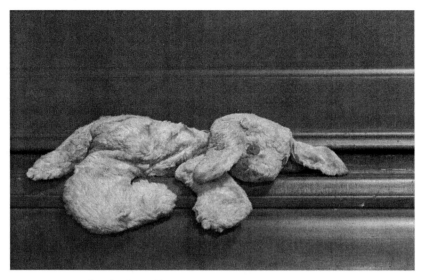

Figure 3.14: Elizabeth Hallam and Jenny Hockey have observed that personal, everyday objects may allow closer links with the dead than public objects like plaques and monuments. Photo Julia Freeman-Woolpert.

Baktaman ritual experiences, which render them impossible to translate into words. Indeed, Barth clearly anticipates performance theory when he states that for the Baktaman, "[t]]he rite's aspect of 'doing something'... clearly predominates for the actors over its 'saying something'" (ibid.: 221). Baktaman rituals evoke intense experiences of danger, fear, awe, pain, and secrecy and involve the use of colourful, tactile, and sensual material objects that accordingly become powerful, and powerfully experienced, ritual symbols. Barth stresses the importance of material symbols in particular within the context of a non-literate society:

> A correlate of non-literacy is the special importance of concrete symbols as uniquely durable symbols of uniquely durable messages. Such concrete objects serve as anchors, not only of abstract thought but of ephemeral communications in general. Persons hold on to the memory of a deceased parent, spouse, sibling, or child by tying and wearing mourning bands and often attaching objects associated

with the dead person to them . . . Several women who wore their mothers' taro scrapers (yom) in this way, explained that the sound of them "made them sorrowful". As concrete representations of emotion, they serve to add reality both to the memory and the feeling. Likewise, a woman makes first degree insignia for a boy she feels close to "to see him better", i.e. to aid them both in experiencing their durable relationship. And the sacred marsupials clearly function in the same way for worshippers, as concrete aids to comprehend and retain the comprehension of ancestors and fertility. (ibid.: 230–31)

For Harvey Whitehouse, however, the Baktaman case highlights not so much the contrast between literate and non-literate societies and their reliance on text versus memory, but between two fundamentally different types of memory and knowledge transmission systems (Whitehouse 1992). He has contrasted Baktaman religion with another Papua New Guinean religion, the Pomio Kivung, in which verbal exegesis, logical integration, and extensive discussion and commentary play an extremely central role. Since neither religion is text-based, Whitehouse argued that the fundamental difference between them is actually in the character and frequency of knowledge transmission. Amongst the Baktaman, transmission is irregular and infrequent, but effective because rituals bombard the senses and elicit intense emotional experiences – in Baktaman initiation, for example, he observes that "anything from sudden pain and extended torture to peculiar aromas and loud noises are unleashed upon the unprepared novices" (ibid.: 782). In contrast, Kivung religious doctrine is transmitted with extraordinary frequency and does not excite the senses. Instead, the focus is on logical integration, routine, and predominantly linguistic communication.

Whitehouse's analysis contrasted sensory and language-oriented experience, reaffirming the distinction that this chapter has attempted to highlight between the representational and sensual aspects of engagement with the material world. The sensory and emotional aspects of material experience are not directly comparable to linguistic experience; instead, they demand that we consider various non-linguistic, supposedly 'irrational' aspects of being human. Just as it has been impossible to understand the role of religion within society in the absence of a consideration of experience, so is it impossible to understand the role of the material world without giving due consideration to the full variety of ways in which it is experienced.

Neurophenomenology

Attention to the senses and emotions invites consideration – as we have seen – of ritual, a sphere of human activity that often fully engages both of these aspects of human experience. And it is undoubtedly because it is characterised by such obviously non-linguistic, bodily experience that ritual has, more often than other areas of interest, encouraged some degree of engagement between scientific and humanities-based approaches to human behaviour. While such attempts at consultation and even occasionally collaboration have been perceived as anathema by some researchers on both sides of the academic divide, others have seen them as essential to any real understanding of the complex interweaving of thought and experience that characterises ritual and religious activity. I would argue that such interdisciplinary approaches are not only critical to the study of ritual, but also of potential interest to scholars trying to unravel the complexities of the relationship between the material world and society.

One early anthropological attempt to address the more physiological and cognitive aspects of ritual can be found in Rodney Needham's discussion of the relationship between percussion and transition in the journal *Man* during the mid-1960s (Needham 1967). Needham was fascinated by the recurrent use, in a variety of societies across the world, of percussive noise in rituals aimed at communicating with the spirit world (Figure 3.15). While sociologists like Durkheim had argued against the use of psychological methods to address sociological phenomena, Needham was convinced that the cross-cultural regularities he had observed with

Figure 3.15: Priest hammering a drum during a Shinto ritual at the Meiji Shrine in Tokyo, Japan. Percussion is a common feature of rituals across the world. Photo Katherine de Vera.

respect to the use of percussion to communicate with the spirit world demanded consideration of the psychological and neurological foundations of experience. The paper presents a preliminary, still speculative and uncertain attempt to grapple with the fact that cultural activities like music and ritual have bodily and emotional dimensions not adequately addressed by anthropological methods. Needham reached the conclusion that percussion was actually linked to the formal passage from one status or condition to another in rites of passage, and gathered that this had something to do with the fact that "sound-waves have neural and organic effects on human beings" (ibid.: 610), but was not able to move far beyond these preliminary insights. Nonetheless, he realised that it would be necessary "to transcend conventional academic distinctions and to account for human phenomena, psychic and social, in their integrity" (ibid.: 612) by collaborating with natural scientists studying cognition and the physiology of the brain. To some degree, further development of these insights and aims had to await subsequent developments in the cognitive and neurological sciences.

Remarkably, however, attempts to construct the kinds of bridges that Needham recommended have remained relatively rare, despite significant advances since Needham's day in the study of the mind. In the early 1980s, for example, a few anthropologists like Donald Tuzin and Alfred Gell drew on scientific studies to explore the physiological and neurological dimensions of acoustic (Tuzin 1984) and sensori-motor (Gell 1980) ritual experience, but such attempts were infrequent, and – as commentary on Tuzin's paper suggests – not always positively received by the wider anthropological community. More recently, a few scholars from both sides of the divide have undertaken more systematic attempts to bring the sciences and humanities together in the study of religion. In particular, researchers like Charles Laughlin, Francisco Varela, and their colleagues have tried to link studies of experience with neurological and cognitive analyses using an approach that is sometimes described as neurophenomenology (Laughlin et al. 1990; Varela 1996; Varela et al. 1991). This involves undertaking more systematic, phenomenologically inspired research into experience in conjunction with more traditional cognitive science studies of the mind and the brain. While such studies remain relatively isolated, and have often focused on altered states of consciousness rather than everyday religious experience, they have nonetheless been very valuable in highlighting the range of types of consciousness and associated experiences, and also in bringing together two of the key kinds of approaches to the senses and emotions that have been addressed in this chapter.

Within the field of archaeology, a few researchers have drawn on work in neurophenomenology and other areas of cognitive science in order to interpret aspects of the material record of a number of diverse societies. Looking into the deep past at Palaeolithic communities in western Europe, David Lewis-Williams, for example, has used neurophenomenological findings to assist in the interpretation of the still enigmatic paintings and engravings found on cave walls throughout the region (Lewis-Williams 2002). He has provided a new interpretation of the paintings, arguing that several of their features and characteristics are highly suggestive of the way the world is experienced by shamans and others during states of altered consciousness (ASC). For example, he has famously suggested that some of the non-representative, geometric designs on cave walls are identical to the kinds of entoptic visual patterns cross-culturally observed during certain stages of altered consciousness. Furthermore, the location of some cave art in deep, nearly inaccessible parts of caves suggests the kind of journeying into a realm deep underground that often characterises shamanistic trance experience. The cave art in many cases also seems to engage with the cave wall. Some of it, for example, takes advantage of natural undulations or crevices in the rock, which are only accentuated with paintings or engravings. These examples suggest that the wall was seen as a kind of living support in which shamans saw and felt for visions of powerful animals that were already there. Other common features, like finger marks and handprints, suggest a similar interaction with the rock. They also suggest the rock was seen as more than just a support for the images; Lewis-Williams argues that the rock, as in other ethnographically documented cases, and as discussed in the section on rock art, was probably a permeable boundary between this world and the worlds accessed during ASC. Thus, rock art is as much about experiences as images, and rather than just representing experiences during ASC, cave art materialised them and became part of them. While not everyone is happy with Lewis-Williams' interpretations (as discussed in Chippindale 2003), it is clear that they are laudable at least for their attention to multi-sensorial and emotional experience, and to the materiality of rock art, so often lost in discussions of images and of representation in rock art studies.

Neurophenomenological approaches have also been applied in later archaeological settings. Jennifer Dornan, for example, has recently drawn attention to the utility of neurophenomenological studies in understanding archaeologically documented changes in the Maya religious system (Dornan 2004). She draws on studies in cultural neurophenomenology that demonstrate how religious experience – even everyday religious experience – induces shifts in brain activity. These shifts can, for example, alter the individual's ability to distinguish between self and other, and are argued to be at the root of many experiences of the sacred, in which people 'feel God' or feel at one with the universe. Such experiences are drawn into a 'cycle of meaning' in which shared religious meaning is constructed through the integration of cultural knowledge and individual experience in a dynamic, ongoing feedback process.

Dornan argues that the collapse of Classic period lowland Maya state religion can be linked to the failure of an increasingly elite-focused religion to provide an experiential element to the religious life of the larger populace. Dornan observes that support for the Maya state religious system was built upon Mayan individuals' subjective experiences (ibid.: 32), which are materially evidenced in a Preclassical architecture characterised by household alters and open, public plazas that acted as the setting for domestic and local religious practices, respectively. Experience of the divine was open to all and provided the foundation for a strong system of religious belief. When the elite subsequently tried to appropriate the power associated with the sacred by restricting access to ritually induced religious experience, they were able to legitimate and strengthen their rule, but also gradually eroded the foundations of a system built upon subjective experience and a degree of equality in access to the sacred. Eventually, the disillusionment of the populace with an increasingly distant state religion, argues Dornan, led to the collapse of the Classic Maya state.

Dornan's perceptive analysis successfully weaves material evidence, neurophenomenological findings, and a consideration of subjective experience in a way that should serve as a model for archaeologists. Her analysis demonstrates that attention to shared physiological regularities in the human body does not preclude consideration of culturally variable experience, nor confine investigation only to the most unusual kinds of religious experience. Most importantly, it demonstrates that material symbols are also experienced materials that require analysis from multiple perspectives. Archaeology will be at its best when it not only takes into consideration, but furthermore links, the representational and experiential dimensions of the material culture remains it studies.

More Than Words Can Say

I began this chapter with a consideration of the semiotic-style analysis I carried out on domestic architecture, space, and material culture in Rajasthan as part of my doctoral research. The various case studies discussed in this chapter demonstrate just how far the insights and studies of individual scholars have pushed the analysis of the material world beyond this limited perspective. If I could go back to Balathal and start over again, I would take my inspiration from these studies, and embark on a very different kind of research program. I would ask questions not only about meaning and what people do, but also about how they feel and what they experience. Perhaps more importantly, I would also spend less time even asking questions. I would devote more attention to simply experiencing and participating in domestic life. For it is very clear that material spaces and objects do much more than offer up a kind of code for living and behaving, or a material version of a cosmological or social scheme. The material world is effective in doing these things, but it also does so much more. Indeed, one of the most interesting things about the material world is the way in which it *differs* from language, from code, and from representation.

Established research on cognition, sensory perception, emotion, and feelings offers up some ways of beginning to understand precisely how material culture does differ from language, but it is also clear that such research is limited in this regard because it usually only briefly touches on the material world. It is invariably predominantly *about* something else. The envelope now needs to be pushed further. Studies of material culture and the role of the material world in general in human society have up to this point been overwhelmingly influenced by trends in the wider humanities and social sciences. Far more interesting developments are likely to come about when those interested in artefacts, material culture, and the material world in general take their inspiration and their direction from their subject matter. This means not just studying the sensory, emotional, and phenomenological aspects of material experience, but also keeping an open mind, and recognising that the material world is going to do things to people that no non-material-oriented field is going to be able to tell us about. It means engaging in new ethnographic, experimental, and phenomenological studies that focus specifically on the material world. The studies discussed in this chapter, predominantly from anthropology, archaeology, and the cognitive sciences, suggest some interesting departures from established ways of thinking about the material world, but they also challenge us to go further in exploring the materiality of the world that societies and individuals inhabit.

CHAPTER 4
The Agency of Matter

The Near Eastern Neolithic and the Materiality of Soil

Few ideas about the material world have provoked as much controversy as the notion that matter may have agency. Indeed, it is the assumption that it is deeply misguided to attribute agency to things themselves, rather than the humans behind them, that has led everyone from seventeenth-century European traders in West Africa to twentieth-century psychoanalysts to decry so-called fetishistic beliefs. And yet in this chapter, and also the next one, I want to go even further than I have so far in exploring the ability of material things to affect human lives. I want to suggest that things impact us not only emotionally and sensually, but also socially and biologically – genetically even. Such ideas fit uneasily with the notion that human beings are masters of their own destiny, or at the very least masters of the passive matter with which they are surrounded. Nonetheless, if we are to do any justice to the story of human involvement with the material world, it is necessary to move beyond the traditional boundaries of humanistic and idealistic thought, and give a little more due to the brute force that is matter.

It is materiality – the physicality of matter – that gives things agency, and hence it is unsurprising that the idealist strands of thought that dominate the social sciences, and that have lately reduced artefacts to reified thoughts, have given little consideration to the degree to which things can act as agents independently of people. Accordingly, my own awareness that matter might have agency was only gradually awakened when I began to give more thought to the materiality of material culture. Once again, therefore, I wish to return briefly to rural Rajasthan. For it was within the context of an analysis of my ethnoarchaeological data on domestic space in rural Rajasthan that I first began to give real consideration to the physical side of material culture. This consideration was no doubt encouraged by the fact that I went to Rajasthan originally not only as a symbolically/interpretively oriented ethnoarchaeologist, but also as a geoarchaeologist. This strange combination of professional interests led me to take more of an interest in the real materiality of domestic space than I otherwise might have, and kept me constantly aware not only of the symbolic and social readings that could be attached to space, but also of the building materials, methods, and practices that went into the physical creation of houses.

In rural Rajasthan, as I have already hinted, houses are expressive creations steeped in symbolic meaning. In particular, they serve, in part, as material means of articulating and reproducing important Rajasthani cultural ideas concerning purity, auspiciousness, and the sacred. As Bourdieu already observed several decades ago, the engagement children have with houses and the way they learn to behave in relation to them provide important means through which the ideas and values of a society, as well as its social relations, are subconsciously passed on in everyday activities. In Balathal, different axes of and spaces within the house are attributed with different social and symbolic values, that are then inculcated in part through the learning, most often by imitation, of how to behave appropriately in these different spaces. Given the paucity of furnishings in rural Rajasthani houses, it is in particular the division of space through the creation of walls, platforms, and various other types of moulded boundary lines, and the use of different types of plaster and building materials, that creates and signals the diverse spaces to which meanings are attached. It is also changes in these material entities – the knocking down of walls, platforms, and boundary lines, and creation of new ones, and the plastering and re-plastering of spaces, for example – that allow Balathal houses to be closely aligned to the temporal rhythms of social, economic, and ritual life in rural Rajasthan (Boivin 2000). Houses are not static entities, but malleable, constantly changing spaces that draw people and houses into ever closer association (Table 4.1). This in turn reinforces the degree to which houses act as powerful symbols within society, and furthermore gives them a role in the creation of the social rhythms that mark and structure time. Houses and the activities carried out within and directed towards them are the means, in part, through which both space and time are differentiated for human purposes.

This is the crux of my analysis of Balathal houses. In addition to ethnographically documenting the social and symbolic aspects of rural Rajasthani houses, however, I also studied their material make-up, and in particular applied geoarchaeological methods to the investigation of the relationship between this rich ethnographic tale and the much more mundane remains that archaeologists normally dig up. Perhaps because I was at the same time examining house floors, walls, and other components under the microscope, and using various chemical and physical techniques to investigate their materiality, it occurred to me during the course of carrying out this interpretive analysis that much of the way that houses assumed a social and symbolic role relied on the use of soil to create them (by soil, I refer to a general category encompassing clay, mud, sediment, etc.). Mud houses are infinitely malleable, and are constantly plastered and re-plastered in ways that enable them to acquire a new appearance, texture, and feel. New mud walls and divisions can be created in as little as a day, and knocked down just as easily. Different colours and textures of mud plaster can be and are applied to different spaces to accentuate or change their meaning (Figure 4.1). While all houses carry meaning, mud houses seem to do so in a way that enables them to be particularly closely linked to the people that occupy them, and the rhythm of their lives. It occurred to me that it is thus probably the case that the material from which a house is made has implications for the way that it is caught up in symbolic and social schemes, and the role that it plays in the lives of humans. The relationship between idea and material is not one way – the material as a simple medium for the idea – but instead involves an interesting play between the two.

From there I thus began to think about the first mud houses, and how they may accordingly have played a role in generating new symbolic and social possibilities within prehistoric society

Table 4.1. *Examples of some house changes associated with human life-cycle changes in Balathal village. There are also other kinds of changes associated with the annual lifecycle and the domestic lifestyle.*

STAGE OF LIFECYCLE	PARTICULAR EVENT OR RITUAL	EXAMPLE OF CHANGE TO MUD SURFACE OF HOUSE
Birth	End of confinement period of mother	Ideally all walls and floors are replastered (with regular plaster), but in practice is usually only floor of room where mother confined.
Marriage	*Bhairū pūjā*	All floors (inside and out) replastered, using very fine quality red soil (non-local source). All walls replastered with white soil.
Widowhood	N/A	Floors plastered less often or not at all and degenerate. Upper floor layers may be lost. Build-up of occupation debris may occur.
Death	Cremation (occurs on day of death)	Red soil is plastered in front of the doorway of the inner room in the shape of a sub-rounded rectangle slightly larger in size than the body.
	Mausar (Death Feast) (12 days after cremation)	All floors, or at least those in room where body lay, are replastered, in most cases using regular plaster. Some individuals insist that black soil is more appropriate.
Post-death	*Pūrbaj pūjā* (for 'untimely' death)	Floor of inner room, or at least area within room where *pūjā* will be performed, plastered with red soil.

CULTURAL SIGNIFICANCE

Purification of pollution associated with birth; often accompanied by other purifying acts, such as the replacement of all ceramic cooking and eating vessels with new ones.

Marks occasion as special and auspicious. Also associated with conferment of temporary liminal status on bride and groom.

Not common occurrence, but if widow/widower living alone and in poor health, may not be able to maintain house. More likely for widow, who is often considered a burden and inauspicious.

Various interpretations: 1) Red soil, as both an auspicious and a pure substance, is appropriate for departing soul; 2) Red soil and cow dung, as well as act of plastering itself, mark space and hence body as liminal.

Purification of pollution associated with death. May also be associated with the reintegration of mourners after a liminal period during which regular acts of purification and maintenance are temporarily suspended.

Various interpretations possible: 1) One of a series of ritual acts designed to placate the 'ghost' of the dead individual; 2) A means of conferring temporary liminal status on space and thus on individual who will 'communicate' with dead; 3) Marks occasion as 'special'.

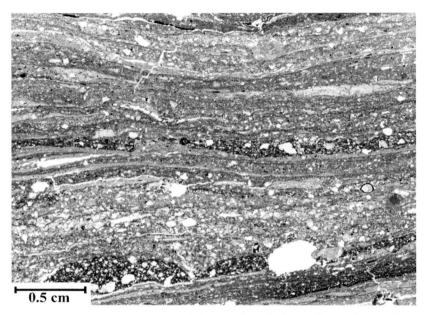

Figure 4.1: Microscopic image of layers of mud plaster from a house floor in Balathal village. Floors are plastered and replastered in association with changes in the lives of a house's occupants. Photo Nicole Boivin.

(Boivin 2004b, 2004d). In particular, I was drawn to a consideration of the world's earliest permanent dwellings, which can be found on archaeological sites in various parts of the south-eastern Mediterranean region (Figure 4.2). Many of them are made partially or wholly of mud, and they are frequently richly elaborated, and divided into a multitude of different spaces through many of the same techniques used in rural Rajasthan – walls, platforms, boundaries, and coats of plaster amongst them. These early mud houses were constructed beginning in the Neolithic period. This Early Holocene period also ushered in a number of other major new developments in the region: the first pottery, the first domestic plants and animals, the first settled societies, and a major boom in material culture and material symbols.

Having become by this point quite interested in mud and soil, and the materiality of things, I could not help noticing that soil seemed crucial to many of these developments. Soil was used,

*Figure 4.2: Building 65 at the Neolithic site of Çatalhöyük in Turkey,
where archaeologists have unearthed some of the earliest mud-built
dwellings in the world. Photo Jason Quinlan, courtesy of the Çatalhöyük
Research Project.*

beginning in this period, to make pottery, to create a built environment, and to fabricate material implements, furnishings, and
surroundings. It was also used to fashion an unprecedented array
of symbols and artistic items, including jewellery, seals, decorative
pieces, figurines, reliefs, sculptures, paintings, and plaster coatings
(see Figure 4.3). Soil was furthermore the medium in which the first
domestic plants were cultivated, and the distribution of appropriate soils would have affected where the first villages were located.
In addition, it was integral to the growth of a familiar Neolithic
and Chalcolithic entity in the south-eastern Mediterranean: the
tell. These early village mounds are composed almost entirely of
soil, and in particular the remains of mud houses and clay-made
items of material culture. While the importance of soil during
this crucial period of development in the Mediterranean has been
surprisingly overlooked by archaeologists, a few, including most
notably Mirjana Stevanovic (1997) and Dave Wengrow (1998), have
attempted to draw attention to it. Indeed, Stevanovic has referred
to the Neolithic in this region of the world as 'the Age of Clay'

in recognition of the overwhelming dominance of this material on Neolithic sites.

What did it matter that people turned to this new material and made it such a focus? Well, as I have argued in more detail elsewhere (see Boivin 2004b), the use of soil as a major resource within Neolithic society may have linked in with, and encouraged, some of the important changes that took place during this period. For example, the eminently malleable nature of soil enabled the rapid and efficient creation of an unprecedented range of containers, enclosures, and spatial divisions when it became a focus of human effort during the Neolithic period. It was therefore a useful means of expressing, reinforcing, and even creating the new types of order and social difference that began to emerge at this time. As Peter Wilson has argued in the *Domestication of the Human Species*, 'domesticated' societies like those that first arose in the Neolithic period exhibit an emphasis on enclosure – through boundaries, categories, and compartments – that is not seen in 'open' (foraging) societies (Wilson 1988). Soil would have provided an ideal substance for mapping and encouraging these new divisions, assisting in the creation of new categories and groups.

Beyond this, the malleability of soil may also have fed into a new fascination with transformation in the Neolithic. This period witnessed an unprecedented shift in both the scale and nature of the transformations humans imposed on the surrounding world. It saw the development, for example, of a number of transformative technologies that, unlike those in the preceding Palaeolithic period, were not effected primarily through physical force (as when stone is transformed into a tool), but rather through the addition of heat and water (Childe 1965; Rollefson 1990). Soil technologies in the eastern Mediterranean may be seen as part of this overall shift. Soil was mixed with water to create structural changes that allowed it to be transformed into furnishings, figurines, houses, and village landscapes, and it was further heated in order to create chemical changes that resulted in lasting ceramic containers and other items. Modifications to soil that allowed it to become such a focal resource during the Neolithic derived from a growing interest in the human capacity to create substantial, durable changes to the natural world.

As I and others have also noted, soil also had a key role to play in the development of a range of new symbolic and communicative

Figure 4.3: Many of the new symbolic media that emerged during the Neolithic in the eastern Mediterranean – like these clay objects from Çatalhöyük – were formed out of soil. (Objects are not to scale.) Mother goddess photo Jason Quinlan, all photos courtesy of the Çatalhöyük Research Project.

processes (see also Stevanovic 1997; Wengrow 1998). The Neolithic period in the eastern Mediterranean featured an explosion of material symbols – many of them made out of soil – that suggests a significant increase in the distances over which symbolic communication was possible, the sizes of the audiences which participated in such communication, and perhaps also the stability of symbolic meanings. But soil did not only enable new possibilities; it also imposed new constraints. For example, the intensive use of soil probably helped to more or less permanently link people to particular places, since items made out of soil are not very transportable. Pottery constrains mobility (Figure 4.4; see also Haaland 1997), as does the creation of other items made out of soil, particularly dwellings. It is said that the cultivation of crops, another technology reliant on soil, also "ties people to the land" and encourages sedentism, which probably explains why soil is often a metaphor for ownership and belonging in various cultural contexts (see Carsten & Hugh-Jones 1995; Lovell 1998, for example). Investing in soil means investing in place. Therefore, just as we can say that settling down encouraged the use of soil as a resource, we can probably also say that, conversely, using soil as a resource encouraged people to settle down. The south-eastern Mediterranean Neolithic may not be so much about which one came first, but rather about the dialectical relationship between the two factors that encouraged and subsequently reinforced sedentarisation.

In effect, while soil did not single-handedly create the various changes to which it is linked in the Neolithic, it was not a passive medium for their simple 'expression' either. People chose to use soil, but its use also opened up a series of new possibilities and imposed a set of new constraints, not all of which would have been intended or expected. The unique material properties of soil helped to create a new world, and once people began to experiment more systematically and frequently with it, these properties helped channel and distribute human energy along particular lines and according to particular patterns. Soil encouraged certain changes and resisted others. It can accordingly be understood to have exerted a kind of agency in human affairs. This agency was not conscious or willed in the sense that many forms of human agency are, but it is an agency nonetheless. Soil was an active agent in the process of Neolithisation in the eastern Mediterranean, among many other active agents, both human and non-human. It was probably partly responsible for the distinctive character of the Neolithic of the eastern Mediterranean compared to other parts of the world. The course of human history is therefore a process not only of human decisions, choices, and ideas, but also of the material forces with which humans are surrounded, and with which they engage. If material is alive only because humans interact with it, it is also true that humans are alive only because they have material to engage with. Indeed, the opposition of human and material is misleading, since humans are themselves material, and their own agency is enabled and constrained by the specifics of that materiality – the fact that they have hands and legs, rather than scales or wings, to provide several obvious examples.

Material Agency in Historical Perspective

The argument that material artefacts can be agents is not of course new. It was, for example, recently taken up by the late anthropologist Alfred Gell, whose interest in materiality has

Figure 4.4: Late Neolithic ceramic vessel from the site of Tabaqat al-Buma in Wadi Ziqlab, northern Jordan. Pottery constrains mobility, as Randi Halaand has also noted. Photo K. Gibbs, provided courtesy of Ted Banning.

already been discussed in several previous chapters. In *Art and Agency*, a book he finished shortly before he died, Gell focused in particular on the agency of art objects, which he claimed should be considered as social agents (Gell 1998). Gell was specifically concerned to move the anthropology of art beyond a focus on symbolism and meaning, and emphasised that art should be seen as a system of action, "intended to change the world rather than encode symbolic propositions about it" (ibid.: 6). Art objects, Gell argued, could be seen as the equivalent of persons, and acted as agents in social processes. For Gell, any object indeed, be it a gun, a car, or even a doll, could be a social agent (Figure 4.5). However, Gell was also clear that art objects and artefacts were not 'primary' but rather, as he described them, 'secondary' agents. They did not have agency of their own, but were in fact only the media of human agency, which could be distributed through them. For Gell, the facts of intention and will were critical to the definition of real agency, and since material objects obviously lack such characteristics, they were automatically exempted from the status of real agents. Indeed Gell's discussion of the agency of artefacts makes it clear that he actually saw objects as mere passive media for the distribution of human-derived agency. His approach is "preoccupied with the practical *mediatory* role of art objects in the social process" (ibid.; my emphasis). Thus, even Gell, the materialist sympathiser that he was, shied away from the notion that things themselves could have agency, though one might also add that this is because Gell's concerns in *Art and Agency* were of a particular sort, to which his notion of agency was well-suited.

At any rate, if Gell resisted attributing real agency to artefacts, others have not. Looking back historically we may in particular note the appearance, in the 1950s, 1960s, and 1970s, of a range of new studies, theories, and schools of thought, in such diverse fields as anthropology, history, sociology, philosophy, and archaeology, that gave pride of place to artefacts, technology, the environment, and the material world in general. In many of these studies, material things assumed the role of active agents, influencing the social and political organisation of society, its values, and its future. The technology-oriented studies of Marshall McLuhan and his lesser-known Canadian colleague Harold Innis may be taken as illustrative of this trend. Both scholars were interested in technology in general, as well as communicative technology in particular, and gave it a central explanatory role in models of social change. One of McLuhan's most lasting dictums – "the medium is the message" – highlights their perspective (ibid.). By it, McLuhan meant to emphasise the pivotal role that technological media play in shaping understanding and social relationships – thus the medium in which a message is sent is more important than its content (ibid.). Accordingly, and in characteristic style, McLuhan asserted that "in terms of the way the machine altered our relations to one another and to ourselves, it mattered not in the least whether it turned out cornflakes or Cadillacs" (ibid.: 7–8). Down the page he elaborated further:

Figure 4.5: Gun. The late anthropologist Alfred Gell argued that objects like guns could function as social agents. However, for Gell, objects lacked primary agency, which was unique to humans. Photo Jason Conlon.

> The "message" of any medium or technology is the change of scale or pace or pattern it introduces into human affairs. The railway did not introduce human movement or transportation or wheel or road into human society, but it accelerated and enlarged the scale of previous human functions, creating new kinds of cities and new kinds of work and leisure. This happened whether the railway functioned in a tropical or a northern environment, and is quite independent of the freight or content of the railway medium. (ibid.: 8)

McLuhan was particularly interested in the way that diverse media of communication differentially shape sensory experience by altering the ratio of the senses (McLuhan 1962, 1964). For example, he argued that print media lead to an emphasis on the visual sense, and a transformation in the way knowledge is acquired (Figure 4.6). In oral cultures, knowledge is obtained through contact with other people, while in print cultures, knowledge is often obtained individually and privately. Print cultures thus encourage individualism and specialisation. They also encourage nationalism, according to McLuhan, since visual media like texts and maps allow the visual apprehension of a mother language and a nation, and also enable standardisation and universalisation of the mother tongue. McLuhan also argued that the advent of print technology removed people from the necessity of participating in a tightly knit oral culture, resulting in the detribalisation of society (Carey 2005: 204). According to McLuhan, electronic media in contrast engineer a radically different, more multi-sensory experience, and are currently encouraging a re-tribalisation – the creation of a 'global village'.

McLuhan's work was much inspired by the insights of his senior colleague at the University of Toronto, Harold Innis. While both assumed the centrality of communication technology, however, they differed in the principal kinds of effects they saw deriving from that technology (ibid.: 200). If McLuhan drew significant attention to its role in sensory organisation and thought, Innis was primarily concerned with its impact on social organisation and culture (Carey 2005). Innis perhaps most notably distinguished between time-binding and space-binding communication media (Innis 1950, 1951). Time-binding media were those that were durable and difficult to transport, such as parchment, clay, and stone. Space-binding media, such as paper and papyrus, were less durable, but light, and thus more easily transportable across space. The nature of the dominant communication medium within society would, according to Innis, significantly bias social organisation. James Carey summarises Innis' model succinctly:

> Any given medium . . . will favor the growth of certain kinds of interests and institutions at the expense of others and will also impose on these institutions a form of organization. Media which are space-binding facilitate and encourage the growth of empire, encourage a concern with expansion and with the present, and thus favor the hegemony of secular political authority. Space-binding media encourage the growth of the state, the military, and decentralized and expansionist institutions. Time-binding media foster concern with history and tradition, have little capacity for expansion of secular authority, and thus favor the growth of religion, of hierarchical organization, and of contractionist institutions. (Carey 2005: 196)

Innis' analysis did not end with observation: he also assessed what kind of media biases made for the best society. He argued

Figure 4.6: Newspapers on sale in London. Both Marshall McLuhan and Harold Innis believed that print media had an important role to play in structuring modern Western society. Photo Mark Devitt.

that media favouring time and space must exist as independent traditions, offsetting and checking the biases of one another, or otherwise "politics becomes sacralized or religion secularized; science destroys morality or morality emasculates science; tradition gives way to the notion of progress or chronic change obliterates tradition" (ibid.: 199). For Innis, the biases produced by the modern West's reliance on print media were responsible for many of its problems in the twentieth century.

The French scholar Jacques Ellul, another key writer on technology, presented an even bleaker assessment of the effects of modern technology on society. For him, technology was an all-consuming, transformative, and often malignant force within modern society. The following is typical of Ellul's views on technology:

> Technology has a double effect on society and human existence. On the one hand, it disintegrates and tends to eliminate bit by bit anything that is not technicizable (this has been brutally felt on the level of merriment, love, suffering,

joy, etc.). And it tends to reconstitute a whole of society and human existence *on the basis of* technological totalization. What is being established is no longer the subordination of man to technology, etc., but, far more deeply, a new totality. It is the process that causes such vast malaise in man and such a keen sense of frustration. (Ellul 1980: 203)

Such dark predictions contrast with McLuhan's increasingly optimistic assessment of the potential of modern electronic media to positively transform society, but are generally in line with the view that the American historian Lewis Mumford came to hold. Drawn upon by many of these later writers on technology, Mumford played a key role, beginning in the 1930s, in highlighting the importance of technology to the social and cultural changes that took place in the West during the course of the last thousand years. He divided this period into three phases based on the principal sources of power and characteristic materials that defined their technology: the eotechnic phase, based on a water-and-wood complex; the paleotechnic phase based on iron and coal; and the neotechnic phase, which relied on an electricity-and-alloy complex (Mumford 1963). Nonetheless, and even if Mumford did indeed come to hold a pessimistic view of the effect of modern technology – 'megatechnics' – on human life, his perspective was always, as he himself was keen to emphasise in the introduction to the 1963 edition of *Technics and Civilization*, less deterministic than that of the next generation of technology commentators. For if he asserted that "[t]he vast material displacements the machine has made in our physical environment are perhaps in the long run less important than its spiritual contributions to our culture" (ibid.: ii), he also always emphasised that the effects of social and technological forces were reciprocal. Looking back on his work in 1963, he stated that "[i]n presenting technical development within the setting of a more general social ecology, I avoided the current bias of making it the dominant and all-important factor, as people still do today when they naively characterize our period as the Jet Age, the Nuclear Age, the Rocket Age, or the Space Age" (ibid.: iii). Mumford accordingly defined 'technics' not just as technology, but as technology plus its social milieu.

If the 1950s through 1970s saw an increase in academic attention to the impact of technology, the period also witnessed a related surge in interest in the formative effects on society of ecology and environment. Within anthropology, for example, a number of new, related schools of thought developed, including cultural ecology, ecological anthropology, and cultural materialism, all of which stressed the relationship between societies and their environments. Many studies brought both ecology and technology into the picture, and saw these material bases as the ultimate cause of particular social and cultural formations. Amongst the notable studies of this period, we can point to Roy Rappaport's examination of the role of ritual pig sacrifices in maintaining environmental equilibrium in New Guinea (Rappaport 1967), and Marvin Harris' analysis of the materialist basis for the seemingly irrational practices surrounding the sacred cow in India (Harris 1966). Both studies argued that ritual and symbolic features had evolved out of particular ecological conditions, and hence that the ideal had its roots ultimately in the material.

Tracing these strands of interest even further back, we find clear links to the theories of social evolution that were developed in the 1940s by anthropologists like Julian Steward and Leslie White. Disillusioned with historical particularism and the assertion that cultures were unique and could not be studied comparatively, Steward advocated the detailed comparison of different societies, and analysis of the way they had adapted to their environments. He emphasised that specific cultures evolve their specific forms in the process of adapting to particular environmental conditions, and that the apparent uniformity of evolutionary stages is actually a matter of similar adaptations to similar natural environments in different parts of the world (Ortner 1984: 132). Leslie White, meanwhile, argued that social evolution resulted from the way in which societies gradually increased the quantity of energy they were able to harvest, leading to predictable increases in their degree of social differentiation (White 1959). White viewed cultural systems in terms of three horizontal strata, with the technological layer at the bottom, the philosophical on the top, and the sociological in between. The basal position of the technological layer reflected its role as *the* determinant of the cultural system as a whole.

Moving back ever further in time, we can identify antecedents to these models in the work of the anthropologist Lewis Henry Morgan, who argued long before many others for a link between social and technological change. In his 1877 classic, *Ancient Societies*, Morgan divided ancient history into three eras, each of which was defined by a particular stage of technology: in the savage era, people learned to manage fire, and invented the bow and pottery; in the barbarian era, plants and animals were domesticated and metalworking invented; and then finally in the civilised era, the alphabet and writing were introduced (Morgan 1877). For Morgan, these technological changes were the force behind social progress. His evolutionary and technology-oriented model greatly influenced not only Steward and White, but also the most well-known commentator on the relationship between technology and society, Karl Marx. Marx's historical materialist model can also be seen as an argument for the pivotal role of technology in social change. Arguing against the philosophical and political idealism of his time (Shaw 1979: 172; Winner 1977: 77), Marx asserted that the material conditions of life and their production through human activity were defining features of human life. Productive activity gave form to experience, and created what Marx referred to as a definitive "mode of life":

> As individuals express their life, so they are. What they are, therefore, coincides with their production, both with *what* they produce and *how* they produce. The nature of individuals thus depends on the material conditions determining their production. (Marx & Engels 1977: 42)

This view of human beings, life, and activity gave shape to Marx's understanding of how material production – particularly technological production – shapes social, political, and ideological life (Winner 1977: 78). In *The Critique of Political Economy*, Marx stated his general historical principal: "The mode of production of material life determines the general character of the social, political and spiritual processes of life" (Marx 1964: 51). Subsequently, he divided the mode of production into the forces of production and the relations of production. His writings make clear that he saw the productive forces – human labour power together with the means of production (instruments or technology plus raw materials) – as critical in shaping the economic structure of society, and hence its nature. Thus, a change in the productive forces brought about a change in society, and we get one of Marx's most famous (or infamous) pronouncements:

> Social relations are closely bound up with productive forces. In acquiring new productive forces men change their mode of production; and in changing their mode of production, in changing the way of earning their living, they change all their social relations. The hand-mill gives you the society with the feudal lord; the steam mill, society with the industrial capitalist. (Marx 1979: 109)

If Marx's model was, and indeed to some degree continues to be, the most systematically worked out model of how matter, and specifically human engagement with it, makes history, it was not the first. Not only did Morgan's work foreshadow Marx's pronouncements on technology, so too did many works of literature. In *Autonomous Technology*, Langdon Winner has drawn attention to the expression of ideas about the transforming role of technology in works of art going back at least a century and a half, if not further (Winner 1977). He notes the fascination of nineteenth-century writers like Mary Shelley and Samuel Butler with the notion that human-made machines could develop autonomy and wreak havoc on society. Such works reflect concerns with the growth of industrial society that have continued to this day. However, if art played an important role in initiating discussion concerning the role of technology in social change, then so too did archaeology. Beginning as early as the Roman period, scholars had hypothesised about an evolutionary sequence of human development in which phases were defined by technological developments, and by the nineteenth century archaeology was able to clearly demonstrate such a progression (Trigger 1989). The Danish archaeologist Christian Jürgensen Thomsen carried out a close analysis of prehistoric material in order to argue for a division of prehistory into three progressive stages: the Stone Age, the Bronze Age, and the Iron Age. These technological developments were understood to mirror, and for some determine, wider changes within society. Lewis Mumford has commented on archaeology's role in highlighting the importance of technology:

> [T]he first scholars to give sufficient weight to technological changes were the anthropologists and archaeologists, who dealt with pre-literate societies for which any other data than the bare tools or weapons were largely lacking. Since all the perishable materials of technology had vanished, along with the people who used them, the stone or pottery artifact came to be treated as self-existent, almost self-explanatory objects, influencing and characterizing the societies that used them. (Mumford 1961: 231)

It is clear that, for Mumford, archaeologists were often tempted, due to the material-oriented nature of their study, to attribute too much influence to technological advancement. The early role of antiquarianism and archaeology in the development of technological studies has nonetheless often been overlooked.

The Spectre of Determinism

Following the fluorescence of technology and ecology-oriented studies in the 1950s through 1970s, the social sciences and humanities as a whole have seen a backlash against the kind of materialist orientation they embodied. In particular, a large number of scholars have critiqued the deterministic and monocausal nature of many of the studies that emerged during this period. It has been pointed out, with reference to the analyses of technological impact, that they frequently ignore cultural factors and changes necessary to the acceptance and spread of new technology, and overlook the intricate ways in which technological and socio-cultural factors are intertwined. Single causes are simplified out when in fact causality is multiple and complex. General comments and unsystematic studies present unjustified links between social transformations and technological changes. In many cases, human agency is

Figure 4.7: Auschwitz concentration camp. Langdon Winner has pointed out that Albert Speer employed the notion of runaway technology to explain the horrors of the Nazi regime. Photo Mihai Guby.

ruled out and machines are made to seem autonomous and beyond human control.

Such a perspective can have moral consequences, as Langdon Winner has pointed out. He draws attention to the example of Albert Speer, Hitler's minister of armaments and war production, and the way that he used the notion of runaway technology as a partial excuse for the barbarism of the Nazi regime (Figure 4.7; Winner 1977: 15). Winner quotes the following excerpts from Speer's memoirs:

> "The criminal events of those years," Speer observes, "were not only an outgrowth of Hitler's personality. The extent of the crimes was also due to the fact that Hitler was the first to be able to employ the implements of technology to multiply crime." Quoting from his testimony at the Nuremberg trial, Speer continues, "The more technological the world becomes, the greater is the danger... As the former minister in charge of a highly developed armaments economy

it is my last duty to state: A new great war will end with
the destruction of human culture and civilization. There
is nothing to stop unleashed technology and science from
completing its work of destroying man which it has so ter-
ribly begun in this war." (ibid.)

Winner observes that while Speer's attempted apology does not
succeed, it is nonetheless notable that what is really a very peculiar
defence should have been offered at all, and should furthermore
have been so willingly accepted by Speer's European and American audience. The idea that technology is autonomous has had
a tremendous impact on the public understanding of technology,
even as it has fallen out of favour in academia.

Equally problematic has been the assertion by some hard-line
technological determinists that law-like relationships can be established between technology and society. Robert Heilbroner, for
example, asks whether there is a fixed sequence to technological development, and a necessary path over which technologically
developing societies must travel, and answers thus:

I believe there is such a sequence – that the steam-mill
follows the hand-mill not by chance but because it is the
next "stage" in a technological conquest of nature that follows one and only one grand avenue of advance. (Heilbroner
1994a: 55)

Elsewhere, Heilbroner lays out his views concerning a science of
technology not unlike the science of physics:

The challenge . . . is to demonstrate that technology exerts
its effects in generalizable ways. If technological determinism is to become a useful overlay for history's palimpsest,
it must reveal a connection between "machinery" and
"history" that displays lawlike properties – a forcefield, if
we will, emanating from the technological background to
impose order on human behaviour in a manner analogous
to that by which a magnet orders the behavior of particles

sprinkled on a sheet of paper held above it or by which gravitation orders the paths of celestial objects. (Heilbroner 1994b: 70–71)

It is not surprising that many became disillusioned with perspectives like this that fail to take into account human ideas, decisions, and cultural values, and that seem to specify an impossible goal for technological studies.

Many of the same flaws were seen with respect to ecological approaches. Charges of determinism were levelled at what were often positivistically oriented studies in anthropology, archaeology, and geography. As Aletta Biersack has discussed, these studies strove to apply biological models to society and culture, and accordingly reduced them to mere epiphenomena of environments or ecological factors (Biersack 1999). Culture was seen as an adaptive tool, intelligible in terms of its materialist effects, with functional relationships often being more assumed than clearly demonstrated. Within geography, environmentally deterministic studies in the early part of the twentieth century frequently linked climatic conditions to a racial, economic, and moral hierarchy that demonstrated, amongst other things, that denizens of the mid latitudes were superior to those of the tropics (Frenkel 1994: 290). All of these studies eventually came in for serious criticism.

Critiques against determinism, combined with the pull of the linguistic turn, have led many scholars in the social sciences and humanities to abandon materialist approaches in favour of idealist models. Anthropologists interested in the environment have developed schools of symbolic ecology, historical ecology, and political ecology (Biersack 1999). These have drawn attention to the social and cultural construction of landscapes and the role of the power relations in structuring human usage of the environment, amongst other issues. Marxists, meanwhile, have been anxious to avoid the "spectre of technological determinism" (Shaw 1979: 155), and to demonstrate that Marx was not, as has often been suggested, a technological determinist (Bimber 1990; MacKenzie 1984). The idea that the base (the economy or technology) should determine the superstructure is often dismissed as 'vulgar Marxism', and many

Marxists argue for more interaction between base and superstructure, or indeed the relative autonomy of the superstructure. Meanwhile, studies of technology in fields like history and anthropology have focused on the ways in which technology and technological practices are socially embedded. These studies stress the important place of social and cultural values in technological narratives, and place agency firmly with human beings:

> Agency . . . is deeply embedded in the larger social structure and culture – so deeply, indeed, as to divest technology of its presumed power as an independent agent initiating change. (Marx & Smith 1994: xiv)

These studies strive to demonstrate the interpenetration of technology with social forms and systems of meaning (Pfaffenberger 1988: 244). According to social constructionist studies, technology cannot be analysed as though it were an independent variable; instead, as the anthropologist Bryan Pfaffenberger emphasises, it should be studied as 'humanised nature':

> To say that technology is humanised nature is to insist that it is a fundamentally *social* phenomenon: it is a social construction of the nature around us and within us, and once achieved, it expresses an embedded social vision. (ibid.)

Such studies have accordingly drawn important attention to the way that the adoption, use, and transformation of technology are inevitably structured by socio-cultural variables. Within archaeology, for example, Heather Lechtman and Bill Sillar have examined the various social and cultural factors that led some technologies to be widely adopted in the Andes, while others, like metalworking, which had a substantial impact in European and Near Eastern societies, remained rather peripheral (Lechtman 1984; Sillar 1996). As pointed out in Chapter 2, Sillar emphasises the *philosophical* aspects of technology, and the way they not only imbue techniques with culturally specific meanings, but also influence what people will consider an 'appropriate' technology to apply to a particular problem. In South India, my colleagues and I have looked at the widespread Neolithic evidence for grinding and hammering technology, and similarly argued for a cultural propensity to address technological challenges in a very particular way (Boivin et al. 2007). Dorian Fuller and I have also traced long-term prehistoric continuities in culinary practices and technologies in various parts of the Old World, and argue that these are rooted to some degree in cultural beliefs and value systems (Boivin & Fuller, forthcoming). Within the field of history, parallel kinds of studies have demonstrated the role that social and political factors have played in the adoption and use of industrial technology. Not only did industrialisation require particular social and cultural changes within society before it could be initiated (as Mumford recognised early on), but struggles between workers and factory owners often influenced the course of technological change (MacKenzie 1984). In some cases, workers successfully resisted the imposition of new technologies, while in others, new technology was designed specifically with the aim of undermining the power of workers. A frequently cited example is the new pneumatic moulding machines introduced at the reaper manufacturing plant of the Chicago industrialist, Cyrus McCormick, in the mid-1880s. While the new machines, manned by unskilled labourers, actually produced inferior castings at a higher cost than the earlier process, and were abandoned three years later, they were nonetheless successful in achieving the aim they were designed to achieve – the destruction of the union (MacKenzie 1984; Winner 1986: 24). Technological studies of this nature are now widespread across many fields. As Misa has pointed out, for example, authors writing for the journal *Technology and Culture* "have piled up detailed studies of how social forces shape technological change" (Misa 1988: 318).

The Baby with the Bathwater?

That recent scholarly emphasis on the social and cultural factors affecting material technologies, environments, and practices has produced important insights is indisputable. Across a range of fields, scholars are now much more aware of the capacity for social and cultural variables to impede on what were once seen as the separate or autonomous realms of technology and environment. Nonetheless, it is difficult to escape the feeling that, at the same time, another important insight – the potential power of material things to supercede human design and will – has been lost. This fear is nicely illustrated in William Shaw's discussion of why Marx's technological determinism should not be refuted. Shaw argues that while non-deterministic readings may make Marx more acceptable in today's academic climate, they also rob his theory of both its originality and its bite. As he says of the theory that Marx was no technological determinist:

> No doubt, it makes Marx less contentious and more palat-able, but the price is a less accurate – and less interesting – account of his theory of history. To concede, for instance, that the notion of a determining factor in history is inco-herent and then to argue that Marx must have meant some-thing else in view is to kill Marx with kindness. Marx was surely concerned to say more than simply that technolog-ical factors ought not to be ignored by historians, or that everything is related to everything. (Shaw 1979: 155–56)

Langdon Winner, who also acknowledges the technological determinism within Marx's theory, similarly takes issue with the way that socio-culturally oriented analyses inevitably seem to minimize technological studies. Pointing out some of the prob-lems with many scholarly and public discussions of technological impact, he states:

> Hence, the stern advice commonly given to those who flirt with the notion that technological artifacts have politi-cal qualities: What matters is not technology itself, but the social or economic system in which it is embedded. This maxim, which in a number of variations is the central premise of a theory that can be called the social determi-nation of technology, has an obvious wisdom. It serves as a needed corrective to those who focus uncritically upon such things as "the computer and its social impacts" but

who fail to look behind technical devices to see the social
circumstances of their development deployment and use.
This view provides an antidote to naive technological determinism . . .

But the corrective has its own shortcomings: taken lit-
erally, it suggests that technical *things* do not matter at
all. Once one has done the detective work necessary to
reveal the social origins – power holders behind a particular
instance of technological change – one will have explained
everything of importance. This conclusion offers comfort
to social scientists. It validates what they have always sus-
pected, namely, that there is nothing distinctive about the
study of technology in the first place. Hence, they can return
to their standard models of social power . . . (Winner 1986:
20–21)

The observations of scholars like Shaw and Winner suggest that
in rejecting material determinism and embracing social constructionism, researchers have to some degree thrown out the baby with
the bathwater. Pfaffenberger notes as a positive development of the
social constructionist approach that it makes technology a subject
of interest to symbolic and interpretive anthropology (Pfaffenberger
1988: 237), but the idealist bent of these schools should probably
make us question whether this is indeed really such a positive
outcome. While it is certainly important to recognise that society shapes technology, this should not lead us to overlook the fact
that technology also shapes society. Furthermore, just as studies of
the social construction of the body have come under fire for over-
looking the actual 'bodily-ness' of bodies (as discussed in previous
chapters), so too must we question an approach to technology or
the environment that overlooks their very materiality. In subsum-
ing material studies into general semiotic and social paradigms,
we highlight certain aspects of material meaning, but at the same
time occlude recognition of what makes material things different
from words and signs – indeed, what makes material things really
interesting in their own right.

There are other problems with approaches that focus on social
construction, and insist that the agency of material things is only

ever an agency of people *through* things. In denying things anything but derived agency, scholars provide perhaps unwitting support to the very questionable notion that humans are masters of nature and matter. The anthropologist Tim Ingold has drawn attention to this 'grand narrative' in human history, and highlighted the way that it actually serves to confuse our understanding of how humans relate to nature. He points out that the essence of Western thought is rooted in the notion of a subordination of nature by human powers of reason (Figure 4.8; Ingold 2000: 80). Making things, according to this notion, entails the imprinting of a prior conceptual design upon a raw material substrate – "Human reason is supposed to provide the form, nature the substance in which it is realised" (ibid.). Much of Ingold's work aims to demonstrate firstly that this is a peculiarly Western and modern perspective, and secondly that is also a problematic one. The domestication of plants and animals, for example, is viewed in many societies not as a mastery of nature, but a mutual relationship with nature (see also Rindos 1980). Furthermore, by Ingold's analysis, domesticated species and artefacts are rarely the result of a clear imposition of form from the reasoning mind; instead, they arise as a result of the "mutual involvement of people and materials in an environment" in which outcomes cannot always be anticipated (ibid.: 347).

A similar conclusion is reached by others who have studied the history of technology. David Turnbull, for example, has described how something that looks as planned as a Gothic cathedral may in fact have been built entirely without a plan. The Chartres cathedral, for example, once considered to exemplify "unity, coherence and the unfolding of original essences", has been shown through more detailed recent study to consist of an "ad hoc mess" (Figure 4.9; Turnbull 2000: 108). As demonstrated by the research of the architectural historian John James, the famous cathedral actually consists of a bewildering variety of spires, pinnacles, buttresses, fliers, roofs, doors, and windows, and is composed of bays and axes in the nave and transepts that are completely irregular. The cathedral went through thirteen major design and structural changes during its rapid rebuilding between 1194 and 1230, and is the ad hoc accumulation of the work of many individuals. That coherence which has been achieved is the result not of any plan, but

Figure 4.8: Sixteenth-century-style garden at the Château de Villandry in the Loire Valley, France. The notion that nature provides the substrate and human beings the design is a pervasive one in Western thought, as Tim Ingold has observed. Photo Nicole Boivin.

of the use of the template – "a pattern or mould that permits both the accurate cutting and replication of shaped stone and the transmission of knowledge between workers" (ibid.: 112–13) – and, equally essentially, "talk, tradition, and trial and error" (ibid.: 113). And Chartres is not alone; Turnbull insists that a large proportion of Gothic cathedrals were built without plans. The notion that the cathedrals were created as a result of the enactment of a unified plan actually reflects the imposition of very modern practices on medieval masons. And indeed, even in modern architecture, this ideal is often not fully realised. While 'remote control' of the design and construction process through drawings became technically possible in the sixteenth century, Turnbull notes that the construction of buildings even today involves a degree of on-site problem-solving, experimentation, and unanticipated outcome.

Perhaps one of the most critical of those commentators to assess the notion that construction is all about the imposition of a pre-conceived human design on matter is Langdon Winner. Like Ingold, he notes that not all cultures share the modern Western insistence that the ability to control things is a necessary prerequisite to human survival – indeed many "have lived and prospered under the belief that an inherent harmony or beneficence in nature would provide for their needs" (Winner 1977: 19). The belief that absolute control over nature is not only possible, but desirable, is what has therefore led to such great concern amongst artists, politicians, academics, and social commentators over the idea that we might lose control of technology. The metaphor of master and slave is the dominant Western way of describing the human relationship to technology, and any speculation that the relationship may not be maintainable is greeted with general horror. This theme of mastery is, as Winner points out, even more apparent with respect to our understanding of the human relationship to nature: as Ingold has similarly argued, "there are seldom any reservations about man's rightful role in conquering, vanquishing, and subjugating every-thing natural... Nature is the universal prey, to manipulate as humans see fit" (ibid.: 21). For Winner, the idea that technology has a certain degree of autonomy, or agency, is therefore a useful one, because it debunks "the dream of mastery" (ibid.: 25).

Winner outlines a set of once standard notions that have been brought into doubt as a result of the questioning of the master–slave understanding of human–technology relations. One is the idea that "men know best what they themselves have made" (ibid.). This assumes that since human beings are the creators of technology, they have precise knowledge of their creations. "They know exactly how things are put together and how they can be taken apart" (ibid.). The second is the notion that "the things men make are firmly under their control" (ibid.). This appears to be mere common sense, since control is built into the very design of things. Technologies are built with very definite purposes in mind, and are the mere tools of those who employ them. The third notion is that "technology is essentially neutral, a means to an end; the benefit or harm it brings depends on how men use it" (ibid.). This follows on from

Figure 4.9: The exterior of the Chartres cathedral, which reveals some of the structural diversity of the famous building. David Turnbull has argued that the Chartres cathedral, like other Gothic cathedrals, was built without a plan. Photo Michael Petraglia.

the notion that technology is merely a tool – the end accomplished is thus determined independently of the instrument employed.

Winner notes that all of these once widely accepted ideas about technology have been increasingly brought into question in discussions about modern technology. For example, it is clear that people today actually know very little about the technology they use, even the technology they use every day. Such knowledge is in fact the domain of increasingly specialised specialists. "People work within and are served by technological organizations that by their very nature forbid a perspicuous overview" (ibid.: 28), and are thus increasingly distanced from and confused by the technology that 'happens to them'. In addition, the evidence that people are able to dominate and hold in restraint the technology human beings have created is lacking. Large-scale technological systems – like weapons systems, freeways, skyscrapers, power and communications networks – seem now to expand by some inherent momentum or mechanism of growth, for example (Figure 4.10). These systems make the idea of controlled application and reasonable use seem increasingly 'absurd' (ibid.), as do the unintended consequences that frequently attend the introduction of a new technology. Finally, the idea that technology is a neutral tool can only be affirmed with, at best, "severe qualifications" (ibid.: 29). Winner describes our technologies as "tools without handles" (ibid.) that "[f]ar from being neutral . . . provide a positive content to the area of life in which they are applied, enhancing certain ends, denying or even destroying others" (ibid.). Winner notes that people are no longer the active, directing agents of the technologies they produce, especially as they tend to "obey uncritically the norms and requirements of the systems they allegedly govern" (ibid.).

Material Agents

Despite the disfavour into which so-called deterministic approaches have fallen, it therefore seems difficult to escape the conclusion that they hold some grain of truth, which in the frenzied attack upon them, has been lost. Let us now play the role of the one determined soul, on hands and knees amidst the commotion

Figure 4.10: Freeway system seen from Sears Tower in Chicago. Freeways demand more freeways in a way that gives such technological systems a certain autonomous momentum. Photo James Lin.

of the foray, looking for that grain of truth. That is, where can we find evidence that technology does in fact drive history? That the material objects people use, and the environments they live in, actually shape to some degree their relations to one another and the cultural values they adopt?

Thomas Misa has proposed that we will find such evidence only if we look on the large scale. While he points out that in recent decades, "historians of technology have contributed impressively to our understanding of how society shapes technology but have nearly abandoned the urgent task of understanding how technology concurrently shapes society" (Misa 1994: 116), he nonetheless argues that it is primarily through macroscale analyses – that abstract from individual cases and look at gross historical patterns – that scholars reach the conclusion that technology is determinative. Microscale studies, he argues, meanwhile inevitably demonstrate that social and cultural factors are critical to the perceived transformations wrought by technology. His solution to the extremes of technological and social determinism that the two scales thus entail is a 'middle-level' methodology that directs attention to the actors, institutions, and processes intermediate between the macro and the micro. While such an approach is in spirit applaudable, it is nonetheless open to question that microscale approaches always highlight more contingent, social forces, rather than technological ones. A number of examples can be presented to highlight this fact.

If my analysis of the impact of focusing on soil as a resource during the Neolithic may be considered a macroscale – and indeed somewhat speculative – study, there are other investigations, much more micro in scale, that support the notion that something as seemingly insignificant as a change in materials can lead to significant transformations within society. Several interesting ones pertain to the particular materials employed in constructing houses in several different African societies. One comes from a study by Michael Dietler and Ingrid Herbich of Luo houses in western Kenya (Dietler & Herbich 1998). According to Dietler and Herbich, recent years have seen a gradual transformation in the form, technique of construction, and materials used to build Luo houses, as a result of the influence on Luo society of economic globalisation. These material changes have been the result of new economic and social practices, and have at the same time had an effect on the society and its economic and social relationships. Interestingly, they point out that some of the most profound social consequences of the new houses have resulted not from their change in form, but from changes in the materials from which they are made. Where once locally obtained wattle and daub were used (Figure 4.11), houses are now increasingly constructed out of cement blocks and corrugated iron. As Dietler and Herbich point out, these changes in material have restructured social relationships once seen as fundamental within Luo society:

> Traditionally, thatched roofs can be built and repaired only by men, while [house] walls must be regularly smeared with clay by groups of women at least once a year. The need for periodic roof repair reinforces relations of dependence between women (the "owners" of houses) and men, and the

Figure 4.11: A Luo man repairing the thatched roof of his wife's house, near Ng'iya, Kenya. Such traditional materials are being replaced by new ones that have helped alter social relations in Luo society. Photo Michael Dietler and Ingrid Herbich.

smearing parties reinforce relations of mutual support and dependence among women. As a further illustration, upon the death of a male head of the homestead, none of the other co-wives is allowed to have her house repaired until the first wife's house has been repaired; and this is allowed only after she has undergone a ritual to mark the end of mourning. *It is clear that the more permanent construction materials, by eliminating such practical needs for repair, may have a profound impact on relations of authority and dependence.* (ibid.: 259; my emphasis)

For Dietler and Herbich, who employ the practice model of Bourdieu to understand society, building materials are capable of having such a profound effect on social relations because they affect the "practices that underlie the dispositions governing social relations" (ibid.). That is, as Bourdieu so clearly highlighted (and as discussed in Chapter 1), houses are socially and symbolically rich domains that not only reflect social life, but also help create it. In other words, the material world shapes the socio-cultural one. If Bourdieu's model does not specifically explore the implications of materiality and technological change for society, it certainly does not preclude their investigation.

Another study of African houses suggests the same kind of material shaping of society in a microscale context. In Kenya, nomadic peoples like the Gabra, the Rendille, and the Somalis have traditionally lived in transportable thatch tents that are 1) built by women; 2) closely linked to ritual activities; and 3) rich in symbolic meaning (Prussin 1996). As they have increasingly been forced to settle, various changes have been imposed on their architectural practices, some of which have had, as was the case with the Luo, profound social consequences. Once again, some of these changes concern the building materials used to make houses. For example, nomadic women once embarked on long journeys to fairly remote desert areas as part of the laborious and time-consuming annual collection and preparation of house-building materials. Once they have settled, however, these socially important work parties are no longer possible for the nomads. Cash-purchased substitute building materials therefore enter the building process, and these, having different bending properties and pliability, affect the form of the house, and hence its traditional symbolic and social role within society. In addition, the independence and interdependence of women are affected as control over building materials shifts to those who have access to the means by which materials can be purchased and services hired.

Other studies focusing particularly on new technologies as opposed to new materials also seem to indicate that even at the microscale, societies not only shape technological practices, but are also shaped by them. Marshall McLuhan cites the well-known example of how Indian villagers asked UNESCO to remove water pipes installed to provide better access to water (McLuhan 1964: 86). This unexpected response is due to an unpredicted outcome of the new technology: by making it unnecessary for villagers to visit the local village well each day, the pipes removed a daily gathering that had important social implications for the villagers. The two different systems for obtaining water thus played an important role in shaping distinctive patterns of social interaction.

Winner also describes a microscale study of the effects of the introduction of the snowmobile on the society of the Skolt Lapps of Finland in the 1960s. This study, by Pertti J. Pelto, "reflects in miniature", he argues, "the whole course of the industrial revolution" (Winner 1977: 86). As Winner describes, the simple introduction of the snowmobile, achieved willingly by the Skolts themselves, effected over the course of a very short period a whole host of economic, ecological, and social changes that they had not willed and which were not foreseen. While the new machines made the annual reindeer roundup easier, they also changed herding practices in ways that placed stress on reindeer populations and eventually led to their decline. This, as well as the need for smaller numbers of participants with the new form of herding, led some families to give up herding altogether, and become wage labourers or newly 'unemployed' people in a society in which such a role had traditionally been unheard of. Other families meanwhile prospered, and used their newfound wealth to acquire other modern goods and technologies. As a result, within a short space of time, what had originally been a highly egalitarian society therefore became an inegalitarian and hierarchical one. As Winner observes:

> From one point of view the Skolts knew exactly what they were doing. They adopted the Bombardier "Ski-Doo" to make herding faster and more efficient. From another point of view, however, they never knew what hit them. (ibid.: 87)

Like the others, this example stresses the profound and unintended social consequences that can result from even the most small-scale and local of technological changes.

If the idea that technology determines society is problematic then, it is not because it describes something that appears to be true at one scale, but upon closer examination is false, or at least more complex. Technological determinism is problematic because it errs in attributing agency entirely to things, and ignores the potential for human agency, and for social and cultural factors, to mediate what otherwise cannot be anything but the overwhelming force of things. But the problematic idea that technology determines society should not be confused with the much more acceptable notion that technology shapes and influences society. Nor should the idea that environments determine societies and cultures be confused with the theory that they help to some degree to mould them. Determinism is a dirty word, and should be perceived as such, because it occludes humans, society, and culture – all the very things that social scientists know all too well the importance of. But throwing out determinism should not lead us to throw out the idea of 'shaping' or the insight that the resources and technologies employed by humans can have unintended consequences for their societies.

I also disagree with Misa's arguments concerning micro and macroscale studies because it seems to me that microscale studies – particularly studies of how changes in materials or the adoption of relatively simple technologies transform society – are actually capable at times of providing clearer insight than macroscale studies into the way human–technology relationships are mediated by the very materiality of technologies. Such examples allow us more clearly to see how the actual physical properties of things – rather than just the ideas we hold about them – instigate change, by placing constraints on some activities and behaviours, and making possible, encouraging, or demanding, other types of behaviour. Building with mud and thatch, for example, demands regular maintenance and encourages communal effort amongst the Luo precisely because neither material is particularly durable, and neither demand specialist builders to be formed into houses, only lots of basic labour. The use of particular species of shrub for hut-building by desert women in Kenya allows them to acquire such materials themselves, but also encourages the formation of cooperative work parties since acquiring and processing them are not easy. Furthermore, the precise qualities (softness, pliability) of the wood of the bushes used enable some tent shapes, but not others. Communal wells that consolidate water sources encourage people to gather to acquire water, while pipes that distribute water to individual houses prevent them from doing so. The important social changes that are decided by the basic physical properties of materials or technologies – whether they are hard or soft, pliable or rigid, durable or ephemeral, or mobile or immobile, for example – highlight the point that no amount of social construction can

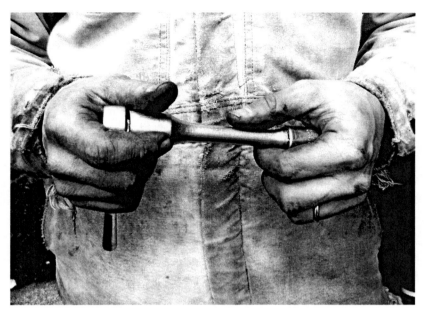

Figure 4.12: Mechanic holding a ratchet. Materiality is not just about matter, but rather about the coming together of matter and embodied humans. Photo Geri-Jean Blanchard.

entirely disguise the fact that technology, materials, or environments transform society because they are material entities with physical effects.

Of course, even at the simplest of levels, material properties are always properties relative to people, as James Gibson's concept of affordances reminds us (Gibson 1986). What a material, artefact, or technology affords an organism depends on the properties of the organism itself. Chairs afford sitting because humans have legs and a backside. Water affords walking for certain water insects, but not for humans, because our density is much higher than that of water. Desert bushes afford the building of tents because humans have hands that can bend branches, not to mention minds that can envision creating a shelter as protection against the elements and a means of privacy. At a basic level, what is important is not just materiality, but the coming together of materiality and embodied humans engaged in particular activities (Figure 4.12). The properties of materials are never objective, but depend on the organism using them. And this is of course where culture comes in, because even the seemingly most insistent of physical properties can be undone by cultural conditioning. Neither bushes nor mud necessarily afford house creating if one has only ever seen houses of concrete and steel, or if bushes and mud are considered impure materials not to be used for building houses. Indeed, systems of metal pipes may afford water acquisition, but not socially acceptable water acquisition, as we have seen. Even at the most basic level, materials and technologies do not act as agents that can be conceptually dissociated from human agents. This does not mean that material agents are only secondary agents that distribute human agency, but it does suggest that locating agency is a complex exercise that probably demands new ways of thinking about it, as well as about humans and things.

The New Materialism

The past few decades have seen a number of new studies and schools of thought that very much challenge scholars to move beyond debates about material determinism versus social constructionism. This is particularly the case in the field of technology studies. Many scholars have taken on board the lessons of the social constructionists, but also argued that we need to avoid an overly ideal approach that fails to do justice to the way technology nonetheless exerts a force within society. The trend towards social constructionism is being offset by a gradual recognition that such approaches have overlooked materiality, and its ability to impose constraints and enable possibilities, as well as lead to unexpected consequences.

The work of Langdon Winner very much illustrates this new approach. In particular, his book *The Whale and the Reactor: A Search for Limits in an Age of High Technology* (Winner 1986) highlights the need to study technologies as 'forms of life' and to develop a philosophy of technology. For Winner, technologies are not separate entities to be studied for their 'impact' upon society, but rather integral aspects of who and what we are. Just as Wittgenstein sought to challenge a popular and restricted view of language as primarily a matter of naming things and events (ibid.), Winner is keen to show that technologies are more than just tools for getting things done. Wittgenstein argued that speaking a language is a form of life, and Winner takes much the same view of technology. In this, he argues, he shares a perspective similar to that of Marx, who, as noted previously, similarly described productive activity as a 'mode of life'. Winner accordingly emphasises that the very act of using the variety of machines, techniques, and systems available to us in society transforms us into particular kinds of beings. As he observes:

> We do indeed "use" telephones, automobiles, electric lights and computers in the conventional sense of picking them up and putting them down. But our world soon becomes one in which telephony, automobility, electric lighting, and computing are forms of life in the most powerful sense: life would scarcely be thinkable without them. (ibid.: 11)

And later:

> As they become woven into the texture of everyday existence, the devices, techniques, and systems we adopt shed their tool-like qualities to become part of our very humanity. In an important sense we become the beings who work on assembly lines, who talk on telephones, who do our figuring on pocket calculators, who eat processed foods, who clean our homes with powerful chemicals. (ibid.: 12; Figure 4.13)

Life then is not separable from the things we use, because they condition (though never in a determinative sense) who we are. Our "individual habits, perceptions, concepts of self, ideas of space and time, social relationships, and moral and political boundaries" (ibid.: 9) are all wrapped up in the technologies we use.

Winner's perspective demands that we therefore consider the ethical and moral implications of technology. He points out that, at least in modern society, decisions about technology have generally been made with little concern for the possibility of the vast social and human transformations that have subsequently followed. As he argues, we have entered into technological contracts blindly, with little awareness of the consequences to follow, allowing ourselves to be preoccupied only with immediate questions of efficiency, cost, and convenience. Winner is thus concerned in *The Whale and the Reactor* to examine the political qualities of things, and specifically the "ways in which they can embody specific forms of power and authority" (ibid.: 19). Labelling his approach a "theory of technological politics", he goes on to provide it with a specific methodological framework:

> The theory of technological politics draws attention to the momentum of large-scale sociotechnical systems, to the response of modern societies to certain technological imperatives, and to the ways human ends are powerfully transformed as they are adopted to technical means. This perspective offers a novel framework of interpretation and explanation for some of the more puzzling patterns that have taken shape in and around the growth of modern material culture. Its starting point is a decision to take technical artifacts seriously. Rather than insist that we immediately reduce everything to the interplay of social forces, the theory of technological politics suggests that we pay attention to the characteristics of technical objects and the meaning of those characteristics. A necessary complement to, rather than replacement for, theories of the social determination of technology, this approach identifies certain technologies as social phenomena in their own right. It points us back, to borrow Edmund Husserl's philosophical injunction, *to the things themselves.* (ibid.: 21–22)

Winner's book is full of examples of the ways that technologies have either deliberately or unforeseeably achieved political ends. One of the most oft-cited in the technology literature is the case of Robert Moses' parkways on Long Island. As New York's master builder of roads, parks, bridges, and other public works from the 1920s to the 1970s, Moses was able to use technology to shape a particular social vision. In the case of the Long Island parkways, this

Figure 4.13: A woman works with a computer and a telephone. As Langdon Winner has noted, our technologies gradually lose their tool-like qualities to become part of who we are. Photo Carl Dwyer.

vision was explicitly racist: Moses deliberately designed the parkways to be low, and thus to exclude buses full of working-class and black people from reaching Jones Beach, his widely acclaimed public park (Figure 4.14). Only wealthy and middle-class, car-driving whites could use the parkways and hence reach the park. Of course, as cars gradually became available to a wider and wider swathe of the American populace, Moses' parkways eventually failed to achieve their desired result. Nonetheless, as Winner emphasises, many of Moses' projects have continued to have enduring effects long after his death. The highways and bridges he built to favour the

Figure 4.14: Sign just before one of Robert Moses' parkways, warning of the low bridge height. The Jones Beach water tower can be seen in the background. Moses deliberately built the bridges low so as to prevent buses from reaching the beaches. Photo Nicole Boivin.

use of the automobile over the development of mass transit have and will continue to shape the city of New York in important ways.

The example of Moses' parkways illustrates only one of the ways that technology is political. An otherwise neutral material or technological trait is deployed in such a way as to achieve a particular non-neutral (positive or negative) effect. Equally if not more important to Winner are cases of 'inherently political technologies' – technologies that appear to require, or at least to be strongly compatible, with particular kinds of political relationships (ibid.: 22) irrespective of how they are used. Some, for example, have argued that solar energy technologies are more inherently compatible with a democratic, egalitarian society than energy systems based upon coal, oil, or nuclear power (Figure 4.15). It makes sense, so solar energy advocates argue, to build solar systems as disaggregated, widely distributed systems, rather than in large-scale, centralised plants. Because this leads individuals and local communities to

Figure 4.15: Solar panel. It has been argued that solar panel is more compatible than oil or nuclear power with a democratic society. Photo Eline van den Berg.

deal with systems that are more accessible, comprehensible, and controllable, they are therefore able to manage their own affairs with less need for centralised powers. While the link between solar energy and democracy is not absolute, or predetermined, there is certainly a sense in which the materiality of solar power may at least favour certain types of political organisation over others.

The research of Alfred D. Chandler, described in *The Visible Hand*, provides Winner with another example. Chandler's wealth of accumulated data, according to Winner, convincingly demonstrates that the construction and daily operation of many nineteenth- and twentieth-century systems of production, transportation, and communication have demanded the development of large-scale, centralised, hierarchical organisations administered by highly skilled managers. Just as Plato argued that a ship at sea needs decisive steering by a single captain and an obedient crew, Chandler argues that the properties of large-scale systems require centralised, hierarchical managerial control – a particular social form that is thus closely linked to the distinctive technological forms of recent history.

Winner's approach, which combines an awareness of the potential for societies to shape technology with a strong desire to do justice to "things themselves", is not unique, but is in fact one of an increasing number of studies to operate from a similar platform. Thomas Hughes' concept of technological momentum, which has been picked up by various scholars in the technology and culture literature, is also, for example, of this general strain. Hughes recognises that earlier theories of technological determinism and more recent theories of social construction have both played important roles in the development of studies of technology, but argues that both suffer from important limitations (Hughes 1994). To overcome these limitations, Hughes proposes that scholars explore the area between the two extremes, where the social and technical interact. He describes this sphere of interaction as "technological systems". The Electric Bond and Share Company (EBASCO), an American electrical utility holding company of the 1920s, is one such technological system he illustrates – it consists of both inanimate electrons and animate regulatory boards, for example. In discussing the technological and social effects surrounding EBASCO, Hughes is clear that "on some occasions EBASCO was a cause; on others it was an effect. The system both shaped and was shaped by society" (ibid.: 107). Thus, technology is no out-of-control determinant of society, even if it does gather a certain momentum that enables it to shape society. Hughes argues that this momentum becomes greater as technological systems become larger and more complex over time. Thus, younger, developing systems tend to be more open to socio-cultural influences, while older, more mature systems are more independent of outside forces.

In the same vein as these discussions is Ruth Schwartz Cowan's earlier study of household technology (Cowan 1989). While Cowan does insist that "tools are not passive instruments, confined to do our bidding, but have a life of their own" (ibid.: 9), she is not concerned to enter into the kinds of theoretical debates that have divided idealists and materialists, and that preoccupy the likes of Winner and Hughes. Instead, in *More Work for Mother: The Ironies of Household Technology from the Open Hearth to the Microwave*, we find a detailed study that demonstrates *empirically* the complex ways in which technological and social changes are interwoven in technological systems. Cowan explores in detail the impact of household industrialisation – a long overlooked process – on women's labour and place within American society. Drawing on a range of historical materials spanning the period between 1860 and 1960, Cowan demonstrates that many of the new industrial technologies that replaced manual household technologies during this period actually liberated men rather than women, and not infrequently made women's lives more difficult. For example, one of the first stages of industrialisation of the household involved the transition from home milling of flour to milling at large automated flour mills, and therefore from home-grown to store-bought grains. This transition, however, lightened the workload of men and boys rather than women, since the milling of flour, either at home, or at local grist mills, had been one of their tasks. While men were relieved of one of their most time-consuming household chores, the new fine wheat flour provided by the automated mills led more labour-intensive yeast breads to replace the quickbreads (based on coarse flour) that had previously been common in most households, and thus resulted in more work for women. As the introduction of increasing numbers of new industrialised technologies gradually enabled men to seek work outside the home, women became ever more tied to domestic labour.

While Cowan sees the industrialisation of technology as critical to the creation in the nineteenth century of 'separate spheres' for men and women (ibid.: 69), her analysis never suggests a determinative role for technology. In examining the second stage of industrialisation in the twentieth century, for example, which she again emphasises did not lighten women's workload, she is clear that not just new technologies, but new social conventions were behind the novel labours that fell upon women's shoulders. Thus, for example, the creation of new household appliances designed to facilitate labour often created more work in part because social expectations changed as well. New appliances and conveniences enabled cleaner houses and clothes, more varied diets, and other advances, but also led to new standards of cleanliness and hygiene, more expectations about the varieties and tastes of food that would be served at home, and new types of social competition (Figure 4.16). Thus, there was very much a reciprocal relationship between the possibilities created by new technologies and the demands made by new social conventions. At no point did the new industrialised technologies simply determine the new social arrangements, relationships and practices, or cultural values that were transformed with them. Cowan's study exemplifies the kind of detailed analysis that permits a more holistic, less biased analysis of the relationship between technological change and society.

Finally, we may highlight the discussions, by sociologists of science and technology like Bruno Latour, Michel Callon, and John Law (e.g., Callon & Law 1997; Latour 1993, 2000), of collectives and networks as another, this time more explicitly theoretical, example of how scholars are moving beyond the extremes of technological determinism and social constructionism. In *We Have Never Been Modern*, for example, Latour describes as hybrids the networks of people, politics, things, and discourse that characterise society – the ozone hole, for example, is not just about chlorofluorocarbons and the atmosphere, but also chemists, corporations, international treaties, chief executives, refrigerators, Third World countries, heads of state, and the rights of future generations (Latour 1993). These actors – both human and non-human – associate to form collectives that the social sciences, having invented a divide between society and nature, are ill-equipped to study. Callon and Law (1997) highlight the problem by comparing human society to baboon society. In baboon society, power and the collective are built by bodies alone: "if you want to be a leader in baboon society . . . you cannot mobilize walls, rifles, or social security numbers. You cannot send letters to your baboon colleagues. You have no secret police. All you have is your own body . . . No other materials are involved" (ibid.: 168). Methodological individualism thus "works just fine in the society of monkeys that wander high on the plains in Kenya", Callon and Law write (ibid.), but is problematic for human societies, because human societies are heterogeneous: they involve

Figure 4.16: Vacuum cleaner. Ruth Schwartz Cohen has highlighted the fact that such new domestic technologies helped shape society, but not necessarily in ways that made women's lives easier. Photo Gokhan Okur.

collectives of humans and non-humans. And non-human materials are fundamental to what human society is and how it functions. Such non-human materials have often been assumed to be passive, and therefore possible to bracket off, but as Callon and Law assert:

> Yes, there are differences between conversations, texts, techniques and bodies. Of course. But why should we start out by assuming that some of these have no active role to play in social dynamics? (ibid.)

Indeed, as they go on to argue, we should not. Latour, elsewhere, echoes this sentiment. For him, things and technologies are also agents, and humans and non-humans are inseparable: "Consider things, and you will have humans. Consider humans, and you are by that fact interested in things" (ibid.: 20). Callon and Law therefore do not recognise discrete subjects and objects, but only sets of relations – networks, or collectivities. Their theoretical stance, parallel to that of Latour's, very much challenges conventional thinking about agency and the relationship between humans and things. It bypasses traditional debates, and demands that we see human society in a whole new way, and bring to bear the things human beings have created on our stories of human relationships, politics, and patterns of authority and action.

We Are Not Ghosts

While this chapter has primarily focused on technologies, it is important to point out that many of the same arguments hold for environments. Indeed, when viewed from the perspective of the arguments made by the likes of Tim Ingold and Bruno Latour about the artifice of separating nature and culture, the realms of technology and environment become difficult to differentiate. The materiality of both technology and environment surrounds and defines us, and the two are possible to keep separate only to the degree that we accept that nature and culture are divided by a nice clear boundary line. Our environment is at once natural and technological – the most remote, 'virginal' patch of Antarctic land is digitised and catalogued by satellite surveys, while even the most virtual of computer images must be recognised as the product of the natural pathways pursued by electrons in a force field. Studies of geography and technology draw divisions across what are in fact continuities.

The idea that technologies and environments shape society is not new, as the discussion in this chapter has attempted to highlight. Hinted at in some of the oldest historical records, capitalised upon by nineteenth-century archaeologists and artists, and made famous by Marx, the idea that the things people act upon can act back upon them is deeply rooted in Western thinking about the material world. And yet, for all its long history, this understanding remains deeply underdeveloped. Many scholars in the humanities and social sciences continue to act as though technologies and environments were marginal topics at best, and the linguistic turn and post-modernism have created a scholarly atmosphere in which it sometimes seems that to give even a moment's serious consideration to the things of the world is to demonstrate a disconcerting naiveté. Nonetheless, both the earlier generations of materialist studies and their newer, improved models suggest that what is really naive is to ignore the materiality of human society, and pretend that it can be studied as though we humans were in fact ethereal ghosts living amongst the clouds. Things are not mere epiphenomena of human history, but an integral part of the human story. Certainly there is more to our interaction with the material world than the representation of pre-conceived meanings.

If many of the technological studies that I have highlighted have focused on modern technology, this is because the literature on technology and society is overwhelmingly dominated by a concern for modern technology. This is to be expected, since the consequences of modern technology are so much more obvious and salient to us than the consequences of earlier technological transformations. What is more problematic, however, is the assumption, shared by some authors, that modern (industrial and digital) technology is categorically different than pre-modern technology. Some even go so far as to assume that it is only in the case of modern technology that large-scale, unintended social consequences have been unleashed: prior to this, technology was somehow benign, innocent, and greatly restricted in its influence. This assumption is nicely illustrated by the fact that the further back we go in time, the more studies of technological influence are replaced by studies of environmental influence. This is also the case with space: the farther we travel from the modern West, the more environment replaces technology as a constraining factor in the lives of people. *We* are defined by technology, it seems, while *they* are shaped by environment. This assumption has to some degree prevented more systematic concern with pre-industrial and prehistoric technologies in recent years. The latest theoretical insights into technologies and the ability of things to act as agents are only rarely applied in anthropological and archaeological discussions, which nowadays often remain caught up in idealist post-modern and social constructivist narratives about meaning and interpretation.

Nonetheless, dissatisfaction, even amongst anthropologists and archaeologists, is growing, and the social sciences and humanities are gradually coming to recognise that discussions of materiality – real materiality – have a critical role to play in our understanding of society and culture. It is certainly too early to speak of any détente across the wall that divides the humanities and sciences, but there is at least a growing recognition amongst social scientists that it is not quite so easy as once previously thought to neatly divide nature and society. And in the next chapter we will see that scientists are discovering the same thing. The world of culture, society, and technology created by human beings is not as easy as once thought to bracket off from the world of genes, biology, and human evolution. The hybrid world of things and ideas that we humans have created is, as we shall see, changing the very essence of our biological selves.

CHAPTER 5

A Self-Made Species

The Role of Technology in Evolution

The material world shapes and transforms us. As the previous chapters demonstrate, it shapes our sensory experiences, our emotional responses, our social organisation, our political structures, and our understanding of the world. But how far are we willing to go with this idea? What about our bodies and our minds? Have the material worlds we have created transformed qualities as fundamental as the form of our bodies or the physical structure and functioning of our minds? Have they impacted our very evolution?

These types of questions take us into the realms of biology, molecular genetics, and evolutionary theory, and hence have been largely failed to attract the attention of scholars in the humanities and social sciences. Paradoxically, however, they have also been overlooked by many natural scientists. For when we start to ask about the world that human beings have created, even the material aspects of that world, we enquire about something that is not normally included within the remit of the natural sciences. Culture and material culture are commonly left to social scientists to study. Furthermore, when considered by scholars of human evolution, they are more often than not seen as *markers* of biological, and particularly cognitive, evolution. The first signs of stone tool use, for example, by an early ancestor of ours called *Homo habilis*, are evidence of a smarter hominid (e.g., Schick & Toth 1993). The first cave art, many, many millennia later, is taken (by some) to signify the onset of a 'modern' mind, and the evolution at last of our own species, *Homo sapiens* (e.g., Klein 1999; Mithen 1996). But the role these cultural and technological steps may have played in actually *driving* biological and cognitive evolution is less frequently considered. Oddly enough, material culture is as passive for most evolutionary biologists as it is for social constructionists. Material culture occupies a strange liminal position where its materiality excludes it from a rightful place in current idealism-dominated social science formulations, while its cultural nature prevents it from attracting systematic interest from biologists, anthropologists, and others studying evolutionary processes.

Nonetheless, not all evolutionary scientists have overlooked the role that the worlds we have made have in turn played in shaping us. Indeed, some very innovative new directions in evolutionary biology and evolutionary anthropology have derived their impetus precisely from a consideration of this process. In the interests of achieving a holistic overview in this book of the role of the material world in human life, this chapter will thus explore some of the theoretical and empirical work in this area. It is important to emphasise, however, that the chapter does not pretend to be a thorough overview of evolutionary theory or even of evolutionary approaches to the material and cultural world. Instead, its primary aim is to demonstrate the continuity of the story of how the material world shapes us across the social and natural sciences divide. The study of the material world that humans create for themselves offers a powerful, if largely unexplored, means of bridging the counterproductive barrier that separates natural from social scientist.

Darwin, Mendel, and the Modern Evolutionary Synthesis

A little background on evolutionary theory is probably useful, given that the ideas I will discuss have emerged from debates within this field. And Charles Darwin is a natural place to start. As most scholars are undoubtedly aware, Darwin is widely regarded as the father of evolutionary theory. His ideas, developed in the middle of the nineteenth century, continue to provide an important framework for how evolutionary biologists model evolutionary processes. Darwin's critical insight was that species are not immutable, as the religious doctrine of his time insisted, but have rather been transformed over time through a process he called natural selection (Darwin 1859). Environments, Darwin observed, have altered through time, and nature has produced variants of species that are more or less well suited to these environments. Those variants best adapted to the environment at hand have survived to reproduce, while those less suited have died before having the opportunity to contribute progeny to the subsequent generation. Over long time periods, this cumulative process of new variants and the differential survival of their offspring has led to the gradual transformation of organisms, and, ultimately, the creation of entirely new species.

What Darwin was lacking from his model, however, was a proper *unit* of heredity (Dennett 1995: 20) – an understanding of what it was exactly that organisms inherited from their progenitors, and that was acted upon by the forces of natural selection. Meanwhile, not far away from the island upon which Darwin was pursuing his ideas, the answer to this critical question was being gleaned through the still relatively unknown experiments of an Augustinian monk named Gregor Mendel. In a monastery garden in what is today the Czech Republic, Mendel was cross-breeding pea plants in an attempt to understand how variation was inherited. Mendel discovered that inherited factors were not combined, as Darwin had supposed, but passed on intact, half from each parent. Some factors were dominant and others recessive. Effectively, what Mendel had discovered was the gene, long before its molecular basis became clear, and his work, which remained obscure during his lifetime, eventually set the stage for the modern field of genetics.

Today the modern evolutionary (or Neo-Darwinian) synthesis is built upon the foundations of the insights of both Darwin and Mendel, as well as other evolutionary theorists. It has drawn the critical connection between the units of evolution – genes – and the mechanism of evolution – selection. Evolution occurs, it argues, because selective pressures result in differing gene frequencies in successive generations. The totality of an organism's genes make up its genotype, which specifies its phenotype, or total physical constitution. For Neo-Darwinists like Richard Dawkins, this phenotype is nothing more than a vehicle for the replicator – the gene. 'Selfish' genes propagate themselves through time by creating temporary vehicles, including the bodies of human beings, which are used by genes for their own replication (Dawkins 1976).

Gene, Organism, and Environment

Not all biologists are happy with the very gene-centred and deterministic view of orthodox Neo-Darwinism, however (Bateson & Martin 1999; Gould 2002; Lewontin 2000; Oyama et al. 2001; Plotkin 1988). Despite its success in generating productive research programs, particularly in modern molecular genetics, the perspective suffers from a lack of attention to both organism and environment that in the view of an increasing number of biologists seriously compromises the further development of biological and evolutionary understanding. One of the main proponents of the need for a more holistic approach to biological organisms has been the geneticist Richard Lewontin, who has emphasised that genes, organisms, and environments are in reciprocal interaction with each other, so that each is both cause and effect of the others (Lewontin 1983: 276). Lewontin has focused particularly on the critique of what he sees as two very problematic metaphors in evolutionary biology (see, for example, Lewontin 1983, 2000). One is the notion that development is the *unfolding* of an already specified form that is latent in the genes and requires only an appropriate environment to be realised. In this view, the organism is little more than the passive object of genetic forces. DNA serves as a design 'blueprint', and the organism is constructed through the relatively straightforward translation of code into structure. The other metaphor Lewontin challenges is that of *problem and solution*. According to the Darwinian view of evolution, the environment poses the problem, and organisms posit solutions in the form of variants, with the result that the best solution is finally chosen. That is, "the organism proposes, the environment disposes" (Lewontin 2000: 43). This perspective, Lewontin argues, once again makes the organism a passive object, in this case of environmental forces. Evolutionary change occurs because organisms – and ultimately their genetic blueprints – respond to the problems posed by ongoing environmental change. Environments determine species.

Both of Lewontin's central critiques hold implications for how we understand the relationship between human evolution and the material world. In particular, however, the second critique has led to some challenging new ideas about evolution that are particularly germane to a discussion of human engagement with the material world. For Lewontin has argued that organisms do not so much *adapt to* as *construct* ecological niches for themselves. He notes that the concept of adaptation assumes the pre-existence of ecological niches, to which organisms thus become adapted as a result of the creation through mutation of new variants better fitted to those niches. However, as Lewontin observes, ecological niches cannot exist independently of organisms. He illustrates this point by imagining the ecological niches that might exist in his garden:

> In my garden there are trees, and grass growing around the trees, and some stones lying here and there on the ground. The grass is part of the environment of a phoebe, a bird that makes its nest out of dried grass, but the stones are not part of its environment. If they disappeared it would make not the slightest difference to the phoebe. But the stones are part of the environment of a thrush, a bird that uses the stones as an anvil to break open snails on which it feeds. There are holes high up in the trees which woodpeckers use for nests, but these holes are not part of the environment of either the phoebe or the thrush. *The elements of each bird's environment are determined by the life activities of each species.* (ibid.: 51–52; my emphasis)

Ecological niches then do not exist as abstract entities, but only as defined by the activities of species. As Lewontin points out, there are accordingly many possible niches that are not niches at all because no organism engages with them. For example, he points out, there is no animal that flies through the air, lives in trees in nests made of grass, and uses the vast quantity of leafy vegetation at the tops of trees for food (since perching birds do not eat leaves;

ibid.: 49). And there are furthermore niches that would seem absurd if they did not exist – like the niche of ants, for example. As Lewontin rhetorically observes, "Who could imagine that ants could live by gathering and mulching leaves to make a garden bed in which they would sow the spores of fungi to grow their food?" (ibid.). It is not enough to see the world as containing many once empty niches that have been filled by organisms through the process of adaptation. Instead, organisms create niches by determining what aspects of the outside world are relevant to them by peculiarities of their shape and metabolism (ibid.: 54).

But Lewontin crucially emphasises that organisms do more than this. They also actively construct – in the literal sense of the word – a world around themselves (ibid.). Obvious examples include the way that birds and ants build nests, spiders build webs (Figure 5.1), earthworms live in burrows, and humans make clothes and houses, but the process he emphasises is in fact more widespread than this. Humans and other animals, for example, create a layer of warm, moist air around their bodies that constitutes a self-produced atmosphere that serves to insulate them from the outer air (ibid.). All species destroy their own environment by using resources that are in short supply and transforming them into other materials not usable by other individuals of the same species (ibid.: 55). This is seen very clearly in the process of plant species successions, wherein the growth of one species changes the conditions of an area such that in subsequent periods, the species is out-competed and replaced by others.

Organisms, therefore, help create the conditions to which they adapt. The relationship between organism and environment in this perspective thus becomes one of co-evolution (Lewontin 1983: 284), with organisms and environments bringing each other into being. This important insight has subsequently been drawn upon and substantially developed by various evolutionary biologists who have adapted what is commonly referred to as a 'niche construction' perspective (Day et al. 2003; Laland & Brown 2006; Laland et al. 2000, 2001; Odling-Smee et al. 2003). These biologists highlight the widespread nature of niche construction, and emphasise its importance as a distinctive evolutionary process. They point out

Figure 5.1: Spider web. The material creations of spiders offer an example of niche construction. Photo Greg Macrae.

that conventional evolutionary theory, in focusing strictly on the way environments shape organisms, has overlooked the way organisms in turn shape environments, and thus transform the selection pressures to which they and their descendents are exposed (Laland et al. 2001). Organisms play a role in their own evolution.

Niche Construction and Human Culture

Niche construction has been defined as the way that "all living creatures, through their own metabolism, their activities and their choices, partly create and partly destroy their own niches, on scales ranging from the extremely local to the global" (Day et al. 2003: 81). Common examples of niche construction, some of which were initially highlighted by Lewontin, include the way organisms choose their own habitats, mates, and resources, and construct important components of their local environments such as nests, holes, burrows, paths, webs, dams, and chemical environments (Laland et al. 2000: 133). Examples of negative niche construction, whereby organisms partly destroy their niches, include the stripping from them of valuable resources and the building up of detritus (ibid.).

Kevin Laland, John Odling-Smee, and Marcus Feldman, the three main proponents of niche construction theory, have described two key ways in which niche construction influences the evolutionary process (ibid.). The first is by counteracting natural selection – for example, animals might counteract selective pressures by digging a burrow or migrating to avoid the cold. The way that many ant and termite species regulate temperature by plugging nest entrances at night or in the cold, by adjusting the height or shape of their mounds to optimise the intake of the sun's rays, or by carrying their brood around the nest to the place with the optimal temperature and humidity for their brood's development (ibid.) illustrates this process. As a result of such activities, ants bypass the forces of selection that might otherwise lead to the evolution of cold-adaptive features.

But there is also a second way that niche construction influences evolution: by introducing novel selection pressures. Animals might do this, for example, by exploiting a new food resource that subsequently leads to selection for a new digestive enzyme. One example discussed by Darwin himself is that of earthworms, which, through their burrowing activities, their dragging of organic material into the soil, their mixing of organic material with inorganic material, and their casting (which serves as the basis for microbial activity), dramatically change both the structure and the chemistry of soils (ibid.: 134; Darwin 1881). As a result, Laland and colleagues assert, "contemporary earthworms live in worlds that have been partly niche-constructed by generations of ancestors" (Laland et al. 2000: 134). They hypothesise quite reasonably that other earthworm phenotypes, such as epidermis structure and the amount of mucus secreted by the epidermis, have probably co-evolved with such niche-constructing behaviour.

While many of the niche constructing behaviours that are addressed in the literature are genetically specified, niche construction as a result of learned or cultural behaviour is also discussed,

Figure 5.2: Example of a human cultural niche: the Champs Elysées in Paris. Culture makes humans exceptionally potent niche constructors, and material culture is a major component of the human cultural niche. Photo Nicole Boivin.

both for humans and other animals. It has been emphasised that human beings are particularly potent niche constructors as a result of their capacity for culture (Laland & Brown 2006: 96). Compared to other organisms, humans and their evolutionary ancestors have demonstrated an extraordinary capacity for modifying their local selective environments (Figure 5.2), and are therefore argued to have been and to continue to be particularly prone to influencing their own evolution (Laland et al. 2001: 23). As long as the cultural traditions that result in environment-modifying activities persist for enough generations to generate a stable selection pressure, then culture too can and does influence human genetic evolution (ibid.: 24). Nonetheless, despite the extraordinary niche constructing activities of human beings, the effect of human cultural activities on human genetic evolution has garnered little attention (though see Boyd & Richerson 1985; Cavalli-Sforza & Feldman 1981; Durham 1991). Instead, as Laland and colleagues point out, the relationship between genetic evolution and culture has more often been seen as one-way, with contemporary human cultures understood as constrained or directed by our biological evolutionary heritage (Laland et al. 2001: 22). This is the perspective that has been adopted within the schools of sociobiology, human behavioural ecology, and evolutionary psychology, for example (ibid.).

If the ability of human cultural activities to influence human genetic evolution has received little attention, the specific capacity of human-created material and technological environments and activities to exert an evolutionary effect has received even less. Anthropologists, primatologists, and others have come up with some very interesting ideas about the role of the intensely social environments of primates in generating novel evolutionary pressures during the course of primate and human evolution (Byrne & Whiten 1988; Dunbar 1998, 2003; Dunbar & Shultz 2007; Humphrey 1976; Whiten & Byrne 1997), but have generally devoted significantly less attention to the potential role that material environments would also have played in this process. For archaeologists, evolutionary anthropologists, and others interested in human evolution, significant technical and material developments have more often been considered as *signifiers* of biological – and particularly cognitive – evolution. In particular, there has been much discussion of the possibility of using developments in stone tool technologies to trace changes in the capacity for language (e.g., Dibble 1989; Gibson & Ingold 1993; Wynn 1988, 1999). Tools, technologies, and other aspects of the material world of humans and their predecessors have largely been seen as the *outcome* of evolutionary developments, and little attempt has been made to investigate their potential role as selection forces during the course of human evolution.

The Self-Made Species

And yet, if niche construction theory is correct, the remarkable, indeed incomparable, material achievements of hominids must have had an effect on their subsequent evolutionary development. Humans and their ancestors have been making material culture, and substantially altering their environments, for several million years at least. They have constructed extraordinary new niches that it is difficult to imagine have not had an impact on their evolutionary history. Indeed the unique material and technological developments of hominids over the past two million years might well be envisioned to have played a role in driving the evolution of the unique cognitive, cultural, and social behaviours that characterise our genus. Changes in each of these areas are likely to have reinforced changes in the others, and to have together generated a kind of co-evolutionary force in which material and technological abilities were at once the impetus for and outcome of other kinds of changes.

One scholar who has acknowledged the potential for such a co-evolutionary spiral is the neuroscientist Terrence Deacon. In his book *The Symbolic Species*, Deacon has drawn attention to the potential impact that the cultural, social, and technological behaviours of individuals can have in modifying the context of natural selection for their future kin (Deacon 1997). Exploring the origins of human language, he has described a process in which not one single factor, but rather a constellation of behavioural changes set the stage for the acquisition of language. In his model, our human ancestors played a major role in generating the new selective pressures that led to language, through their development of increasingly complex technological, social, and cultural environments. Behavioural change led to genetic change that not only reinforced existing behaviours but also generated new ones. Deacon points, for example, to the impact of the first stone tool technologies in generating new evolutionary pressures. He observes that while the increased brain size of the emergent *Homo* genus is often seen as the reason why stone tool technology developed, the chronological relationship is in fact unclear. It is equally possible, he argues, to interpret the archaeological and fossil record as indicating that the first stone tools were the work of australopithecines (Figure 5.3). In this model, the transition from australopithecines to *Homo* was in part a consequence rather than the cause of the foraging innovation introduced by the new technology. Interestingly, more recent chronological findings, which suggest that stone tools were being produced by *Australopithecus garhi* by about 2.5 million years ago (de Heinzelin et al. 1999), seem to support this picture, especially since the earliest known *Homo* fossils only date so far to 2.3 million years ago.

If Deacon has drawn material culture into the "co-evolutionary net" (Deacon 1997: 349), he has nonetheless also taken a fairly conventional view in placing language at the core of the human evolutionary story. One writer who has given a more central role to material culture, however, is Jonathon Kingdon. In Kingdon's view, human technological achievements have not only defined but also shaped our species, creating new worlds for future generations (Kingdon 1993). Because of technology, we are, in Kingdon's view, the "self-made" species:

> Few may care to identify technology with the fruit of the Tree of Knowledge but eating this apple had many biological consequences for the path of human evolution: the human form, human diversity, language and our relationship with nature have all been shaped by technology. Humans have become intrinsically different from apes by becoming, in a very limited but real sense, artefacts of their own artefacts. (ibid.: 3)

Like Deacon, Kingdon has argued that the emergence of the first stone tool technology was pivotal in generating new selection pressures. While he does not specifically identify stone tool use as catalytic in the origins of *Homo*, he does see it as having had implications for the subsequent evolution of the genus. In particular, the first stone technologies – which likely coincided with the development of other technological industries, based on poorly preserved materials like bone, horn, sinew, skin, shell, wood, bark, fibres, and grass (ibid.: 47) – suggest to Kingdon the emergence of a new kind of primate, which could assume a specialised diet without the need to evolve specific modifications of anatomy, physiology, or behaviour. Through the use of technology, ancestral humans thus rapidly multiplied the number of ecological niches they could invade – as Kingdon has argued, "each new tool opened possibilities that were formerly the prerogative of very specialised animals" (ibid.: 37). And the use of tools was probably self-reinforcing,

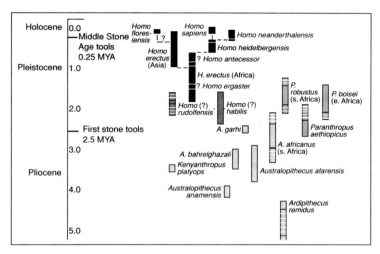

Figure 5.3: Diagram of human evolution showing species that have evolved during the Pliocene and Pleistocene epochs, and associated technologies.

leading to improvements in the natural anatomical versatility of primate arms, palms, fingers, and fingernails (ibid.: 47). It may also, I would argue, have encouraged the trend towards improved learning of new skills that Kingdon argues necessarily accompanied the first archaeologically evidenced tool technologies.

Kingdon also speculates that the modern human features identified in the fossil record in Africa beginning around 190,000 years ago may have been created, at least in part, through the use of new technologies (Figure 5.3). As he states:

> The sudden appearance of a new technology need not be matched by any strikingly novel form of human. Indeed, it is not necessary to expect that progressive changes in anatomy (notably, the thinning bones, lighter build and more 'childlike' heads that are typical of Modern humans) need always be associated with Middle Stone Age tools. If my basic hypothesis of "self-making" is correct these changes could have been the *products* of a new technology and its associated behaviour. Should this be the case, gross anatomical changes could have trailed well behind the

technical achievements of a genetically and intellectually
unique population. (ibid.: 95–96)

Thus, Kingdon sees technology as potentially having had a critical role to play in the evolution of new human species. Kingdon's argument is that the new technology of the Middle Stone
Age (Figure 5.4), together with associated changes in the human
social system at this time, may well have played a role in generating anatomical and genetic alterations in the forerunners to modern
humans. Such changes would have been part of a longer-term trend,
he emphasises, but one whose tempo and intensity was increased
in the Middle Stone Age. He argues not only that powerful, heavily boned people would have been at less of an advantage in the
context of the larger, more cooperative and more efficient social
groups that he suggests developed at this time, but also that a more
thorough artificial processing of food led to a similar decline in the
size of teeth, chewing muscles, and their associated bony anchor-
age (ibid.: 96). Such changes would have occurred slowly however,
he notes, and also irregularly, depending on what technologies and
practices were adopted locally. Such irregularities in the pattern of
anatomical change, as well as the trailing of biological adaptation
behind technological innovation, may, in Kingdon's view, help to
explain the emergence of distinctive human 'races': "When locally
adapted technologies dominated the existence of a distinct people,
they became a major influence on the further evolution of that
population" (ibid.).

The role of technologies in shaping modern human diversity is
indeed a significant topic of interest for Kingdon. Even climate-
derived genetic changes, such as alterations in skin pigmentation,
need to be viewed as technology-driven, he argues, because technology was the factor that allowed human beings to colonise new environments in the first place. As humans radiated out of Africa, into
new habitats, they employed and developed new technologies and
practices to do so. The need to meet the inbuilt nutritional requirements and physiological limitations of humans would then have
led to a certain conservatism once new foods and places had been
adapted to through technological innovations. As Kingdon notes,
such specialisation can become very specific and self-perpetuating.

Figure 5.4: Middle Stone Age (MSA) points from Hollow Rock Shelter, South Africa (the two larger points are about 2 cm across). New MSA technologies may have led to anatomical changes in humans. Images courtesy of Chris Clarkson.

Long-term specialisation also has the potential to yield associated anatomical and genetic changes that eventually serve to differentiate populations. Kingdon is cautious, however, in attributing too much power to technologies. As he emphasises, "many scores of generations had to live and die before artefacts could influence the genetics of their makers, and even then the influence was indirect" (ibid.: 166). Nonetheless, more recent evidence from molecular genetics studies supports many of Kingdon's assertions, as we shall see.

Beyond stone tools and other artefacts, another technology that likely had a role to play in evolution was that which surrounded the control of fire. Kingdon suggests that the effective control and setting of fire probably long predates the first evidence for hearths at about one million years ago, presumed to have been made by *habilis'* successor, *Homo erectus*. He argues that cave-dwelling and human colonisation of cold northern latitudes were dependent on the prior development of fire-controlling techniques farther south (ibid.: 57). Richard Wrangham and colleagues, meanwhile, have placed both fire and cooking at the centre of a hypothesis that suggests that they had a role to play in driving anatomical and social change in *Homo erectus* (Wrangham et al. 1999). In contrast to those who have argued that hunting and meat eating were key factors in human evolution (e.g., Aiello & Wheeler 1995; Bunn & Kroll 1986; Washburn & Lancaster 1968), Wrangham and colleagues suggest instead that it was the cooking of plant foods that led to crucial changes, including most notably the speciation of *erectus* from an earlier *Homo* population. The cooking of plant foods is argued to have led to a large increase in plant digestibility and in energy yielded, and thus a decrease in the size and robustness of the masticatory apparatus, as well as an increase in especially male but also female absolute body size. More controversially, they also suggest that cooking led to delayed food consumption, and hence increased competition for food that resulted in social changes, particularly in the relationship between males and females. Hypotheses and debates like these, while often highly speculative, have nonetheless focused attention on the role of technology in driving, rather than just reflecting, human evolution.

Quite appropriately then, niche construction theorists have emphasised that part of the power of the niche construction model lies in its ability to generate exciting new hypotheses and approaches in evolutionary studies (Laland et al. 2000). They argue, for example, that according to niche construction theory we can expect more technically advanced cultures to display a greater capacity for counteractive niche construction (which, as indicated above, would counteract natural selection pressures). Such a suggestion generates, they observe, a number of testable hypotheses. For example, we would accordingly thus expect hominids to show less response to fluctuating climates than other mammals, and would similarly expect that cultures with more technology and material culture would in general exhibit less of an adaptive response to fluctuating climates than cultures with less technology. They also examine the implications of counteractive niche construction for Bergmann's and Allen's rules, which lead us to expect that populations in warmer climates will be smaller bodied and have larger extremities than those in cooler climates. Again, hominids would be expected, according to niche construction theory, to demonstrate less adherence to these rules than other mammals, as would human societies (e.g., modern humans) with more technology compared to those with less (e.g., Neanderthals). They also propose that we should expect an inverse relationship between robustness and the capacity for counteractive niche construction (the idea being that more robust physiology is necessary in the absence of material culture). The latter appears to some degree to be borne out by the fact that some of the most robust modern or recent-day populations (such as the Australian Aboriginal peoples at the time of first colonial contact, and the Fuegians) possessed), some of the most basic material culture repertoires known. Finally, Laland et al. also propose that it may be possible to reverse the inference, and use the fossil record to infer something about the niche constructing capabilities of hominids. For example, they hypothesize that the greater the response to environmental change that is exhibited by a hominid, the more restricted must have been its capacity for niche construction.

Not all of these proposals are new of course, but, as Laland and his colleagues emphasise, a niche construction perspective allows them to be more systematically formulated and empirically tested. Niche construction theory accordingly has much to offer not only to our general understanding of evolutionary processes, but also the specific evolutionary trajectories that led to modern humans, and the role that material culture played within them. Moreover, as we shall see, it also holds the potential to shed light on how technology has impacted on people during more recent periods of the human past.

Self-Domestication

The idea that not just animals and plants, but also human beings, became domesticated with the advent of the Neolithic period has recently become a popular one in archaeology (e.g., Hodder 1990; Thomas 1999; Wilson 1988). The Neolithic appears to have ushered in not only a series of economic and material changes, but also a range of social and ideological changes that altered our relationships to the natural world as well as to each other. People, it is argued, began during the Neolithic period to domesticate themselves, by generating new patterns of living that differed dramatically from any that had appeared before. These recent arguments, made by the likes of Ian Hodder and Peter Wilson, focus not so much on the evidence for morphological domestication as *social* domestication, and propose major transformations in the social and conceptual frameworks of human societies, leading to profound changes in human behaviour and lifestyle.

One of the main catalysts for these new patterns of living is argued to be the house (Hodder 1990; Watkins 1990; Wilson 1988). The Neolithic is not only about settling down and living in permanent dwellings, but also about all the symbolic and social baggage that seems to come with living in houses. One of the main signs of the importance of social and symbolic factors in the domestication process is the way that they seem, in some very early contexts, to actually precede the domestication of plants and animals. Contrary to traditional perspectives, which saw changes in the social and cultural sphere as secondary to those in the economic sphere, some archaeologists accordingly argue now that they were, at least to some degree, the impetus for some of the economic changes that have been taken as characteristic of the Neolithic (Bender 1978; Cauvin 2000; Hayden 1990; Wilson 1988).

Regardless of what type of change came first, the idea that humans domesticated themselves socially and culturally is a compelling one that seems amenable to extension to the biological and genetic realms. That is, if humans domesticated themselves socially and culturally through the Neolithic process, perhaps they also, at the same time, domesticated their bodies, creating equally notable changes in human morphology, as the term domestication implies. This is an argument that has been made by the archaeologist Helen Leach, in an article entitled "Human Domestication Reconsidered" (Leach 2003). However, as Leach observes, consideration of such changes by archaeologists and anthropologists has been minimal, probably in part because the beginning of the Neolithic is seen as marking a boundary, after which biological evolution is only rarely considered. She notes that:

> Following the lead of widely used introductory textbooks, we have taught the Palaeolithic stages largely as a narrative of biological evolution, with brief excursions into stone technology and subsistence. In contrast, we present Holocene prehistory as the story of cultural evolution, and the standard texts (which happily discuss such details as the retromolar gap in Neanderthals) generally ignore the physical anthropology of Halafians, Sumerians, Egyptians, and others as they move on to the origins of civilization. The physical changes occurring in post-Pleistocene *Homo sapiens* are relegated to textbooks on physical anthropology, where they are considered as examples of human variation. (ibid.: 364)

The anthropologist Tim Ingold has made similar arguments about the problematic way in which the human past is dichotomised into evolutionary and historical phases (Ingold 2000). Leach has pointed out that culture is seen as something that "increasingly buffered humans from the cold winds of natural selection" (Leach 2003: 364), rendering biological evolution unimportant.

And yet the early stages of some very significant cultural transformations – at the end of the Pleistocene and beginning of the Holocene – appear to be associated with significant changes in human morphology. Many studies suggest that during this period, human beings underwent a series of morphological changes, including reduction in size and stature, cranial gracilization, alterations in post-cranial robusticity, shortening of the face and jaws, tooth crowding and malocclusion, and tooth-size reduction and simplification (ibid.: 355). Interestingly, these are many of the same changes that animals also underwent during the process of domestication. The changes appear to coincide with the late Palaeolithic and early Neolithic periods, when major transformations in human subsistence, sedentism, material culture, and technology took place. Leach has accordingly argued that these changes led to new selection pressures on humans, many of which overlapped with the new selection pressures acting on animal morphologies during the process of domestication. Thus human evolution was affected by, for example, increased concentrations of people, conscious or unconscious interference in breeding, decreased mobility, changes in diet breadth, and an artificial, protected environment (Figure 5.5). The overlap in selection factors is particularly apparent for animals, like pigs, dogs, mice, and sparrows, that were likely living in close proximity to humans (and in some cases even sharing their dwellings) and consuming the same foods.

The fact that while Leach's arguments have been foreshadowed in the work of others – for example, the anthropologist Frans Boas, as she herself observes – and yet remain unconventional suggests of course that the story is not entirely straightforward. And there are problems. For one thing, it is rarely clear to what degree changes in morphology, in both animals and humans, have derived from genetic factors or environmental influences during the course of development. In most cases, it is probably to some degree a case of both having been influential, and this naturally clouds the picture. On the other hand, few commentators would deny that genetic selection has had a role to play in the case of both the human and animal transformations associated with the late Palaeolithic and/or early Neolithic. In addition, however, there is the problem of chronology. In many cases, the morphological changes seen in humans occur in the late Palaeolithic and Mesolithic periods, while those undergone by animals occur in the Neolithic period. However, as the Neolithic 'package' is gradually broken down into component parts (e.g., Smith 2001; Verhoeven 2004), it is becoming increasingly clear that sedentism, built environments, dietary changes, and new forms of technology and material culture often significantly preceded the advent of agriculture and husbandry (e.g., Bender 1978; Byrd 2005; Kelly 1992; Watkins 1990). It may thus perhaps be less surprising that human morphological domestication would be initiated in many cases prior to animal domestication – that we domesticated ourselves before we domesticated other species. As the discussion in the preceding section suggests, this was indeed simply a continuation of a long-term process of self-shaping that had already been going on for millions of years.

Figure 5.5: A modern European farm. The kinds of practices that led to agriculture and the domestication of animals in the Neolithic are argued to have had a comparable impact on humans. Photo Ekaterina Boym.

Perhaps the greatest resistance to the idea of self-domestication comes from the perseverance of biases generated by an increasingly outdated, but still influential, notion of domestication (Leach 2003). According to the traditional view, domestication is a process achieved through deliberate interference with natural patterns by human agents. Domesticates are seen as purposeful human creations, fashioned through a process of human 'mastery' of nature (as discussed in Chapter 4). Animals that live with humans as unwelcome guests, and that have been transformed as a result of this proximity – such as mice and sparrows – are not seen as synonymous with domesticates. Instead, their adaptation is described as commensalism. But increasingly a very different view of domestication has taken hold, which views it not as deliberate, but rather as unconscious selection. Thus selection during domestication is similar to natural selection, only occurring in a human-modified environment. Rather than being masters of the domestication process, humans have more commonly been unaware that it is occurring. Domestication has accordingly been increasingly recognised as a kind of co-evolutionary process, in which humans and other species alter the selective forces acting on each other in unintentional and unanticipated ways (Rindos 1980). Within such a view, processes like commensalism and mutualism are actually akin to domestication, and indeed some have seen these terms as preferable for at least the early stages of the domestication process.

Leach uses the example of several common commensals to illustrate how human-modified environments may have influenced humans themselves. The house mouse, she notes for example, has adapted to commensalism with humans by developing changes in pelage, a longer tail, shortening of the face and molar row, and possible size reduction (Tchernov 1984). One domesticated variety, *Mus musculus domesticus*, spread through the Fertile Crescent in association with human sedentism beginning in the Epipalaeolithic (Boursot et al. 1993). Agriculture was not a key factor in the dispersal of the species, which was associated in the Middle East with pre-Neolithic human dwellings. It was therefore living in these dwellings with humans that likely shaped the mice into initial domestic forms. The importance of the human built environment in generating new selection pressures also appears to be clear for the house sparrow (*Passer domesticus*), which underwent a size decrease with the introduction of commensalism (Morales-Muñíz et al. 1995). The species clearly required human shelter and a winter feed supply to spread, as it eventually did, into northern Europe. Leach therefore asks why, if such commensal species could have undergone specific evolutionary changes as a result of living in the modified environments and eating the modified diets created by humans, we too may not have been altered by the same novel pressures. Whatever the complications, it seems difficult to accept the conclusion that the novel material and environmental changes introduced by human beings beginning in the late Pleistocene had no effect on their morphology and genetic evolution.

Molecular Genetics and Recent Human Evolution

Indeed, the impression that Leach is right is reinforced by recent findings within the field of molecular genetics. These findings tend to confirm the idea, already expressed in the evolutionary literature, that rates of biological evolution can be extremely fast, particularly when culture is involved. Laland and Brown, for example, point out that biologists have recently been able to measure rates of selection in animals and plants, and have found that selection may operate more rapidly than hitherto conceived, with significant genetic and phenotypic change sometimes observable in a handful of generations (Laland & Brown 2006: 101). They suggest, based on calculations from selection rates data, that significant human evolution could even be measured in hundreds of years or less, opening up the possibility that humans could realistically have evolved solutions to self-imposed problems over the last few millennia (ibid.). In another paper in which evolution rates are addressed, Laland and colleagues also observe that the rapidity with which cultural niche construction can alter environments relative to most natural environmental changes would suggest that culture can generate atypically strong selection, and hence cause particularly rapid evolutionary change (Laland et al. 2000).

Preliminary but pioneering genetic studies over the past few years support these conclusions by demonstrating significant recent change in the human genome. A variety of studies that have scanned the human genome for signs of strong, recent selection have found widespread evidence of late – in some cases possibly Holocene period – change in those populations sampled (Akey et al. 2004; Voight et al. 2006; Wang et al. 2005). That is, a surprising number of genetic changes seem to have appeared in humans since the – on an evolutionary scale – relatively recent adoption of agriculture and a sedentary existence. The fact that many of the observed genetic changes are found only in particular populations supports the idea that they are of recent origin, and furthermore accentuates the degree to which local environments – natural, but also human-made – have shaped human genetic diversity.

It will take time for scientists to locate systematically the many genes that have evolved relatively recently in our history, and, more importantly, to understand the evolutionary forces that shaped them. However, one significant impetus for such research derives from the fact that many of the genetic changes so far identified hold medical implications. For example, several of the genetic changes that can be clearly linked to the adoption of agricultural practices since the Neolithic period are tied to diseases that severely impact upon modern populations. The genes associated with malaria resistance provide an excellent illustration. As Sarah Tishkoff and her colleagues observe, malaria is a leading cause of death, whose approximately 500 million cases each year result in about two million fatalities (Tishkoff et al. 2001). The link between malaria prevalence and the frequency of certain blood diseases (e.g., sickle cell anaemia and thalassaemia) has been understood for some time, and shown to relate to the ability of several different blood molecule disorders to confer resistance to malaria. These disorders are significantly more common in regions in which malaria is prevalent, and the genes that cause them are thus argued to have been selected for as a means of preventing malaria.

It is now widely recognised that both malaria, and the genetic blood disorders and other genetic mutations that help prevent it, have arisen relatively recently, in response to human activities and new technologies. While some of these activities, such as expansion into tropical forest and settlement of riverbanks in association with new technologies, probably date back to the Middle Stone Age (Webb 2005), other varieties of malaria and/or genetic adaptations to it appear to have emerged in response to the new agricultural technologies of the Holocene. For example, a recent genetic study by Tishkoff and colleagues of several alleles (genetic variants) that confer resistance to malaria suggests that they evolved relatively recently, and certainly within the Holocene (ibid.). This supports the notion that malaria has had a significant impact on human populations in the last 10,000 years or so, and is consistent with the hypothesis that forest-clearing as a part of agricultural activities significantly increased malaria prevalence by creating abundant pools of standing water that served as excellent breeding grounds for the mosquito vector that carries the parasite associated with severe malaria. In the Sahara and north-east Africa, malaria may also have increased in somewhat earlier periods when fishing industries and incipient cattle domestication concentrated people near lake shores and water pools (ibid.). Either way, it was the Neolithic technological practices associated with plant and animal domestication, and with settling down, that likely made malaria more prevalent in the

Holocene, and that led to increased genetic adaptation to the disease. Malaria resistance thus provides an excellent, and very clear illustration, of the way in which humans have ultimately shaped their own genomes through cultural and technological practices in recent evolutionary history.

Another medical problem that seems to be at least partially attributable to the development and spread of agriculture during the Holocene is the modern prevalence of obesity-related diseases. The classic example of such a disease is type 2 diabetes mellitus, which currently affects over 150 million people worldwide, and appears set to become one of the world's most common diseases and biggest public health problems (Diamond 2003). The incidence of diabetes has increased dramatically in the last half century amongst many world populations, and appears to be related to lifestyle factors, including in particular a high calorie intake and low exercise. The classic, and probably still the most convincing, explanation for this trend in diabetes incidence, as well as other obesity-related diseases, is James Neel's 'thrifty gene hypothesis' (Neel 1962). Neel argued that thrifty genes, like the gene responsible for type 2 diabetes, would previously have helped buffer against food shortages by ensuring more efficient food utilisation, fat deposition, and rapid weight gain when food was available. Such genes were selected for in our evolutionary history, to buffer us against unstable food reserves, but now prove deleterious when faced with the plentiful, rich, high-calorie diets now common in many parts of the world (see also Di Rienzo & Hudson 2005).

Most explanations for the evolution of thrifty genes have simply attributed them to the hunter-gatherer lifestyle of the Palaeolithic, when it is assumed that food availability would have been more sporadic than today. There may be some truth to this explanation, but there is also evidence that the situation is more complex than such accounts recognise, and that pre-modern agricultural lifeways also contributed to the selection of thrifty genes. Useful discussion of the various evolutionary factors that may have contributed to the selection of thrifty genes, and fatness, in the human genome has been offered by the medical researcher, Jonathan Wells (Wells 2005, 2006). Noting that the human phenotype is generally fatter than that of other mammals occupying similar environmental niches, Wells sets out to investigate why. He notes, firstly, that early hominids were increasingly exposed to seasonal environments (Foley 1993) that would have favoured selection for thrifty genes. Then, with the evolution of *Homo* and its expensive brain, increased energy stores in the reproducing female and in the offspring early in life would have been favoured. But this is not the end of the story. With the introduction of agriculture, argues Wells, further selection pressures were introduced that continued to favour the genetic trend towards fatness. One of these was regular famines. Wells notes that while hunter-gatherers traditionally exploit a wide variety of food sources, and can migrate in order to avoid severe energy stress, sedentary farmers specialising in a few crops are much more susceptible to environmental deterioration (Wells 2005: 20). Wells also notes the effect of social differentiation as a result of new storage technologies in the Neolithic and subsequently (Figure 5.6), which enabled certain individuals and groups to dominate food resources, and thus left others more prone to resource instability.

Wells' arguments are strengthened and supplemented by studies of ethnic variability in susceptibility to obesity-related diseases. The fact that different ethnic groups vary tremendously in their susceptibility to such diseases seems to confirm the operation of relatively recent economic, social, and technological selection factors on the human genome. Geneticist Yasuo Kagawa and colleagues, for example, have highlighted the regional variation evidenced for a range of thrifty genes that confer susceptibility to obesity-related disease (Kagawa et al. 2002). They suggest that ethnic differences in energy metabolism, and hence lifestyle-related diseases, are the result, in large part, of the evolutionary effects of novel environments created by different agricultural complexes. Such an argument, while speculative, also fits with the picture derived from the various recent genome-scanning exercises discussed above. Benjamin Voight and colleagues, for example, describe a number of genes that have undergone recent selection as a result of the transition to new food sources subsequent to the colonisation of new habitats and the advent of agriculture, including the alcohol dehydrogenase cluster (in East Asians); genes involved in metabolising mannose (in Yoruba and East Asians), sucrose (in East Asians), and

Figure 5.6: Mud-built grain storage container in Rajasthan, India. Similar storage technologies emerged in the Neolithic, and enabled new social and political relationships that probably led to differential access to food resources. Photo Nicole Boivin.

lactose (in Europeans); and genes responsible for various aspects of the processing of dietary fatty acids (Voight et al. 2006).

That the genes responsible for the metabolism of lactose have undergone recent selection in Europeans, as well as certain other populations, is already of course a well-known fact (see Bersaglieri et al. 2004) that is only confirmed by the study of Voight and colleagues. Indeed, the recent evolution of lactose-tolerance is one of the clearest and most oft-cited examples of how cultural niche construction has altered the human genome (Durham 1991; Feldman & Cavalli-Sforza 1989). The evolution of lactose-tolerance also exemplifies the manner in which novel technologies and practices introduced in the Neolithic period led to human self-domestication. Lactose is a protein found in milk that is metabolised by an enzyme called lactase normally only available in childhood (Figure 5.7). However, in certain populations, and particularly amongst Europeans, lactase continues to be produced in adults, thus enabling the continued digestion of milk and its products. Studies of the geographic distribution of lactase persistence indicate that it coincides with the distribution of dairy farming. Hence, it seems clear that lactase persistence was selected for amongst early cattle pastoralists, to enable utilisation of the rich food resources in cow's milk.

This scenario is confirmed by archaeological and ancient DNA evidence suggesting that early cattle pastoralists in North Central Europe, for example, were dependent on milk, but still lacked the lactase enzyme (Burger et al. 2007). Not only are early Neolithic sites in the region rich in cattle remains (Bökönyi 1988), but analysis of intratooth change in nitrogen isotope ratios from cattle teeth dating to this period also demonstrates that cattle herds were managed for early weaning of calves, in order to make cow's milk more available for human consumption (Balasse & Tresset 2002; Dudd & Evershed 1998). In addition, a recent genetic study also indicates that cattle genes have undergone evolution in parallel with human ones, as a result of selection for increased milk yield and altered milk protein composition (Beja-Pereira et al. 2003). Thus, animal domestication, as Leach argued, is not a one-way process, but a complex trajectory in which animals and humans have often co-evolved. The example of lactase persistence also highlights the important role played by technologies in cultural niche construction: not only did systematic dairying involve new cultural practices, but it also relied on new technologies, and in particular the invention of ceramic containers in which milk could be collected and stored. Developments in ceramic technology, such as the creation of strainers, would have subsequently enabled intensification of reliance on milk through the creation of milk products like yogurt and cheese.

As regional and ethnic differences in the human genome are unravelled, it is becoming increasingly clear that the specific evolutionary trajectories that generated them may be very complex and difficult to reconstruct. For example, Jared Diamond has argued that the well-known susceptibility of Nauruans to diabetes is

Figure 5.7: Milk in container. The recent evolution of lactose persistence in populations with a history of dairying technology is one of the clearest known examples of Holocene period niche construction leading to genetic evolution in humans. Photo Jim Broughton.

the result of evolutionary pressures deriving from diverse sources (Diamond 2003). Nauru is a remote island in the Pacific which has one of the highest known diabetes rates in the world. Diabetes seems to have been unknown on the island until as recently as 1925, but increased rapidly following adoption of a Western diet and lifestyle. Diamond cites three different reasons why the thrifty genes that lie behind the resultant diabetes epidemic would likely have been selected for. First, in the initial colonisation period, when boat technology enabled people to settle the Pacific islands, those who were fattest were often the only ones to survive the starvation situations sometimes encountered on long voyages. Subsequently, the island's frequent droughts and poor soil led to recurrent famines that maintained the earlier selection pressure. Finally, during the Second World War, the island was occupied by Japanese forces, who imposed forced labour and reduced rations on the population, and then deported most of the population to Truk, where half of them died of starvation. Thus, the enrichment of the population's diabetes-susceptibility genes was the result of a range of different technologies, processes, and historical events that acted over varying time periods.

Europeans, meanwhile, were susceptible to very different forces that decreased their risk of diabetes, in spite of a diet and lifestyle that in other populations have proven so disabling. Diamond suggests that Europeans became much less susceptible to famines beginning around 1650, due to key technological, economic, and political developments, including increasingly efficient state intervention and grain redistribution, increasingly efficient food transport by land and sea, and increasingly diversified agriculture after AD 1492. These developments reduced selection for thrifty genes, which indeed would likely have been selected *against* as Europeans became more affluent, and acquired richer, more stable diets. The importance of such counter-selection is perhaps illustrated by the rate of diabetes in European immigrants of British and German ancestry in the United States and Australia, which at 7–8 percent is significantly higher than the 2 percent for British and German people still living in Europe today under similar lifestyles (ibid.: 602). Diamond suggests that this pattern reflects the socially stratified emigration that is often discussed by historians. Thus, Europeans who stayed at home tended to be of a more affluent class than those who emigrated, and hence had already undergone several centuries of selection against diabetes thrifty genes by the time they split from the poorer, more starvation-prone populations who sought better conditions abroad.

The discovery of increasing numbers of thrifty genes, as well as others that confer disease for similar reasons (Di Rienzo & Hudson 2005; Thompson et al. 2004; Young et al. 2005), would seem to suggest that human beings are poorly adapted to post-Palaeolithic and/or post-Neolithic lifestyles. However, it is important to bear in mind that evolution is an ongoing process, and that post-Neolithic niche construction, right up to the present day, has also generated its own selection pressures and genetic changes. The example of obesity-related disease provides an illustration of this process. Not only modern diets, but also the incredible variety of technologies that have removed the need for human labour, have generated novel selection pressures that have in fact acted to *decrease* the prevalence of thrifty genes in recent human evolutionary

history. This has been documented most clearly for the Nauruans, who have, in the past thirty or forty years, begun to see
a decline in their once catastrophic diabetes rates (Dowse et al.
1991). This has not happened because Nauruans have returned to
a more traditional diet or eschewed the mechanised technologies
that together have made them prone to both obesity and diabetes,
but rather because selection has already acted to remove a high
proportion of genetically susceptible individuals from the Nauruan
gene pool (ibid.). That is, cultural niche construction in the form
of a rich diet and advanced technology appears to have generated
extremely rapid genetic change. Diamond describes it as "the most
rapid instance known to me of natural selection in a human population – an occurrence of detectable population-wide selection
within less than 40 years" (Diamond 2003: 600). Of course, the
description of the selection as natural is a misnomer, since it is in
fact entirely cultural, but the point remains that evolution can happen extremely rapidly in human populations under the influence of
cultural selection pressures, just as Laland and his colleagues have
proposed.

Cognitive Evolution

It seems clear then that various types of human activities, and in
particular technological and material activities, have had an impact
on human evolution, right up until the present day. Up to this
point, however, my discussion has focused largely on the pressures
that technologies have exerted upon aspects of our bodies like our
skeletal morphology, enzymes, and the cellular features that confer
and resist disease. Of equal, if not greater interest, however, is the
question of what impact material culture has potentially had on the
evolution of our brains and minds. Have technology and material
culture contributed to shaping the developed cognitive faculties
that characterise our species?

This is of course a more difficult question to answer. As the discussion in Chapter 2 suggested, the mind continues to evade simple
understanding, and the complexities of studying it are amplified
multifold for the past. Furthermore, relatively few studies have

considered the impact of the technological niche on human cognitive evolution. Nonetheless, there are researchers who have begun to consider how our brains may have adapted to our technologies. In particular, a number of them have focused on the earlier stages of human and even primate evolution, when some of the earliest technologies likely began to emerge.

Though stone tool technologies provide the first irrefutable evidence for the creation of artefacts by a primate ancestor, increased recognition of the widespread presence of tool-making abilities amongst modern-day primates and indeed other animals (Beck 1980; Hunt 1996; McGrew 1992; van Schaik et al. 2003; Whiten et al. 1999) has drawn attention to the likelihood of pre-hominid material technologies. The fact that non-human tools and artefacts are generally made of materials that either have poor preservational potential or would be difficult to distinguish archaeologically from non-cultural materials implies the possibility of a significant range of unrecognised technologies leading up to the first archaeologically visible manifestations of tool-making in the archaeological record (e.g., Panger et al. 2002). Hence, as some have argued, we need to consider the potential role of pre-hominid technological innovations in driving the behavioural and anatomical changes that eventually generated the first hominids.

One scholar who has considered precisely this issue is the primatologist Richard Byrne (see Byrne 1997). Looking more closely at the Machiavellian (or social) intelligence hypothesis, which suggests that the evolution of cognitive capacity in primates was driven by the need to handle the social complexity and competition characteristic of primate groups (e.g., Byrne & Whiten 1988; Dunbar 1998), Byrne notes that it does not appear to apply to all stages of primate evolution (Figure 5.8). While increased neocortex investment does appear to relate to social complexity, and particularly social manipulation, in monkeys and apes, for example, and to explain their evolutionary split from other primates like the lemur and the loris, the same pattern of differentiation does not hold for the great ape–monkey split. Though the great apes – including the modern orangutan, gorilla, chimpanzees, and ourselves – do appear to be rather cognitively different compared to other Haplorhine primates (including Old World monkeys), they do not appear to live in bigger

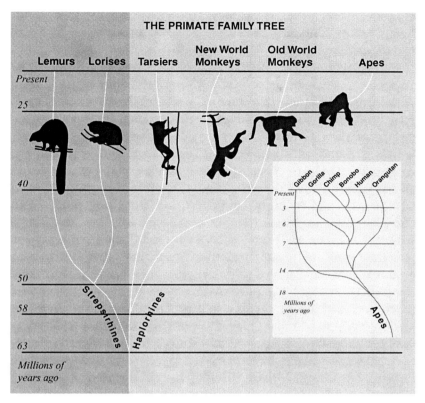

Figure 5.8: Primate family tree. Richard Byrne has pointed out that cognitive ability was increased at several points in the ancestral line leading to humans, and has argued that different catalysts may have been involved in driving increased intelligence at different stages.

or socially more complex groups. Both the great apes and monkeys exhibit significant species diversity in group size and social structure, and no systematic correlations with neocortical enlargement have been demonstrated. Thus, Byrne suggests that rather than viewing the social intelligence hypothesis as a general explanation for primate brain evolution, we need to take into account the likelihood that intellectual capacity was increased at several points in the ancestral line leading to humans, and that in each case, different circumstances precipitated the cognitive change. While social complexity may at some stages have served as a spur for further brain evolution, other stages may have seen the dominance of different factors. One important alternative factor suggested by Byrne is technical intelligence.

Byrne's technical intelligence hypothesis was foreshadowed by an earlier consideration of nest-building behaviour in great apes, which suggested its importance as a potential evolutionary catalyst. Primatologists Barbara Fruth and Gottfried Hohmann speculated that the building of nests (or beds as they are also known), which is found only amongst the great apes, and is indeed the most pervasive form of material skill in apes, may have served as an important stimulus to the further evolution of material skill and cognitive ability in this group (Fruth & Hohmann 1996). Fruth and Hohmann suggest a number of reasons why nest building – which they argue must have evolved in the Miocene – might have benefited apes and given them an evolutionary edge. Firstly, nest groups would have served as 'information centres' that facilitated the transfer at night of information concerning the quality of food patches visited during the day, and hence improved foraging efficiency. They would also have allowed food resources to be more easily monopolised, since apes could sleep in their vicinity. Nests themselves would also have enabled better-quality sleep and hence improved learning abilities. In addition, as the first products of exploratory behaviour with twigs and sticks, nests may well have provided the foundation for the subsequent development of tool use ability. Nest building, they suggest, may have promoted higher levels of tool use that helped to open up new food resources. Overall, they see nest building as a potentially critical impetus to further behavioural and cognitive changes in the great apes.

Byrne's technical intelligence hypothesis takes into account nest building in the great apes, but also looks more generally at the technical behaviour of apes. Byrne notes that the great apes are defined not only by their constructional abilities, but also by their common ability, at least in captivity, to use and make tools (Figure 5.9). Great apes also exhibit more complex foraging behaviours in general, showing food extraction or processing techniques that are technically demanding in some way. They build complex programs of action for plant or insect gathering that Byrne argues differ qualitatively from anything seen in monkeys. Byrne suggests that these

Figure 5.9: A chimpanzee mother at Bossou, Guinea, uses a stone hammer and anvil to crack open oil palm nuts, while her daughter looks on. Fieldwork by the primatologist Bill McGrew, amongst others, has been critical in highlighting the importance of material culture in chimpanzee societies (McGrew 1992). Photo Susana Carvalho, courtesy of Bill McGrew.

various technical and foraging skills enabled great apes to compete successfully with monkeys, despite their need for higher-quality food sources, and their lack of cheek pouches, which enabled monkeys to rapidly collect and remove food items. They also selected for the evolution of new cognitive skills. For example, the complexity of foraging and technical skills in apes may have resulted in the need for a long period of apprenticeship and 'social information donation', which fits with the evidence for imitation and perhaps occasional teaching in great apes but not monkeys (Byrne 1997: 305). In addition, Byrne argues that the great apes exhibit unique abilities for representational thinking that may have been selected for in the technical sphere and subsequently applied to other areas. He thus sees "the undoubted sophistication of apes in the social area (including theory of mind and mirror self-representation) as a secondary effect, derived from possession of a representational format for knowledge that evolved in the technical sphere" (ibid.: 306).

The technical intelligence hypothesis has now been offered some support through a more recent comparative study, looking at the correlation between social learning, innovation, tool use, and brain size in a range of non-human primates (Reader & Laland 2002). The study observes that the reported incidence of tool use amongst individual primate species correlates with their executive brain ratio. The study's authors accordingly suggest that the ability to use tools, as well as to learn from others and invent new behaviours, likely played a pivotal role in primate brain evolution. Nonetheless, the technical intelligence hypothesis requires further systematic investigation in order to achieve widespread support.

Some speculation has also focused on later stages of primate cognitive evolution, and its relationship to tool use. As outlined earlier, for example, Terrence Deacon has suggested that tool use may have had a role to play in the emergence of language. Others have implicated stone tool use in the emergence of increased intelligence (e.g., Gibson & Ingold 1993). There are, however, very few studies that have specifically explored the way in which the novel niches created through the production and use of material culture led to new evolutionary pressures that helped to shape human cognitive abilities. One recent notable exception that deserves mention is a paper by Mathias Osvath and Peter Gärdenfors (Osvath & Gärdenfors 2005) that explores the co-evolution of cognition and Oldowan material culture (Figure 5.10). Specifically, Osvath and Gärdenfors argue that the new cultural niche that arose in the Oldowan, and that was characterised by stone tool manufacture, the transport of tools and food over long distances, and the use of specific places in the landscape for the accumulation of materials (Plummer 2004), selected for the emergence of anticipatory cognition. That is, as the hominid lifestyle became increasingly extended in time and space – with ever longer delays, for example, between the acquisition and use of a tool – the ability to form representations of the distant future became progressively more useful, conferring an evolutionary advantage on those

Figure 5.10: Granite core dating to the Oldowan period, from Excavation 1 at Kanjera South, an approximately two-million-year-old Oldowan site in south-western Kenya. Mathias Osvath and Peter Gärdenfors, drawing upon the research of Thomas Plummer, argue that Oldowan technology and human cognition co-evolved. Photo Thomas Plummer.

individuals with specific genetic changes that improved it. As people made and used Oldowan tools then, they shaped the minds of their descendents.

Material culture may also have shaped cognition in other ways. Some cognitive scientists, for example, have argued that culture, including material culture, has selected for a mind that actively relies on culture to function normally. Within this perspective, already introduced in Chapter 2, cognition does not take place in a mental black box, but is instead deeply informed, and indeed to some degree part of, an external environment. This kind of perspective on cognition has led Andy Clark to refer to the mind as a 'leaky' organ that is 'extended' into its environment (Clark 1997). That is, he argues, much of our thinking is scaffolded by a range of tools, both conceptual (like language) and material (like technologies), that make us smarter. Humans are able to demonstrate the remarkable cognitive achievements they do not only because they have big, unique brains, but also because they have an entire cultural corpus of artefacts, texts, media, cultural practices, and cultural institutions to draw upon (Clark 1999). We are, argues Clark, like bluefin tuna, whose remarkable ability to turn sharply, to accelerate quickly, and to reach high speeds derives not from special adaptations of their morphology, but rather their exploitation of both naturally and self-created currents, vortices, and pressure gradients. A human being employing a paper and pen to solve a multiplication problem that would baffle our unaided brains, points out Clark, employs parallel tactics (Figure 5.11). He or she, raised in a "sea of cultural tools", will develop strategies for problem solving that factor in such external resources as "profoundly and deeply as the bodily motions of the tuna factor in and maximally exploit the reliable properties of the surrounding water" (ibid.: 349).

Given this profound and deep factoring in of a human-generated external environment, it seems reasonable to ask whether it has resulted in any evolutionary pressures on human cognition. Clark certainly thinks so. As he and David Chalmers argue:

> [I]t may be that the biological brain has in fact evolved and matured in ways that factor in the reliable presence of a manipulable external environment. It certainly seems that evolution has favored on-board capacities which are especially geared to parasitizing the local environment so as to reduce memory load, and even to transform the nature of the computational problems themselves. (Clark & Chalmers 1998: 11)

As humans have increasingly altered their external environment then, it seems likely that they have altered their cognitive abilities and even the evolutionary pathways by which cognition has changed. One obvious example, highlighted by Clark and Chalmers, of an external environment that has possibly been increasingly factored in by evolution is language (ibid.). Another example, frequently addressed in Clark's work, is material culture.

Figure 5.11: Person holding pencil. Such material culture helps make humans smarter, and some researchers argue that our minds may have evolved to factor in our tools. Photo Dimitris Kritsotakis.

As human beings have evolved, so too has their material culture, until it has reached the phenomenal levels of abundance, diversity, and pervasiveness that characterise its place in the modern world. Material culture – that is, everything from stone tools, to fishing rods, to portable works of art, to monuments, and pens and paper – has clearly been instrumental in making humans smarter and more capable animals.

The fact that once technology emerges – during the Oldowan period about 2.5 million years ago – it never goes away, and instead becomes increasingly more complex through time, would seem to support the notion that material culture is fundamental to the type of animal that we are. Oldowan hominids adapted to their stone (and probably other less well-preserved) tools, and human beings then went on to use tools for another 2.5 million years. It seems probable that early humans began to factor tools regularly into problem-solving by at least the Oldowan period, and that through time, the relationship between people and their tools simply became increasingly close. The notion that our brains adapted to and came to rely upon the presence of these tools, while still speculative, is thus a compelling one that merits further attention.

A Word of Warning: The Role of Development and Cognitive Plasticity

While it is clear that the mind evolved substantially since the Oldowan, highlighting the possibility that the earliest and simplest technologies created a niche for cognitive evolution, it is less clear when the brain stopped evolving. Some evolutionary anthropologists have suggested that major cognitive changes occurred up until relatively recently. Archaeologists like Richard Klein, for example, have argued – controversially – that a genetic change as recently as around 50,000 years ago finally enabled the acquisition of language (Klein & Edgar 2002). Others, however, place the origins of language substantially earlier (Deacon 1997; Falk 1983; Kay et al. 1998). The debate over whether our brains continued to evolve until recently has now been fuelled by controversial molecular genetic findings that suggest that brain genes have continued to evolve into the Holocene (Evans et al. 2005; Mekel-Bobrov et al. 2005). If this were the case, it might suggest that our minds have adapted not only to Oldowan tools, but also the houses, villages, symbols, artistic items, and even possibly writing systems of later times. Problematically, however, it also suggests that the brains of different peoples with varying recent histories might be different, which is not only politically inflammatory, but does not fit with the evidence for worldwide parallels in the intelligence and cognitive capabilities of humans from very different environments.

The controversy over recent brain evolution reminds us that we need to proceed cautiously when it comes to studying cognitive evolution. In particular, genes are not everything, nor are all adaptations genetic. As I noted at the outset of the chapter, evolutionary biologists like Richard Lewontin (1983, 2000) have stressed the role that organisms and environments play in shaping not only evolution (phylogeny), but also development (ontogeny) (see also Bateson & Martin 1999; Hinde 1996; Oyama et al. 2001). They have taken

Figure 5.12: The author's daughter in her cultural learning environment. Material culture is part of all-pervasive cultural environment that plays a critical role in shaping human cognitive development. Photo Nicole Boivin.

great exception to the gene-centred view that has shaped molecular biology, and much of our understanding of evolution. Organisms, they stress, are not just the products of genes, but also of the processes through which they develop and grow, which are also dependent on both environments and organisms themselves. Phenotypes, that is, are not directly determined by genotypes. There is, accordingly, a great deal of plasticity in an organism's development that is not pre-figured by genes. And this plasticity may be nowhere more evident than in the development of the brain and of our cognitive processes.

One important pioneer in the study of epigenetic (i.e., non-genetic) effects on the development of organisms was the embryologist Gilbert Gottlieb (for a summary, see Gottlieb 2001). Studying bird embryos, and a variety of mammalian foetuses, including humans in the 1960s, Gottlieb noted that the sensory system begins to function while the embryo or foetus is still undergoing maturation, and that accordingly, an organism contributes to its own normal development (see also Bateson & Martin 1999). Gottlieb also discovered, for example, while studying bird embryos, that chicks not exposed to their species' calls during development do not learn to recognise them. Based on these and a myriad of other studies, he argued that both organism and environment have a major impact on the development of the organism (Gottlieb 2001), as a wealth of other studies have now similarly demonstrated. And, as we now know, such positive influence of functional activity on the nervous system is not restricted to the prenatal environment, but continues into adulthood (ibid.). Organisms are products of their actions and environments in ways that cannot be underestimated. This is not just to say that a normal, minimal suite of environmental factors must be present for development to occur, but rather to argue that the organism's final form is fundamentally shaped by the specific environment to which it is exposed, and the way the organism uses that environment.

In humans, development is shaped not just by a natural, but also by a cultural environment that is all-pervasive and indeed critical to what we now consider 'normal development' (Figure 5.12). Thus, as Lewontin has emphasised, the human ability to speak is contingent not only on having the appropriate suite of genetic characteristics, but also the necessary social environment for learning language (Lewontin 2000). Another scholar who has emphasised the importance of the cultural environment to human cognition is the psychologist Merlin Donald (e.g., Donald 1991, 1998, 2000). Arguing for a central role for culture in human cognition and cognitive development, Donald has stated:

> Our brains and minds can be deeply affected by the overwhelming influence of symbolic cultures during development. I mean this, not in the superficial sense intended, for

instance, by the Whorfian hypothesis about the influence of language on the way we think, but on a much deeper, architectural, level. Some cultural changes can actually remodel the operational structure of the cognitive system. The clearest example of this is the extended and widespread effect of literacy on cognition. In this case, we know that the brain's architecture has not been affected, at least not it its basic anatomy or wiring diagram. But its functional architecture has changed, under the influence of culture. (Donald 2000: 19)

Thus, while certain brain modifications during human evolution are obviously a precondition for the emergence of complex culture, including material culture, a number of important usages to which the human brain is put cannot occur in the absence of such cultural factors. Donald also stresses the extreme plasticity of the human brain during epigenesis, and suggests that it is this trait in particular that has allowed the human brain to adopt to the ever-faster rates of change that have become typical of our modern society (ibid.: 20). Thus, as argued in the previous section, brains may have evolved as a result of exposure to human-made cultural and material environments, but it is also the case that they may often have not needed to. The remarkable cognitive achievements of human beings likely have as much to do with their self-made environments and cognitive plasticity as their genes. That this is the case is highlighted by the fact that certain chimpanzees have achieved remarkable levels of language understanding, and tool creation and use in the presence of an appropriate, human-generated cultural environment (Donald 1998).

Overall then, it is clear that our self-made environments and our actions have helped to shape the course of our own evolution, for many millions of years and up to the present day. We are indeed the 'self-made species', with everything from our distinctive morphology to our unique brains having been shaped in some measure by our own activities and by the increasingly complex material and cultural environment we have generated. But the fact that our species is no passive genetic construct is illustrated by the way that we have played a role not only in our own genetic evolution as a species, but also in our own development as individual organisms within that species. The role of our cultural and material culture heritage in influencing development is probably nowhere more apparent than in the realm of cognition, where human beings appear to exhibit particularly notable plasticity. And it is this cognitive plasticity that has likely led us to achieve many of the things we have in the absence of any evolutionary change whatsoever. In addition, this plasticity also makes any individual or group variation in something like brain genes less potentially important than we might initially think. Thus, no easy interpretation of new data on genetic evolution, like that outlined earlier, will likely be possible. Instead, we can expect that the interplay between genes, organisms, and environments will prove an exciting, and controversial, area of study, particularly where human cognition is concerned, for many years to come.

CHAPTER 6

Conclusion

This book started in a rural Indian village, and has ended in the high-tech laboratories where molecular genetics research is carried out. Along the way, it has visited a range of fields, from anthropology to cognitive science, and addressed a range of perspectives, from post-modernism to niche construction theory. Despite the diversity of disciplines and the variety of approaches, however, the book has focused on a single message: that the material world, including, and perhaps especially, the material world that we as humans have created, plays and has long played a fundamental role in shaping human thought, society and, over the long term, evolution.

Material culture is everywhere. From the moment we are born, we engage in an ongoing and increasingly intensive interaction with environments that are to varying degrees natural and human-made. From the moment we started to diverge from our primate ancestors, and probably long before, we have interacted with environments that we have played a significant role in shaping. The archaeological record traces a sequence of 2.5 million years of cultural artefacts. Museums worldwide display just a minute sample of the diverse and abundant array of things that have been created over this period. And today, global industry sees the production of many millions of additional cultural artefacts on a daily basis.

The material world surrounds us and shapes us, and yet in many ways, we have barely begun to study its role in our lives. Some of the reasons for this paradoxical state of affairs have already been discussed in the opening chapter: the long, idealist tradition in

Western thought, the emergence of an understanding of culture as non-material, and the recent dominance of linguistic models in the social sciences and humanities, for example. But it is undoubtedly also in part the very pervasiveness of the material world that has led it to escape our notice. Things surround us and are so remarkably fundamental to our lives that, like our bodies, they really only attract our attention when they go wrong. They are also so specialised and diverse that no one type of person can possibly understand them all. We have computer technicians to deal with computers, photocopy machine designers and repairmen to handle photocopiers, scientists to deal with electrons and nuclear reactors, librarians to address books, industrial designers to create new artefacts, and museum curators and archaeologists to deal with old artefacts. No one type of person really deals with all things, including the things we make, the environments we live in, and the bodies we think and move with, except in the most abstract way. But the abstraction of the material world, as when philosophers discuss the 'material', comes at a price. An abstracted material world inevitably loses part of what distinguishes it in the first place: its physicality. It is this physicality, what I have termed 'materiality', that is, accordingly, missing from many discussions of material culture and the material more generally.

So how is this situation to be rectified? This book has outlined a myriad of ways in which the material world impacts on us because of its very materiality, and yet at the same time, it is clear that only a small minority of studies in the humanities, social sciences, and natural sciences has examined the role of the material world in the development and transformation of humans and their societies. Clearly, there is a critical need for more focused analysis of how people engage with and are transformed by the materiality that surrounds them. Material culture needs to be recognised as a valid and important topic of study by scholars from a range of disciplines.

But beyond this obvious point, what more is there to recommend? Should we not, for example, develop a more unified and coherent methodology for dealing with material culture? My view on this point would be that no, we should not. I consider the current diversity of approaches to material culture to be a decidedly positive thing, and would not wish to see this diversity diminished by the pursuit of unity. Methodological diversity is, in my view, the way forward for those studying material culture. Different methods clarify different aspects of the material world's impact upon us, and so only through the employment of a range of methods will we gain anything approaching a holistic picture of how the material world impacts human society and thought.

In this book, I have explored a wide array of models and methods for studying material culture. Each of these methods has proven fruitful for looking at particular aspects of our relationship to material culture and the wider material world. Niche construction theory, for example, has helped to clarify how we may have shaped our own evolution through our technologies and cultural practices. Artificial intelligence researchers, meanwhile, have been conducting fascinating studies with robots that help us to understand just how humans use the material world to think with. Linguists, on the other hand, have been starting to provide insights into how the material world shapes both language and thought. Anthropologists, archaeologists, sociologists, psychologists, and cognitive scientists, using a variety of methods, have provided initial clues concerning the ways in which we respond sensually and emotionally to material culture. Historians have drawn upon historical records of various sorts to begin to shed light on how the emergence of new technologies has frequently helped to shape the form that societies take. None of these methods is sufficient in itself for studying the role of material culture in human thought and society. All of them bring something unique to the table, and provide a distinctive perspective on the material world.

What is needed then is not methodological unity, or some kind of specific procedure for studying material culture, but rather a better way to bring the findings of these diverse disciplines and approaches together. What is needed is more effective cross-disciplinary fertilisation. This is not to say that such interdisciplinarity never happens of course – it is clear, for example, that some archaeologists and anthropologists have drawn on the findings of cognitive science to understand material culture, and the new sub-disciplinary title neurophenomenology reveals collaboration in unexpected places. But such examples of interdisciplinarity in material culture studies are rare and frequently one way. Archaeologists and anthropologists have started to draw upon cognitive science, but there is little evidence that cognitive scientists have taken an interest in archaeology and anthropology. Archaeologists have taken a major interest in anthropology, but, despite all of archaeology's recent symbolic and social interest in material culture, anthropologists frequently ignore their sister discipline when they turn to studying material culture.

One scholarly venture that has tried to bring together different disciplines in the study of material culture is of course material culture studies. The tenor of this interdisciplinary enterprise is perhaps best exemplified by the kinds of studies that are published in the journal *Material Culture Studies*. This new interdisciplinary field and journal are to be commended for raising the profile of material culture studies, and for bringing together different disciplines. However, the range of disciplines continues to remain relatively limited within this field, as does the suite of methods and models, which continue to be dominated by linguistically inspired approaches. In particular, the post-modern and cultural constructivist nature of much of the work in material culture studies has prevented engagement with the natural sciences. Only scientifically oriented researchers who make a big effort to engage with humanities paradigms, like Antonio Damasio and Andy Clark, have really been rewarded with much interest from those outside of the natural sciences.

In my opinion, this is a key problem, not just in material culture studies, but throughout the research world. I believe in methodological diversity, but I am also a strong believer in interdisciplinarity, and the wall that has been constructed between humanities and social science approaches on the one hand, and natural sciences approaches on the other, is a major barrier to research progress in academics. This wall, which half a century after Charles Percy Snow critiqued the mutual incomprehensibility of the "two cultures" in his University of Cambridge lecture (Snow 1993), shows no sign of coming down, is also part of the reason why so many studies of the body and of material culture in the humanities and social sciences have overlooked their actual materiality. The idea that only natural scientists engage with the actual physicality of matter, and only humanities and social sciences scholars study culture and society, has meant that the latter have been studied as etherealised, disembodied, abstract entities. The fact that biology and culture, and mind and matter, are deeply interwoven, indeed inseparable, has been an inconvenient truth that has only rarely been acknowledged.

Thus, in my opinion, the main way forward for studies of material culture and of materiality is interdisciplinarity, and in particular interdisciplinarity that crosses the "two cultures" divide. We need participant-observation and phenomenological studies of the way that the material world impacts us sensually and emotionally, but we also need measurements of how brains respond to these aspects of the material world. We need integrated psychological, cognitive, anthropological, and biological studies of how children are shaped developmentally by their material surroundings. We need some rigorous testing of Bourdieu's ideas about the house and the habitus. We need molecular biologists to consult with historians and archaeologists about the role that culture may have played in driving the recent evolutionary changes they are starting to recognise in the human genome. We need niche construction theorists to talk to social anthropologists. We need doctors and biologists to start to quantify the responses of the body to the diverse qualities of the material world, and anthropologists and cognitive scientists to help factor the mind into these studies. We need less suspicion, we need openness, and we need all-together more mixing.

The natural sciences have excelled in developing methods and models for studying matter, including the physical particulars of objects, the wet tissue and hard bone of the body, and the physical activity of the brain. The social sciences and humanities, meanwhile, have developed a valuable set of research techniques and theories for dealing with people, including their behaviour, social formations, cosmological beliefs, and experience. Material culture, which by very definition straddles these two major perspectives, demands an integrated approach that brings these very different methods and models together. In addition, however, for real progress to be made, it will also be necessary to develop new methods and new models, that derive from efforts that are multidisciplinary from the outset. In particular, researchers need to develop and work with a concept of mind–matter–body that recognises that they are not the strictly segregated entities that these individual terms suggest. The sites of overlap between the diverse and very different disciplines that study the material world and its impact on humans will constitute a rich and fertile spawning ground for the birth of new perspectives and research initiatives. But for this to happen, interdisciplinarity needs to be encouraged and minded. Not only do researchers need to take an interest in what other disciplines are doing and saying, but they must also interact and engage with these disciplines.

This, in my view, is where studies of material culture need to go next. The new horizon lies not in a unified strategy, but simply in an interdisciplinary effort that can begin to piece the diverse findings of different fields together into a more holistic picture, and at the same time suggest new models and directions. Coupled with more studies of material culture in general, such a strategy holds the potential to yield important new insights into the role of material culture, and the material world more generally, in human life. This book has demonstrated that materiality has a powerful role to play in the human story, but researching it also led me to recognise just how dispersed studies of materiality are, and just how many opportunities for cross-disciplinary fertilisation are lost out on because researchers remain deeply wedded to antagonistic views of what their colleagues on the other side of the humanities–sciences fence are doing.

It is also clear to me that there is a certain urgency to the need to undertake more focused study of material culture, and to bring down the walls that divide researchers from one another. This urgency derives from the fact that the material world is currently being altered at an unparalleled rate. Not only has global capitalism led to the creation of an overwhelming and unprecedented diversity of new material objects and technologies, whose effects on individuals and societies continue to go largely unstudied, but traditional material landscapes, artefacts, and bodies are being transformed faster than ever before. The human material story is also, and increasingly so, a tale of environmental degradation, resource depletion, and the loss of traditional technologies, practices, and ways of life, as well as the destruction of cultural

Figure 6.1: Smoking power plant in Hungary. The role of environmental degradation and the loss of traditional technologies in the present-day human material story add urgency to the need to study our material world. Photo Constantin Jurcut.

heritage and archaeological sites (Figure 6.1). At just the moment that new material cultures threaten to overwhelm us, we are witnessing the disappearance of a range of traditional technologies and archaeological resources that hold keys to understanding how we have been shaped and may continue to be shaped by the material world. As we watch technologies spread faster and further than ever before, we see material ways of life disappear that may have greater emotional, moral, health, and social value than those with which they are being replaced.

So we need to stop treating material culture and the material world either as if it were neutral, as the natural sciences generally do, or as if it were simply a question of meaning and representation, as the humanities and social sciences have recently been inclined to do. We need to really start to understand our relationship to the material world. There are not just social and cultural facets to this relationship, but also biological and health ones. There are not just academic issues at stake, but also public and political ones. There is not just a past that has shaped us, but a future that we can help to shape. To do so, however, we must look beyond the extraordinary to the everyday, beyond the lofty to the near, and focus on the mundane but powerful objects and environments that surround us and that create us as we create them. We need to turn our attention to the things that go unnoticed – the pots and pans, the highways and pens, and teacups and computers, fishing hooks, doorways, building blocks, religious relics, conveyor belts, spears, carpets, parks, antennae, pendants, perfumes, appliances, museum objects, lace curtains, skyscrapers, tombstones, tribal masks, houses, agricultural fields, lampposts, picket fences, artworks, quarries, pacemakers, and duffel coats. The usualness of the material world is greatly surpassed by its ubiquity. The myriad of ways in which this mass of simple things has shaped and transformed our thoughts, emotions, bodies, and societies has only just begun to be explored.

Bibliography

Ader, R. & N. Cohen. 1993. Psychoneuroimmunology: Conditioning and stress. *Annual Review of Psychology* **44**, 53–85.

Aiello, L. C. & P. Wheeler. 1995. The expensive-tissue hypothesis: The brain and digestive system in human and primate evolution. *Current Anthropology* **36**, 199–221.

Akey, J. M., M. A. Eberle, M. J. Rieder, C. S. Carlson, M. D. Shriver, D. A. Nickerson & L. Kruglyak. 2004. Population history and natural selection shape patterns of genetic variation in 132 genes. *PLos Biology* **2**, e286.

Allchin, F. R. 1963. *Neolithic Cattle-Keepers of South India*. Cambridge: Cambridge University Press.

Appadurai, A. (ed.). 1986. *The Social Life of Things: Commodities in Cultural Perspective*. Cambridge: Cambridge University Press.

Balasse, M. & A. Tresset. 2002. Early weaning of Neolithic domestic cattle (Bercy, France) revealed by intra-tooth variation in nitrogen isotope ratios. *Journal of Archaeological Science* **29**, 853–59.

Barth, F. 1975. *Ritual and Knowledge among the Baktaman of New Guinea*. New Haven, CT: Yale University Press.

Bateson, P. & P. Martin. 1999. *Design for a Life: How Behaviour Develops*. London: Jonathon Cape.

Baudrillard, J. 1981. *For a Critique of the Political Economy of the Sign*. St. Louis, MO: Telos Press.

Bauer, A. A. 2002. Is what you see all you get? Recognizing meaning in archaeology. *Journal of Social Archaeology* **2**, 37–52.

Beck, B. B. 1980. *Animal Tool Behavior: The Use and Manufacture of Tools by Animals*. New York: Garland.

Beja-Pereira, A., G. Luikart, P. R. England, D. G. Bradley, O. C. Jann, G. Bertorelle, A. T. Chamberlain, T. P. Nunes, S. Metodiev, N. Ferrand & G. Erhardt. 2003. Gene-culture coevolution between cattle milk protein genes and human lactase genes. *Nature Science* **35**, 311–13.

Bell, C. 1997. *Ritual: Perspectives and Dimensions*. Oxford: Oxford University Press.

Bender, B. 1978. Gatherer-hunter to farmer: A social perspective. *World Archaeology* **10**, 204–22.

―――. 1993. *Landscape: Politics and Perspectives*. Oxford: Berg.

―――. 1998. *Stonehenge: Making Space*. Oxford: Berg.

Bersaglieri, T., P. C. Sabeti, N. Patterson, T. Vanderploeg, S. F. Schaffner, J. A. Drake, M. Rhodes, D. E. Reich & J. N. Nirschorn. 2004. Genetic signatures of strong recent positive selection of the lactase gene. *American Journal of Human Genetics* **74**, 1111–20.

Biersack, A. 1999. Introduction: From the 'New Ecology' to the new ecologies. *American Anthropologist* **10**, 5–18.

Bimber, B. 1990. Karl Marx and the three faces of technological determinism. *Social Studies of Science* **20**, 333–51.

Bloch, M. 1991. Language, anthropology and cognitive science. *Man (N.S.)* **26**, 183–98.

―――. 1992. What goes without saying: The conceptualization of Zafiminary society. In *Conceptualizing Society* (ed.) A. Kuper, pp. 127–46. London: Routledge.

―――. 1993. Domain-specificity, living kinds and symbolism. In *Cognitive Aspects of Religious Symbolism* (ed.) P. Boyer, pp. 111–20. Cambridge: Cambridge University Press.

―――. 1995. Questions not to ask of Malagasy carvings. In *Interpreting Archaeology: Finding Meaning in the Past* (eds.) I. Hodder, M. Shanks, V. Buchli, J. Carman, J. Last & G. Lucas, pp. 212–15. London: Routledge.

―――. 1998. Review of Edwin Hutchin's *Cognition in the Wild*. *Journal of the Royal Anthropological Institute* **4**, 150–51.

Boivin, N. 2000. Life rhythms and floor sequences: Excavating time in rural Rajasthan and Neolithic Çatalhöyük. *World Archaeology* **31**, 367–88.

―――. 2001. 'Archaeological science as anthropology': Space, time and materiality in rural India and the Ancient Past. University of Cambridge.

―――. 2003. Heat, colour and sound: Experiencing ritual in the South Indian Neolithic. Paper presented at the 'Embodied Histories: Bodies, Senses, Memories in Archaeology and Anthropology' Conference in Southampton, UK, 24–25 January 2003.

————. 2004a. From veneration to exploitation: Human engagement with the mineral world. In *Soils, Stones and Symbols: Cultural Perceptions of the Mineral World* (eds.) N. Boivin & M. A. Owoc, pp. 1–29. London: UCL Press.

————. 2004b. Geoarchaeology and the goddess Laksmi: Rajasthani insights into geoarchaeological methods and prehistoric soil use. In *Soils, Stones and Symbols: Cultural Perceptions of the Mineral World* (eds.) N. Boivin & M. A. Owoc, pp. 165–86. London: UCL Press.

————. 2004c. Landscape and cosmology in the South Indian Neolithic: New perspectives on the Deccan ashmounds. *Cambridge Archaeological Journal* **14**, 235–57.

————. 2004d. Mind over matter? Collapsing the mind-matter dichotomy in material culture studies. In *Rethinking Materiality: The Engagement of Mind with the Material World* (eds.) E. DeMarrais, C. Gosden & C. Renfrew, pp. 63–71. Cambridge: McDonald Institute for Archaeological Research.

————. 2004e. Rock art and rock music: Petroglyphs of the south Indian Neolithic. *Antiquity* **78**, 38–53.

Boivin, N., A. Brumm, H. Lewis, D. Robinson & R. Korisettar. 2007. Sensual, material, and technological understanding: Exploring prehistoric soundscapes in south India. *Journal of the Royal Anthropological Institute (N.S.)* **13**, 267–94.

Boivin, N. & D. Q. Fuller. forthcoming. Niche construction and cultural practice: Bridging evolutionary and cultural perspectives on human society.

Boivin, N. & M. A. Owoc (eds.). 2004. *Soils, Stones and Symbols: Cultural Perceptions of the Mineral World*. London: UCL Press.

Bökönyi, S. 1988. *History of Domestic Mammals in Central and Eastern Europe*. Budapest: Akademiai Kiado.

Bourdieu, P. 1973. The Berber house. In *Rules and Meanings* (ed.) M. Douglas, pp. 98–110. Harmondsworth: Penguin.

————. 1977. *Outline of a Theory of Practice*. Cambridge: Cambridge University Press.

————. 1990. *The Logic of Practice*. Cambridge: Polity Press.

Boursot, P., J.-C. Auffray, J. Britton-Davidian & F. Bonhomme. 1993. The evolution of house mice. *Annual Review of Ecology and Systematics* **24**, 119–52.

Boyd, R. & P. Richerson. 1985. *Culture and the Evolutionary Process*. Chicago: University of Chicago Press.

Brooks, R. A. 1991a. Intelligence without reason. In *Proceedings of the 12th International Joint Conference on Artificial Intelligence, Sydney, Australia, August 1991*, pp. 69–95.

———. 1991b. Intelligence without representation. *Artificial Intelligence Journal* **47**, 139–59.

Buchli, V. (ed.). 2002. *The Material Culture Reader*. Oxford: Berg.

Bunn, H. T. & E. M. Kroll. 1986. Systematic butchery by Plio/Pleistocene hominids at Olduvai Gorge, Tanzania. *Current Anthropology* **27**, 431–52.

Burger, J., M. Kirchner, B. Bramanti, W. Haak & M. G. Thomas. 2007. Absence of the lactase-persistence-associated allele in early Neolithic Europeans. *Proceedings of the National Academy of Sciences USA* **104**, 3736–41.

Byrd, B. F. 2005. Reassessing the emergence of village life in the Near East. *Journal of Archaeological Research* **13**, 231–90.

Byrne, R. W. 1997. The technical intelligence hypothesis: An additional evolutionary stimulus to intelligence? In *Machiavellian Intelligence II: Extensions and Evaluations* (eds.) A. Whiten & R. W. Byrne, pp. 289–311. Cambridge: Cambridge University Press.

Byrne, R. W. & A. Whiten (eds.). 1988. *Machiavellian Intelligence: Social Expertise and the Evolution of Intellect in Monkeys, Apes and Humans*. Oxford: Oxford University Press.

Callon, M. & J. Law. 1997. After the individual in society: Lessons on collectivity from science, technology and society. *Canadian Journal of Sociology* **22**, 165–82.

Carey, J. W. 2005. Harold Adams Innis and Marshall McLuhan. In *Marshall McLuhan: Critical Evaluations in Cultural Theory* (ed.) G. Genosko, pp. 193–220. London: Routledge.

Carsten, J. & S. Hugh-Jones. 1995. Introduction. In *About the House: Lévi-Strauss and Beyond* (eds.) J. Carsten & S. Hugh-Jones, pp. 1–46. Cambridge: Cambridge University Press.

Cauvin, J. 2000. *The Birth of the Gods and the Origins of Agriculture* (trans.) T. Watkins. Cambridge: Cambridge University Press.

Cavalli-Sforza, L. L. & M. Feldman. 1981. *Cultural Transmission and Evolution: A Quantitative Approach*. Princeton: Princeton University Press.

Chandler, D. 2002. *Semiotics: The Basics*. London: Routledge.

Chiel, H. J. & R. D. Beer. 1997. The brain has a body: Adaptive behavior emerges from interactions of nervous system, body and environment. *Trends in Neurosciences* **20**, 553–57.

Childe, V. G. 1965. *Man Makes Himself*. Suffolk: Chaucer.

Chippindale, C. 2003. Trying to test a trance hypothesis in its social context. *Cambridge Archaeological Journal* **13**, 218–19.

Churchland, P., V. S. Ramachandran & T. Sejnowski. 1994. A critique of pure vision. In *Large-Scale Neuronal Theories of the Brain* (eds.) C. Koch & J. Davis, pp. 23–60. Cambridge, MA: MIT Press.

Clark, A. 1997. *Being There: Putting Brain, Body and World Together Again.* Cambridge, MA: MIT Press.

———. 1998. Where brain, body and world collide. *Daedulus* **127**, 257–80.

———. 1999. An embodied cognitive science? *Trends in Cognitive Sciences* **3**, 345–51.

Clark, A. & D. J. Chalmers. 1998. The extended mind. *Analysis* **58**, 7–19.

Classen, C. 1991. Creation by sound/creation by light: A sensory analysis of two South American cosmologies. In *The Varieties of Sensory Experience: A Sourcebook in the Anthropology of the Senses* (ed.) D. Howes, pp. 239–55. Toronto: University of Toronto Press.

Connerton, P. 1989. *How Societies Remember.* Cambridge: Cambridge University Press.

Coote, J. 1992. 'Marvels of everyday vision': The anthropology of aesthetics and the cattle-keeping Nilotes. In *Anthropology, Art and Aesthetics* (eds.) J. Coote & A. Shelton, pp. 245–73. Oxford: Clarendon Press.

Coote, J. & A. Shelton. 1992. Introduction. In *Anthropology, Art and Aesthetics* (eds.) J. Coote & A. Shelton, pp. 1–11. Oxford: Clarendon Press.

Corn, J. J. 1996. Object lesson/object myths? What historians of technology learn from things. In *Learning from Things: Method and Theory of Material Culture Studies* (ed.) W. D. Kingery, pp. 35–54. Washington and London: Smithsonian Institution Press.

Costall, A. 1997. The meaning of things. *Social Analysis* **41**, 76–85.

Costall, A. P. 1984. Are theories of perception necessary? A review of Gibson's *The Ecological Approach to Visual Perception. Journal of the Experimental Analysis of Behavior* **41**, 109–15.

Cowan, R. S. 1989. *More Work for Mother: The Ironies of Household Technology from the Open Hearth to the Microwave.* London: Free Association Books.

Csordas, T. J. 1990. Embodiment as a paradigm for anthropology. *Ethos* **18**, 5–47.

———. 1994. Introduction: The body as representation and being-in-the-world. In *Embodiment and Experience: The Existential Ground of Culture and Self* (ed.) T. J. Csordas, pp. 1–24. Cambridge: Cambridge University Press.

Cunningham, C. E. 1973. Order in the Atoni house. In *Right and Left: Essays on Dual Symbolic Classification* (ed.) R. Needham, pp. 204–38. London: University of Chicago Press.

Damasio, A. 1994. *Descartes' Error: Emotion, Reason and the Human Brain*. New York: Grosset/Putnam.

———. 2003. *Looking for Spinoza: Joy, Sorrow and the Feeling Brain*. London: William Heinemann.

Darwin, C. 1859. *On the Origin of Species by Means of Natural Selection*. London: Murray.

———. 1881. *The Formation of Vegetable Mold through the Action of Worms with Observations on Their Habits*. London: Murray.

Dawkins, R. 1976. *The Selfish Gene*. Oxford: Oxford University Press.

Day, R. L., K. N. Laland & J. Odling-Smee. 2003. Rethinking adaptation: The niche-construction perspective. *Perspectives in Biology and Medicine* **46**, 80–95.

de Heinzelin, J., J. D. Clark, T. White, W. Hart, P. Renne, G. WoldeGabriel, Y. Beyene & E. Vrba. 1999. Environment and behavior of 2.5-million-year-old Bouri hominids. *Science* **284**, 625–29.

Deacon, T. 1997. *The Symbolic Species: The Co-evolution of Language and the Human Brain*. London: Penguin.

DeMarrais, E., C. Gosden & C. Renfrew. 2004. *Rethinking Materiality: Engagement of Mind with the Material World*. Cambridge: McDonald Institute for Archaeological Research.

Dennett, D. C. 1995. *Darwin's Dangerous Idea*. London: Penguin.

Derrida, J. 1976. *On Grammatology* (trans.) G. C. Spivak. Baltimore: Johns Hopkins University Press.

———. 1978. *Writing and Difference*. Chicago: University of Chicago Press.

Descola, P. 1996. Constructing natures: Symbolic ecology and social practice. In *Nature and Society: Anthropological Perspectives* (eds.) P. Descola & G. Pálsson. London: Routledge.

Descola, P. & G. Pálsson (eds.). 1996. *Nature and Society: Anthropological Perspectives*. London: Routledge.

Diamond, J. 2003. The double puzzle of diabetes. *Nature* **423**, 599–602.

Dibble, H. L. 1989. The implications of stone tool types for the presence of language during the Lower and Middle Pleistocene. In *The Human Revolution: Behavioural and Biological Perspectives on the Origins of Modern Humans* (eds.) P. Mellars & C. Stringer, pp. 415–31. Edinburgh: Edinburgh University Press.

Dietler, M. & I. Herbich. 1998. Habitus, techniques, style: An integrated approach to the social understanding of material culture and boundaries. In *The Archaeology of Social Boundaries* (ed.) M. T. Stark, pp. 232–63. London: Smithsonian Institution University Press.

Di Rienzo, A. & R. R. Hudson. 2005. An evolutionary framework for common diseases: The ancestral-susceptibility model. *Trends in Genetics* **21**, 596–601.

Donald, M. 1991. *Origins of the Modern Mind: Three Stages in the Evolution of Culture and Cognition*. Cambridge, MA: Harvard University Press.

———. 1998. Hominid enculturation and cognitive evolution. In *Cognition and Material Culture: The Archaeology of Symbolic Storage* (eds.) C. Renfrew & C. Scarre, pp. 7–17. McDonald Institute Monographs. Cambridge: The McDonald Institute for Archaeological Research.

———. 2000. The central role of culture in cognitive evolution: A reflection on the myth of the 'isolated mind'. In *Culture, Thought and Development* (eds.) L. Nucci, G. Saxe & E. Turiel, pp. 19–38. Mahwah, NJ: Lawrence Erlbaum Associates.

Dornan, J. L. 2004. Beyond belief: Religious experience, ritual, and cultural neuro-phenomenology in the interpretation of past religious systems. *Cambridge Archaeological Journal* **14**, 25–36.

Douglas, M. 1966. *Purity and Danger: An Analysis of the Concepts of Pollution and Taboo*. London: Routledge.

———. 1996. *Natural Symbols*. London: Routledge.

Douglas, M. & B. Isherwood. 1996. *The World of Goods: Towards an Anthropology of Consumption*. London: Routledge.

Dowse, G. K., P. Z. Zimmet, C. F. Finch & V. R. Collins. 1991. Decline in incidence of epidemic glucose intolerance in Nauruans: Implications for the 'thrifty genotype'. *American Journal of Epidemiology* **133**, 1093–104.

Dudd, S. N. & R. P. Evershed. 1998. Direct demonstration of milk as an element of archaeological economies. *Science* **282**, 1478–81.

Dunbar, R. I. M. 1998. The social brain hypothesis. *Evolutionary Anthropology* **6**, 178–90.

———. 2003. The social brain: Mind, language, and society in evolutionary perspective. *Annual Review of Anthropology* **32**, 163–81.

Dunbar, R. I. M. & S. Shultz. 2007. Evolution in the social brain. *Science* **317**, 1344–47.

Durham, W. H. 1991. *Coevolution: Genes, Culture, and Human Diversity*. Stanford, CA: Stanford University Press.

Ellen, R. 1988. Fetishism. *Man (N.S.)*, vol. 4, pp. 213–35.

Ellen, R. & K. Fukui. 1996. *Redefining Nature: Ecology, Culture and Domestication*. Oxford: Berg.

Ellul, J. 1980. *The Technological System* (trans.) J. Neugroschel. New York: Continuum.

Evans, J. G. 2003. *Environmental Archaeology and the Social Order*. London: Routledge.

Evans, P. D., S. L. Gilbert, N. Mekel-Bobrov, E. J. Vallender, J. R. Anderson, L. M. Vaez-Azizi, S. A. Tishkoff, R. R. Hudson & B. T. Lahn. 2005. *Microcephalin*, a gene regulating brain size, continues to evolve adaptively in humans. *Science* **309**, 1717–20.

Fagg, M. C. 1997. Rock music. *Pitt Rivers Museum Occasional Paper on Technology* **14**.

Falk, D. 1983. Cerebral cortices of East African early hominids. *Science* **221**, 1072–74.

Feld, S. 1982. *Sound and Sentiment: Birds, Weeping, Poetics and Song in Kaluli Expression*. Philadelphia: University of Pennsylvania Press.

Feldman, M. W. & L. L. Cavalli-Sforza. 1989. On the theory of evolution under genetic and cultural transmission with application to the lactose absorption problem. In *Mathematical Evolutionary Theory* (ed.) M. W. Feldman, pp. 145–73. Princeton, NJ: Princeton University Press.

Fernandez, J. W. 1972. Persuasion and performances: On the beast in every body . . . and the metaphors of everyman. *Daedulus* **101**, 39–60.

Ferro-Luzzi, G. E. 1977. Ritual as language: The case of South Indian food offerings. *Current Anthropology* **18**, 507–14.

Foley, R. A. 1993. The influence of seasonality on human evolution. In *Seasonality and Human Ecology* (eds.) S. J. Ulijaszek & S. S. Strickland, pp. 17–37. Cambridge: Cambridge University Press.

Foucault, M. 1972. *The Archaeology of Knowledge*. New York: Harper & Row.

———. 1977. *Discipline and Punish*. New York: Pantheon Books.

———. 1980. *The History of Sexuality* **1**. New York: Pantheon Books.

Frank, A. W. 1990. Bringing bodies back in: A decade review. *Theory, Culture and Society* **7**, 131–62.

Freedberg, D. & V. Gallese. 2007. Motion, emotion and empathy in esthetic experience. *Trends in Cognitive Sciences* **11**, 198–203.

Frenkel, S. 1994. Old theories in new places? Environmental determinism and bioregionalism. *Professional Geographer* **46**, 289–95.

Freund, P. E. S. 1988. Bringing society into the body: Understanding socialized human nature. *Theory and Society* **17**, 839–64.

Fruth, B. & G. Hohmann. 1996. Nest building behavior in great apes: The great leap forward? In *Great Ape Societies* (eds.) W. C. McGrew,

L. F. Marchant & T. Nishida, pp. 225–40. Cambridge: Cambridge University Press.

Geertz, C. 1973. *The Interpretation of Cultures*. New York: Basic Books.

Gell, A. 1980. The gods at play: Vertigo and possession in Muria religion. *Man (N.S.)* **15**, 219–48.

———. 1992. *The Anthropology of Time*. Oxford: Berg.

———. 1995. The language of the forest: Landscape and phonological iconism in Umeda. In *The Anthropology of Landscape: Perspectives on Place and Space* (eds.) E. Hirsch & M. O'Hanlon, pp. 232–54. Oxford: Clarendon Press.

———. 1996. Language is the essence of culture: Against the motion. In *Key Debates in Anthropology* (ed.) T. Ingold, pp. 159–65. London: Routledge.

———. 1998. *Art and Agency: An Anthropological Theory*. Oxford: Oxford University Press.

———. 1999. *The Art of Anthropology: Essays and Diagrams* (London School of Economics Monographs on Social Anthropology 67). London: Athlone Press.

Gibson, J. J. 1966. *The Senses Considered as Perceptual Systems*. London: George Allen & Unwin Ltd.

———. 1986. *The Ecological Approach to Visual Perception*. London: Lawrence Erlbaum Associates.

Gibson, K. R. & T. Ingold (eds.). 1993. *Tools, Language and Cognition in Human Evolution*. Cambridge: Cambridge University Press.

Goldhahn, J. 2002. Roaring rocks: An audio-visual perspective on hunter-gatherer engravings in northern Sweden and Scandinavia. *Norwegian Archaeological Review* **35**, 29–61.

Gosden, C. 2004. Aesthetics, intelligence and emotions: Implications for archaeology. In *Rethinking Materiality: The Engagement of Mind with the Material World* (eds.) E. DeMarrais, C. Gosden & C. Renfrew, pp. 33–40. Cambridge: McDonald Institute for Archaeological Research.

Gottlieb, G. 2001. A developmental psychobiological systems view: Early formulation and current status. In *Cycles of Contingency: Developmental Systems and Evolution* (eds.) S. Oyama, P. E. Griffiths & R. D. Gray, pp. 41–54. Cambridge, MA: MIT Press.

Gould, S. J. 2002. *The Structure of Evolutionary Theory*. Cambridge, MA: Belknap/Harvard University Press.

Graves-Brown, P. M. 2000. Introduction. In *Matter, Materiality and Modern Culture* (ed.) P. M. Graves-Brown, pp. 1–9. London: Routledge.

Haaland, R. 1997. Emergence of sedentism: New ways of living, new ways of symbolizing. *Antiquity* **71**, 374–85.

Hahn, R. A. & A. Kleinman. 1983. Belief as pathogen, belief as medicine: 'Voodoo death' and the 'placebo phenomenon' in anthropological perspective. *Medical Anthropology Quarterly (N.S.)* **14**, 16–19.

Hallam, E. & J. Hockey. 2001. *Death, Memory and Material Culture*. Oxford: Berg.

Hamilakis, Y., M. Pluciennik & S. Tarlow (eds.). 2002. *Thinking through the Body: Archaeologies of Corporeality*. New York: Kluwer Academic/Plenum.

Harris, M. 1966. The cultural ecology of India's sacred cattle. *Current Anthropology* **7**, 51–64.

Harrison, S. 2004. Emotional climates: Ritual, seasonality and affective disorders. *Journal of the Royal Anthropological Institute* **10**, 583–602.

Haudricourt, A.-G. 1968. La technologie culturelle: Essai du méthodologie. In *Ethnologie Générale* (ed.) J. Poirier, pp. 731–822. Paris: Gallimard.

Hayden, B. 1990. Nimrods, piscators, pluckers, and planters: The emergence of food production. *Journal of Anthropological Archaeology* **9**, 31–69.

Hedges, K. 1993. Places to see and places to hear: Rock art and features of the sacred landscape. In *Time and Space: Dating and Spatial Considerations in Rock Art Research, Occasional AURA Publication No. 8*. (eds.) J. Steinbring, A. Watchman, P. Faulstich & P. Taçon, pp. 121–27. Melbourne: Australian Rock Art Research Association.

Heil, J. 2004. *Philosophy of Mind: A Guide and Anthology*. Oxford: Oxford University Press.

Heilbroner, R. L. 1994a. Do machines make history? In *Does Technology Drive History? The Dilemma of Technological Determinism* (eds.) M. R. Smith & L. Marx, pp. 53–65. Cambridge, MA: MIT Press.

————. 1994b. Technological determinism revisited. In *Does Technology Drive History? The Dilemma of Technological Determinism* (eds.) M. R. Smith & L. Marx, pp. 67–78. Cambridge, MA: MIT Press.

Hinde, R. A. 1996. The interpenetration of biology and culture. In *The Lifespan Development of Individuals: Behavioral, Neurobiological and Psychosocial Perspectives* (ed.) D. Magnusson, pp. 359–75. Cambridge: Cambridge University Press.

Hirst, P. & P. Wooley. 1982. *Social Relations and Human Attributes*. London: Tavistock Publishers.

Hodder, I. (ed.). 1982a. *Symbolic and Structural Archaeology*. Cambridge: Cambridge University Press.

———. 1982b. *Symbols in Action: Ethnoarchaeological Studies of Material Culture*. Cambridge: Cambridge University Press.

———. 1982c. Theoretical archaeology: A reactionary view. In *Symbolic and Structural Archaeology* (ed.) I. Hodder, pp. 1–16. Cambridge: Cambridge University Press.

———. 1985. Postprocessual archaeology. In *Advances in Archaeological Method and Theory 8* (ed.) M. B. Schiffer, pp. 1–26. New York: Academic Press.

———. (ed.). 1987. *The Archaeology of Contextual Meanings*. Cambridge: Cambridge University Press.

———. 1988. Material culture texts and social change: A theoretical discussion and some archaeological examples. *Proceedings of the Prehistoric Society* **54**, 67–76.

———. 1989. This is not an article about material culture as text. *Journal of Anthropological Archaeology* **8**, 250–69.

———. 1990. *The Domestication of Europe: Structure and Contingency in Neolithic Societies*. Oxford: Blackwell.

———. 1991. *Reading the Past*. Cambridge: Cambridge University Press.

———. 1992. *Theory and Practice in Archaeology*. London: Routledge.

Hollan, D. 2000. Constructivist models of mind, contemporary psychoanalysis, and the development of culture theory. *American Anthropologist* **102**, 538–50.

Hoskins, J. 1998. *Biographical Objects: How Things Tell the Story of People's Lives*. London: Routledge.

Howes, D. 1991. 'To summon all the senses'. In *The Varieties of Sensory Experience: A Sourcebook in the Anthropology of the Senses* (ed.) D. Howes, pp. 3–21. Toronto: University of Toronto Press.

Hughes, T. P. 1994. Technological momentum. In *Does Technology Drive History? The Dilemma of Technological Determinism* (eds.) M. R. Smith & L. Marx, pp. 101–13. Cambridge, MA: MIT Press.

Humphrey, N. K. 1976. The social function of intellect. In *Growing Points in Ethology* (eds.) P. Bateson & R. A. Hinde, pp. 303–17. Cambridge: Cambridge University Press.

Hunt, G. R. 1996. Manufacture and use of hook-tools by New Caledonian crows. *Nature* **379**, 249–51.

Ingold, T. 2000. *The Perception of the Environment: Essays in Livelihood, Dwelling and Skill*. London: Routledge.

Innis, H. A. 1950. *Empire and Communications*. Toronto: University of Toronto Press.

———. 1951. *The Bias of Communication*. Toronto: University of Toronto Press.

Jackson, M. 1977. *The Kuranko: Dimensions of Social Reality in a West African Society*. London: C. Hurst.

———. 1983. Knowledge of the body. *Man (N.S.)* **18**, 327–45.

———. 1989. *Paths toward a Clearing: Radical Empiricism and Ethnographic Inquiry*. Bloomington and Indianapolis: Indiana University Press.

———. 1996a. Introduction: Phenomenology, radical empiricism, and anthropological critique. In *Things as They Are: New Directions in Phenomenological Anthropology*, pp. 1–50. Bloomington and Indianapolis: Indiana University Press.

———. (ed.). 1996b. *Things as They Are: New Directions in Phenomenological Anthropology*. Bloomington and Indianapolis: Indiana University Press.

———. 2002. Familiar and foreign bodies: A phenomenological exploration of the human-technology interface. *Journal of the Royal Anthropological Institute (N.S.)* **8**, 333–46.

Joerges, B. 1988. Technology in everyday life: Conceptual queries. *Journal for the Theory of Social Behaviour* **18**, 219–37.

Johansen, P. G. 2004. Landscape, monumental architecture, and ritual: A reconsideration of the South Indian ashmounds. *Journal of Anthropological Archaeology* **23**, 309–30.

Jones, A. 2002. *Archaeological Theory and Scientific Practice*. Cambridge: Cambridge University Press.

Kagawa, Y., Y. Yanagisawa, K. Hasegawa, H. Suzuki, K. Yasuda, H. Kudo, M. Abe, S. Matsuda, Y. Ishikawa, N. Tsuchiya, A. Sato, K. Umetsu & Y. Kagawa. 2002. Single nucleotide polymorphisms of thrifty genes for energy metabolism: Evolutionary origins and prospects for intervention to prevent obesity-related diseases. *Biochemical and Biophysical Research Communications* **295**, 207–22.

Kay, R. F., M. Cartmill & M. Balow. 1998. The hypoglossal canal and the origin of human vocal behavior. *Proceedings of the National Academy of Sciences USA* **95**, 5417–19.

Kelly, R. L. 1992. Mobility/sedentism: Concepts, archaeological measures, and effects. *Annual Review of Anthropology* **21**, 43–66.

Kemper, T. D. 1978. Toward a sociology of emotions: Some problems and some solutions. *American Sociologist* **13**, 30–41.

Kingdon, J. 1993. *Self-Made Man and His Undoing*. London: Simon & Schuster.

Kirmayer, L. J. 1992. The body's insistence on meaning: Metaphor as presentation and representation in illness experience. *Medical Anthropology Quarterly (N.S.)* **6**, 323–46.

Klein, R. & B. Edgar. 2002. *The Dawn of Human Culture*. New York: Wiley.

Klein, R. G. 1999. *The Human Career: Human Biological and Cultural Origins*. Chicago: University of Chicago Press.

Knappett, C. 2005. *Thinking through Material Culture*. Philadelphia: University of Pennsylvania Press.

Korzybski, A. 1933. *Science and Sanity: An Introduction to Non-Aristotelian Systems and General Semantics*. Lancaster: The Science Printing Company.

Kroeber, A. L. 1917. The superorganic. *American Anthropologist* **19**, 163–213.

Lakoff, G. 1987. *Women, Fire, and Dangerous Things: What Categories Reveal About the Mind*. Chicago: University of Chicago Press.

Lakoff, G. & M. Johnson. 1999. *Philosophy in the Flesh: The Embodied Mind and Its Challenge to Western Thought*. New York: Basic Books.

————. 2003. *Metaphors We Live By*. Chicago: University of Chicago Press.

Laland, K. N. & G. R. Brown. 2006. Niche construction, human behavior, and the adaptive-lag hypothesis. *Evolutionary Anthropology* **15**, 95–104.

Laland, K. N., J. Odling-Smee & M. W. Feldman. 2000. Niche construction, biological evolution, and cultural change. *Behavioral and Brain Sciences* **23**, 131–75.

————. 2001. Cultural niche construction and human evolution. *Journal of Evolutionary Biology* **14**, 22–33.

Lambert, H. 1994. The homeless goddess: Cosmology, sickness and women's identity in Rajasthan. *Journal of the Anthropological Society of Oxford* **25**, 21–30.

Latour, B. 1993. *We Have Never Been Modern* (trans.) C. Porter. London: Harvester Wheatsheaf.

————. 2000. The Berlin key or how to do words with things. In *Matter, Materiality and Modern Culture* (ed.) P. M. Graves-Brown, pp. 10–21. London: Routledge.

Laughlin, C. D., J. McManus & E. G. d'Aquili. 1990. *Brain, Symbol and Experience: Toward a Neurophenomenology of Human Consciousness*. Boston: Shambhala.

Layton, R. 1997. *An Introduction to Theory in Anthropology*. Cambridge: Cambridge University Press.

Leach, E. R. 1976. *Culture and Communication: The Logic by Which Symbols Are Connected. An Introduction to the Use of Structuralist Analysis in Social Anthropology*. Cambridge: Cambridge University Press.

Leach, H. M. 2003. Human domestication reconsidered. *Current Anthropology* **44**, 349–68.

Lechtman, H. 1984. Andean value systems and the development of prehistoric metallurgy. *Technology and Culture* **15**, 1–36.

Lemonnier, P. 1992. *Elements for an Anthropology of Technology*. Ann Arbor: University of Michigan Press.

Leroi-Gourhan, A. 1943. *Evolution et Techniques: L'Homme et la Matière*. Paris: A. Michel.

———. 1945. *Evolution et Techniques: Milieu et Techniques*. Paris: A. Michel.

———. 1964. *Le Geste et la Parole I: Technique et Langage*. Paris: A. Michel.

———. 1965. *Le Geste et la Parole II: La Mémoire et les Rythmes*. Paris: A. Michel.

———. 1968. *The Art of Prehistoric Man in Western Europe*. London: Thames & Hudson.

———. 1976. Interprétation esthétique et religieuse des figures et symboles dans la préhistoire. *Archives de Sciences Sociales des Religions* **42**, 5–15.

Lévi-Strauss, C. 1972. *Structural Anthropology* (trans.) C. Jacobson & B. Grundfest Schoepf. Harmondsworth: Penguin.

Levin, D. M. (ed.). 1993. *Modernity and the Hegemony of Vision*. Berkeley: University of California Press.

Lewis-Williams, J. D. 2002. *The Mind in the Cave: Consciousness and the Origins of Art*. London: Thames & Hudson.

Lewis-Williams, J. D. & T. A. Dowson. 1988. The signs of all times: Entoptic phenomena in Upper Palaeolithic art. *Current Anthropology* **29**, 201–45.

———. 1990. Through the veil: San rock paintings and the rock face. *South African Archaeological Bulletin* **45**, 5–16.

Lewontin, R. 1983. Gene, organism and environment. In *Evolution from Molecules to Men* (ed.) D. S. Bendall, pp. 273–85. Cambridge: Cambridge University Press.

———. 2000. *The Triple Helix: Gene, Organism and Environment*. Cambridge, MA: Harvard University Press.

Lovell, N. 1998. Wild gods, containing wombs and moving pots: Emplacement and transience in Watchi belonging. In *Locality and Belonging* (ed.) N. Lovell, pp. 53–77. London: Routledge.

Lutz, C. 1988. *Unnatural Emotions: Everyday Sentiments on a Micronesian Atoll and Their Challenge to Western Theory*. Chicago: University of Chicago Press.

Lyon, M. L. 1990. Order and healing: The concept of order and its importance in the conceptualization of healing. *Medical Anthropology* **12**, 249–68.

————. 1995. Missing emotion: The limitations of cultural construction-ism in the study of emotion. *Cultural Anthropology* **10**, 244–63.

MacKenzie, D. 1984. Marx and the machine. *Technology and Culture* **25**, 473–502.

Marx, K. 1964. *Selected Writings in Sociology and Social Philosophy* (trans.) T. B. Bottomore. London: McGraw-Hill.

————. 1979. *The Poverty of Philosophy*. New York: International Publish-ers.

Marx, K. & F. Engels. 1977. *The German Ideology*. London: Lawrence & Wishart.

Marx, L. & M. R. Smith. 1994. Introduction. In *Does Technology Drive History? The Dilemma of Technological Determinism* (eds.) M. R. Smith & L. Marx, pp. ix–xv. Cambridge, MA: MIT Press.

Mauss, M. 1979. *Sociology and Psychology: Essays* (trans.) B. Brewster. London: Routledge & Kegan Paul.

McBeath, M., D. Shaffer & M. Kaiser. 1995. How baseball outfielders deter-mine where to run to catch fly balls. *Science* **268**, 569–73.

McDade, T. W. 2005. The ecologies of human immune function. *Annual Review of Anthropology* **34**, 495–521.

McGrew, W. C. 1992. *Chimpanzee Material Culture: Implications for Human Evolution*. Cambridge: Cambridge University Press.

McLuhan, M. 1962. *The Gutenberg Galaxy: The Making of Typographic Man*. London: Routledge & Kegan Paul.

————. 1964. *Understanding Media*. London: Routledge & Kegan Paul.

Mekel-Bobrov, N., S. L. Gilbert, P. D. Evans, E. J. Vallender, J. R. Anderson, R. R. Hudson, S. A. Tishkoff & B. T. Lahn. 2005. Ongoing adaptive evolution of *ASPM*, a brain size determinant in *Homo sapiens*. *Science* **309**, 1720–22.

Merleau-Ponty, M. 1962. *Phenomenology of Perception* (trans.) C. Smith. London: Routledge.

Meskell, L. M. 1996. The somatization of archaeology: Institutions, dis-courses, corporeality. *Norwegian Archaeological Review* **29**, 1–16.

————. 1999. *Archaeologies of Social Life: Age, Sex, and Class in Ancient Egypt*. Oxford: Basil Blackwell.

Michea, J. 1968. La technologie culturelle: Essai de systématique. In *Eth-nologie Générale* (ed.) J. Poirier, pp. 823–77. Paris: Gallimard.

Miller, D. 1985. *Artefacts as Categories: A Study of Ceramic Variability in Central India*. Cambridge: Cambridge University Press.

————. (ed.). 1995. *Acknowledging Consumption: A Review of New Stud-ies*. London: Routledge.

————. (ed.). 1998a. *Material Cultures: Why Some Things Matter*. London: UCL Press.

———. 1998b. *A Theory of Shopping*. Cambridge: Polity.

Miller, D. & C. Tilley (eds.). 1984. *Ideology, Power and Prehistory*. Cambridge: Cambridge University Press.

Misa, T. J. 1988. How machines make history, and how historians (and others) help them to do so. *Science, Technology and Human Values* **13**, 308–31.

———. 1994. Retrieving sociotechnical change from technological determinism. In *Does Technology Drive History? The Dilemma of Technological Determinism* (eds.) M. R. Smith & L. Marx, pp. 115–. Cambridge, MA: MIT Press.

Mithen, S. 1996. *The Prehistory of the Mind*. London: Thames & Hudson.

Moerman, D. E. 1983. Physiology and symbols: The anthropological implications of the placebo effect. In *The Anthropology of Medicine: From Culture to Method* (eds.) L. Romanucci-Ross, D. E. Moerman & L. R. Tancredi, pp. 156–67. South Hadley, MA: J. F. Bergin.

Moore, H. 1986. *Space, Text and Gender: An Anthropological Study of the Marakwet of Kenya*. Cambridge: Cambridge University Press.

Morales-Muñíz, A., M. A. C. Pecharromán, F. H. Carrasquilla & C. Liesau von Lettow-Vorbeck. 1995. Of mice and sparrows: Commensal faunas from the Iberian Iron Age in the Duero Valley (Central Spain). *International Journal of Osteoarchaeology* **5**, pp. 123–38.

Morell, V. 1993. Anthropology: Nature-culture battleground. *Science* **261**, 1798–802.

Morgan, L. H. 1877. *Ancient Society*. London: Macmillan.

Morphy, H. 1989. From dull to brilliant: The aesthetics of spiritual power among the Yolngu. *Man (N.S.)* **24**, 21–40.

Morton, J. 1995. The organic remains: Remarks on the constitution and development of people. *Social Analysis*, 101–18.

Mumford, L. 1961. History: Neglected clue to technological change. *Technology and Culture* **2**, 230–36.

———. 1963. *Technics and Civilization*. London: Harcourt Brace Jovanovich.

Needham, R. 1967. Percussion and transition. *Man (N.S.)* **2**, 606–14.

Neel, J. V. 1962. Diabetes mellitus: A 'thrifty' genotype rendered detrimental by 'progress'? *American Journal of Human Genetics* **14**, 353–62.

Odling-Smee, J., K. N. Laland & M. W. Feldman. 2003. *Niche Construction: The Neglected Process in Evolution* (Monographs in Population Biology 37). Princeton, NJ: Princeton University Press.

Olsen, B. 2003. Material culture after text: Re-membering things. *Norwegian Archaeological Review* **36**, 87–104.

Ong, W. 1969. World as view and world as event. *American Anthropologist (N.S.)* **71**, 634–47.

———. 2002. *Orality and Literacy: The Technologizing of the Word*. New York: Routledge.

Ortner, S. B. 1984. Theory in anthropology since the sixties. *Comparative Studies in Society and History* **26**, 126–66.

Osvath, M. & P. Gärdenfors. 2005. Oldowan culture and the evolution of anticipatory cognition. *Lund University Cognitive Science* **122**, pp. 1–16.

Ouzman, S. 2001. Seeing is deceiving: Rock art and the non-visual. *World Archaeology* **33**, 237–56.

Oyama, S., P. E. Griffiths & R. D. Gray (eds.). 2001. *Cycles of Contingency: Developmental Systems and Evolution*. Cambridge, MA: MIT Press.

Paddayya, K. 2004–2005. Symbolic approaches to the study of early agropastoral communities of Lower Deccan. *Puratattva* **35**, 1–6.

Panger, M. A., A. S. Brooks, B. G. Richmond & B. Wood. 2002. Older than the Oldowan? Rethinking the emergence of hominin tool use. *Evolutionary Anthropology* **11**, 235–45.

Parker Pearson, M. & Ramilisonina. 1998. Stonehenge for the ancestors: The stones pass on the message. *Antiquity* **72**, 308–26.

Parker Pearson, M. & C. Richards. 1994. Architecture and order: Spatial representation and archaeology. In *Architecture and Order: Approaches to Social Space* (eds.) M. Parker Pearson & C. Richards, pp. 38–72. London: Routledge.

Parrott, W. G. & M. P. Spackman. 2000. Emotion and memory. In *Handbook of Emotions* (eds.) M. Lewis & J. M. Haviland-Jones, pp. 476–90. London: Guilford Press.

Patrik, L. E. 1985. Is there an archaeological record? In *Advances in Archaeological Method and Theory*, vol. 8. Edited by M. B. Schiffer. London: Academic Press.

Peirce, C. S. 1998. *The Essential Peirce: Selected Philosophical Writings*. Bloomington: Indiana University Press.

Pels, P. 1998. The spirit of matter: On fetish, rarity, fact and fancy. In *Border Fetishisms: Material Objects in Unstable Places*. Edited by P. Spyer, pp. 91–121. London: Routledge.

Pfaffenberger, B. 1988. Fetishised objects and humanised culture: Towards an anthropology of technology. *Man (N.S.)* **23**, 236–52.

———. 1992. Social anthropology of technology. *Annual Review of Anthropology* **21**, 491–516.

Pietz, W. 1985. The problem of the fetish, I. *Res* **9**, 5–17.

Plotkin, H. C. (ed.). 1988. *The Role of Behavior in Evolution*. Cambridge, MA: MIT Press.

Plummer, T. 2004. Flaked stones and old bones: Biological and cultural evolution at the dawn of technology. *Yearbook of Physical Anthropology* **47**, 118–64.

Pollard, J. 2001. The aesthetics of depositional practice. *World Archaeology* **33**, 315–33.

Preucel, R. W. & A. A. Bauer. 2001. Archaeological pragmatics. *Norwegian Archaeological Review* **34**, 85–96.

Prown, J. D. 1996. Material culture: Can the farmer and the cowman still be friends? In *Learning from Things: Method and Theory of Material Culture Studies* (ed.) W. D. Kingery, pp. 19–27. Washington, DC, and London: Smithsonian Institution Press.

Prussin, L. 1996. When nomads settle: Changing technologies of building and transport and the production of architectural form among the Gabra, the Rendille, and the Somalis. In *African Material Culture* (eds.) M. J. Arnold, C. M. Geary & K. L. Hardin, pp. 73–102. Indianapolis: Indiana University Press.

Quinn, N. 1991. The cultural basis of metaphor. In *The Theory of Tropes in Anthropology* (ed.) J. W. Fernandez, pp. 56–93. Stanford, CA: Stanford University Press.

Rabinow, P. & W. M. Sullivan (eds.). 1979. *Interpretive Social Science: A Reader*. Berkeley: University of California Press.

Rainbird, P. 2002a. Making sense of petroglyphs: The sound of rock-art. In *Inscribed Landscapes: Marking and Making Place* (eds.) B. David & M. Wilson, pp. 93–103. Honolulu: University of Hawaii Press.

———. 2002b. Marking the body, marking the land. Body as history, land as history: Tattooing and engraving in Oceania. In *Thinking through the Body: Archaeologies of Corporeality* (eds.) Y. Hamilakis, M. Pluciennik & S. Tarlow, pp. 233–47. New York: Kluwer Academic/Plenum Publishers.

Ramachandran, V. S. & E. M. Hubbard. 2003. Hearing colors, tasting shapes. *Scientific American* **288**, 52–59.

Rappaport, R. A. 1967. *Pigs for the Ancestors*. New Haven, CT: Yale University Press.

Reader, S. M. & K. N. Laland. 2002. Social intelligence, innovation, and enhanced brain size in primates. *Proceedings of the National Academy of Sciences* **99**, 4436–41.

Ricoeur, P. 1971. The model of the text: Meaningful action considered as text. *Social Research* **38**, 529–62.

Rindos, D. 1980. Symbiosis, instability, and the origin and spread of agriculture: A new model. *Current Anthropology* **21**, 751–72.

Rollefson, G. O. 1990. The uses of plaster at Neolithic 'Ain Ghazal, Jordan. *Archaeomaterials* **4**, 33–54.

Rorty, R. (ed.). 1967. *The Linguistic Turn: Essays in Philosophical Method.* Chicago: University of Chicago Press.

Rosaldo, M. Z. 1984. Toward an anthropology of self and feeling. In *Culture Theory: Essays on Mind, Self and Emotion* (eds.) R. A. Shweder & R. A. Levine, pp. 137–57. Cambridge: Cambridge University Press.

Sackett, J. R. 1977. The meaning of style in archaeology: A general model. *American Antiquity* **42**, 369–80.

Sahlins, M. 1976. *Culture and Practical Reason.* Chicago: University of Chicago Press.

Saussure, F. de. 1983. *Course in General Linguistics* (trans.) R. Harris. London: Duckworth.

Scheper-Hughes, N. & M. Lock. 1987. The mindful body: A prolegomenon to future work in medical anthropology. *Medical Anthropology Quarterly (N.S.)* **1**, 6–41.

Schick, K. D. & N. Toth. 1993. *Making Silent Stones Speak: Human Evolution and the Dawn of Technology.* New York: Simon & Schuster.

Schiffer, M. B. 1999. *The Material Life of Human Beings: Artifacts, Behavior, and Communication.* London: Routledge.

Seidman, S. (ed.). 1994. *The Postmodern Turn: New Perspectives on Social Theory.* Cambridge: Cambridge University Press.

Seremetakis, C. N. 1994. Implications. In *The Senses Still: Perception and Memory as Material Culture in Modernity* (ed.) C. N. Seremetakis, pp. 123–45. Chicago: University of Chicago Press.

Shanks, M. & C. Tilley. 1982. Ideology, symbolic power and ritual communication: A reinterpretation of Neolithic mortuary practices. In *Symbolic and Structural Archaeology* (ed.) I. Hodder, pp. 129–54. Cambridge: Cambridge University Press.

———. 1987. *Social Theory and Archaeology.* Oxford: Polity Press.

———. 1992. *Re-constructing Archaeology: Theory and Practice.* London: Routledge.

Shaw, W. H. 1979. "The handmill gives you the feudal lord": Marx's technological determinism. *History and Theory* **18**, 155–76.

Shelton, A. 1992. Predicates of aesthetic judgement: Ontology and value in Huichol Material Representations. In *Anthropology, Art and Aesthetics* (eds.) J. Coote & A. Shelton, pp. 209–44. Oxford: Clarendon Press.

Sillar, B. 1996. The dead and the drying: Techniques for transforming people and things in the Andes. *Journal of Material Culture* **1**, 259–89.

Smith, B. 2003. The ecological approach to information processing. In *Mobile Learning: Essays on Philosophy, Psychology and Education* (ed.) J. Nyiri, pp. 17–24. Vienna: Passagen Verlag.

Smith, B. D. 2001. Low-level food production. *Journal of Archaeological Research* **9**, 1–43.

Smith, D. W. 2005. Phenomenology. In *The Stanford Encyclopedia of Philosophy* (ed.) E. N. Zalta. http://plato.stanford.edu/archives/win2005/entries/phenomenology/ (Winter 2005 Edition).

Snow, C. P. 1993. *The Two Cultures*. Cambridge: Cambridge University Press.

Solomon, G. E. 1987. Psychoneuroimmunology: Interactions between central nervous system and immune system. *Journal of Neuroscience Research* **18**, 1–9.

Solomon, R. C. 2000. The philosophy of emotions. In *Handbook of Emotions* (eds.) M. Lewis & J. M. Haviland-Jones, pp. 3–15. London: Guilford Press.

Soper, K. 1995. *What Is Nature? Culture, Politics and the Non-human*. Oxford: Blackwell.

Stevanovic, M. 1997. The age of clay: The social dynamics of house destruction. *Journal of Anthropological Archaeology* **16**, 334–95.

Steward, J. 1955. *Theory of Culture Change: The Methodology of Multilinear Evolution*. Urbana: University of Illinois Press.

Stoller, P. 1989. *The Taste of Ethnographic Things: The Senses in Anthropology*. Philadelphia: University of Pennsylvania Press.

Strathern, M. 1988. *The Gender of the Gift: Problems with Women and Problems with Society in Melanesia*. Cambridge: Cambridge University Press.

Sturrock, J. 1986. *Structuralism*. Oxford: Oxford University Press.

Taçon, P. S. C. 1991. The power of stone: Symbolic aspects of stone use and tool development in western Arnhem Land, Australia. *Antiquity* **65**, 197–207.

Tambiah, S. J. 1969. Animals are good to think and good to prohibit. *Ethnology* **8**, 423–59.

Tarlow, S. 2000. Emotion in archaeology. *Current Anthropology* **41**, 713–46.

Tchernov, E. 1984. Commensal animals and human sedentism in the Middle East. In *Animals and Archaeology, 3: Early Herders and Their Flocks* (eds.) J. Clutton-Brock & C. Grigson, pp. 91–115. British Archaeological Reports International Series 202.

Thomas, J. 1996. *Time, Culture and Identity: An Interpretive Archaeology*. London: Routledge.

———. 1999. *Understanding the Neolithic*. London: Routledge.

Thomas, N. 1991. *Entangled Objects: Exchange, Material Culture and Colonialism in the Pacific*. Cambridge: Harvard University Press.

Thompson, E. E., H. Kuttab-Boulos, D. Witonsky, L. Yang, A. Roe & A. Di Rienzo. 2004. CYP3A variation and the evolution of salt-sensitivity variants. *American Journal of Human Genetics* **75**, 1059–69.

Tilley, C. 1989. Interpreting material culture. In *The Meanings of Things* (ed.) I. Hodder. Cambridge: Cambridge University Press.

———. (ed.). 1990. *Reading Material Culture*. Oxford: Blackwell.

———. 1991. *Material Culture and Text*. London: Routledge.

———. 1999. *Metaphor and Material Culture*. Oxford: Blackwell.

———. 2004. *The Materiality of Stone: Explorations in Landscape Phenomenology*. Oxford: Berg.

Tishkoff, S. A., R. Varkonyi, N. Cahinhinan, S. Abbes, G. Argyropoulos, G. Destro-Bisol, A. Drousiotou, B. Dangerfield, G. Lefranc, J. Loiselet, A. Piro, M. Stoneking, A. Tagarelli, G. Tagarelli, E. H. Touma, S. M. Williams & A. G. Clark. 2001. Haplotype diversity and linkage disequilibrium at human *G6PD*: Recent origin of alleles that confer malarial resistance. *Science* **293**, 455–62.

Trigger, B. 1989. *A History of Archaeological Thought*. Cambridge: Cambridge University Press.

Turnbull, D. 2000. Gothic tales of spandrels, hooks and monsters: Complexity, multiplicity and association in the explanation of technological change. In *Technological Innovation as an Evolutionary Process* (ed.) J. Ziman, pp. 101–17. Cambridge: Cambridge University Press.

Turner, V. 1967. *The Forest of Symbols: Aspects of Ndembu Ritual*. Ithaca, NY: Cornell University Press.

———. 1982. *From Ritual to Theater: The Human Seriousness of Play*. New York: Performing Arts Journal Publications.

Tuzin, D. 1984. Miraculous voices: The auditory experience of numinous objects. *Current Anthropology* **25**, 579–96.

Van Gennep, A. 1960. *The Rites of Passage* (trans.) M. B. Vizedom & G. L. Caffee. Chicago: University of Chicago Press.

van Schaik, C. P., M. Ancrenaz, G. Borgen, B. Galdikas, C. D. Knott, I. Singleton, A. Suzuki, S. S. Utami & M. Merrill. 2003. Orangutan cultures and the evolution of material culture. *Science* **299**, 102–05.

Varela, F. J. 1996. Neurophenomenology: A methodological remedy for the hard problem. *Journal of Consciousness Studies* **3**, 330–49.

Varela, F. J., E. Thompson & E. Rosch. 1991. *The Embodied Mind: Cognitive Science and Human Experience*. Cambridge, MA: MIT Press.

Verhoeven, M. 2004. Beyond boundaries: Nature, culture and a holistic approach to domestication in the Levant. *Journal of World Prehistory* **18**, 179–282.

Voight, B. F., S. Kudaravalli, X. Wen & J. K. Pritchard. 2006. A map of recent positive selection in the human genome. *PLoS Biology* **4**, 446–58.

Wang, E. T., G. Kodama, P. Baldi & R. K. Moyzis. 2005. Global landscape of inferred Darwinian selection for *Homo sapiens*. *Proceedings of the National Academy of Sciences* **103**, 135–40.

Warnier, J.-P. 2001. A praxeological approach to subjectivation in a material world. *Journal of Material Culture* **6**, 5–24.

Washburn, S. L. & C. S. Lancaster. 1968. The evolution of hunting. In *Man the Hunter* (eds.) R. B. Lee & I. DeVore, pp. 293–303. Chicago: Aldine.

Watkins, T. 1990. The origins of house and home? *World Archaeology* **21**, 336–47.

Watson, C. 2003. *Piercing the Ground: Balgo Women's Image Making and Relationship to Country*. Fremantle: Fremantle Arts Centre Press.

Webb, J. L. A., Jr. 2005. Malaria and the peopling of early tropical Africa. *Journal of World History* **16**, 269–91.

Weiner, J. 1991. *The Empty Place: Poetry, Space and Being among the Foi of Papua New Guinea*. Bloomington: Indiana University Press.

Weiner, J. F.. 1996. Language is the essence of culture: Against the motion. In *Key Debates in Anthropology* (ed.) T. Ingold, pp. 171–75. London: Routledge.

———. 2001. *Tree Leaf Talk*. Oxford: Berg.

Wells, J. C. K. 2005. Evolution of the human profile of fatness. *Human Ecology Special Issue No.* **13**, 17–22.

———. 2006. The evolution of human fatness and susceptibility to obesity: An ethological approach. *Biological Reviews of the Cambridge Philosophical Society* **81**, 183–205.

Wengrow, D. 1998. "The changing face of clay": Continuity and change in the transition from village to urban life in the Near East. *Antiquity* **72**, 783–95.

White, L. 1959. *The Evolution of Culture: The Development of Civilization to the Fall of Rome*. New York: McGraw-Hill.

Whitehead, A. N. 1978. *Process and Reality: An Essay in Cosmology*. New York: Free Press.

Whitehouse, H. 1992. Memorable religions: Transmission, codification and change in divergent Melanesian contexts. *Man (N.S.)* **27**, 777–97.

Whiten, A. & R. W. Byrne (eds.). 1997. *Machiavellian Intelligence II: Extensions and Evaluations*. Cambridge: Cambridge University Press.

Whiten, A., J. Goodall, W. C. McGrew, T. Nishida, V. Reynolds, Y. Sugiyama, C. E. G. Tutin, R. W. Wrangham & C. Boesch. 1999. Culture in chimpanzees. *Nature* **399**, 682–85.

Whorf, B. L. 1956. *Language, Thought and Reality*. Cambridge, MA: MIT Press.

Wiessner, P. 1984. Reconsidering the behavioral basis for style: A case study among the Kalahari San. *Journal of Anthropological Archaeology* **3**, 190–234.

Wilson, P. 1988. *The Domestication of the Human Species*. London: Yale University Press.

Winner, L. 1977. *Autonomous Technology: Technics-out-of-control as a Theme in Political Thought*. Cambridge, MA: MIT Press.

——. 1986. *The Whale and the Reactor*. Chicago: University of Chicago Press.

Winston, P. H. 1984. *Artificial Intelligence*. Reading, MA: Addison-Wesley.

Wrangham, R. W., J. H. Jones, G. Laden, D. Pilbeam & N. Conklin-Brittain. 1999. The raw and the stolen. *Current Anthropology* **40**, 567–94.

Wynn, T. G. 1988. Tools and the evolution of human intelligence. In *Machiavellian Intelligence: Social Expertise and the Evolution of Intellect in Monkeys, Apes and Humans* (eds.) R. W. Byrne & A. Whiten, pp. 271–84. Oxford: Oxford University Press.

——. 1999. The evolution of tools and symbolic behaviour. In *Handbook of Human Symbolic Evolution* (eds.) A. Lock & C. R. Peters, pp. 263–87. Oxford: Blackwell.

Yentsch, A. 1996. The symbolic divisions of pottery: Sex-related attributes of English and Anglo-American household pots. In *Contemporary Archaeology in Theory: A Reader* (eds.) R. W. Preucel & I. Hodder, pp. 315–49. Oxford: Blackwell.

Young, J. H., Y.-P. C. Chang, J. D.-O. Kim, J.-P. Chretien, M. J. Klag, M. A. Levine, C. B. Ruff, N.-Y. Wang & A. Chakravarti. 2005. Differential susceptibility to hypertension is due to selection during the out-of-Africa expansion. *PLoS Genetics* **1**, e82.

Index

CPSIA information can be obtained at www.ICGtesting.com
Printed in the USA
BVOW021445240213

314018BV00005B/47/P